MW01640345

THE WORLD

IS AT YOUR DOOR

By Phil Watlington

UNDERSTANDING AND LEVERAGING GLOBALIZATION AND NEW-AGE INNOVATION

ISBN 0-7414-3408-3

Published by:

INFINITY
PUBLISHING.COM

1094 New DeHaven Street, Suite 100
West Conshohocken, PA 19428-2713
Info@buybooksontheweb.com
www.buybooksontheweb.com
Toll-free (877) BUY BOOK
Local Phone (610) 941-9999
Fax (610) 941-9959

Printed in the United States of America

Printed on Recycled Paper

Published August 2006

This book is dedicated to my wife Nicki, whose support, advice, and excellent editing skills made the book come to life for my readers. I also owe gratitude and thanks to my sister-in-law, Rebecca Williams, and my sister, Jan Thompson—each of whom contributed their research, editing, and proof-reading skills. We had some fun along the way—learning, discussing, and debating the many topics incorporated into the book. We look forward to our next journey as we strive to provide readers with books that deal with pertinent issues in this extraordinary time in history in which we live—where every day is tomorrow!

Phil Watlington, June 2006
Leawood, Kansas

CONTENTS

INTRODUCTION

"A focus on globalization as an *opportunity*, rather than a *threat*, is absolutely required for individuals and firms to effectively compete and win in the new global economy!"

Phil Watlington, Author "The World Is At Your Door!"

I'll tell you right up front that this book is about how individuals and businesses can win and prosper in the new *globalized* and, to a degree, economically leveled world in which we now live. This book is also about the rebirth of *innovation* (which I propose we call *new-age innovation*) and the critical interrelationships this process has with *globalization.* Equally important, this book is simply about competition and survival—because for many individuals, organizations, and nations, leveraging (efficiently utilizing) innovative global processes will be the only course of action available for economic survival. While many of the examples used throughout the book are U.S. and "Western World" oriented (53% of the world's largest thirty corporations are located in the United States, 34% in Europe, and 13% in Japan), the conclusions presented and arguments set forth have practical application for all who participate, or have critical need to participate, in the new Internet-driven global economy (Pocket World in Figures, 2006).

Looking forward, not back!

In this book, we will be dealing with understanding *globalization* and *new-age innovation* as they relate to successfully living in the present, as well as planning for the future. However, on occasion, we'll look back at history because knowledge of how problems were solved in the past can help solve problems today and in the future. In the pages that follow, I have included real life examples, supporting research data, and discussions that will help bridge the gap between what is occurring today *(globalization)*, and what businesses and individuals can, and must do *(create and innovate)*, to survive and thrive in the new global economy. This is the central theme of the book! And, as we progress through the pages, I hope you will feel the pull of an underlying theme and emotional tone, as I focus on *globalization* and the *rebirth of innovation* as positive forces that will reshape the world into a better place for all.

At the end of each chapter, I have included a short list of *Recommended Action Items.* These *action items* are intended to help readers turn the concepts and discussions presented in the chapter into "real life" winning operational strategies. The effective execution of these *action items* will bring about added value to all stakeholders in an organization. Many firms—Procter & Gamble, General Electric, Apple Computers, Siemens, Motorola, Samsung, Toyota, IBM—to name just a few, are already confronting the challenges brought about by *globalization*, with innovatively designed organizational structures, investment arrangements, business processes, and products and services. Each has found that the strategic models of the past no longer work in the interconnected global economy in which organizations participate today! In this regard, I have included a chapter to help individuals and organizations formulate and implement global strategies—strategies that will empower businesses and individuals to achieve and sustain a competitive advantage in the new global economy. The chapter is called "Global Strategy, Hedgehogs, Martha Stewart, and Others" (Collins, 2001).

But first . . .

I won't take a lot of your time discussing how certain countries in the new global economy, such as India and China, have supposedly taken jobs from the "developed countries." At this point, it is a given that much of the world's manufacturing output has moved to *China*—perhaps unavoidably (perhaps even rightly so), I will argue. It is also true that *India* has become the world's major provider and location for outsourced and offshored services. Furthermore, in the past fifteen years, manufacturing jobs in the U.S. have declined about 18%, primarily due to globalization. Japan's manufacturing jobs have declined 22%, Britain's 27%, and France's 20% (Bernanke, 2004). And today, "one in every ten jobs in the U.S." is in jeopardy of being outsourced to an offshore location (Sarfatti, 2004). After all, many countries around the world have now been converted to capitalism, or some form thereof, and that's exactly what capitalism is all about—competition, free/fair trade, and balancing resources to drive prices to their lowest level of sustainability.

Additionally, I'm not going to focus on the history of how we got to *globalization* and a *"flat world,"* since Mr. Thomas Friedman, writer for the *New York Times* and author of *The World is Flat, A Brief History of the Twenty-first Century,* has done an excellent job of this (Friedman, 2005). His work, I believe, is having a profound impact on our understanding of the new globally connected, economically leveled, and collaborative world in which we now find ourselves. Another writer on the subject, Mr. Clyde Prestowitz, President of the Economic Strategy Institute in Washington, D.C., in his recent book titled *Three Billion New Capitalists,* has also made a significant contribution to the historical perspective of globalization. He vividly lays out for us that China, India, Eastern Europe, and much of Asia have now come onto the level economic playing field and changed the world's supply chains and economic models, forever (Prestowitz, 2005). Both authors seem to agree that the new *flat world* is being driven by the continued growth of the Internet/World Wide Web, and the relaxing of many national and political barriers around the world.

From my perspective, several key historical and current day events support these assumptions. They are: (1) the fall of the Berlin Wall (1989); (2) China becoming a member of the World Trade Organization in 1986 (official acceptance 2001) and opening its commercial borders to the rest of the world; (3) the demise of the old Soviet Union regime (1991); (4) the continued rise of large multinational (global) corporations; (5) the expanding role of global organizations such as the World Trade Organization, The United Nations, The World Bank, and The International Monetary Fund to foster fair trade and interconnectedness among the nations of the world, and (6) the Internet/World Wide Web and, to a greater extent, global computer hardware and software platforms that provide the backbone for vast numbers of people to easily communicate, engage in commercial transactions, and exchange information and ideas. Which of these events will prove to be the most powerful will be a subject of debate for some time.

However, it is generally accepted that the Internet and World Wide Web have been major enablers of the *globalization* process. In fact, I will argue in this book that *globalization* and the leveling of the world's economic playing field are two of the most significant *unintended consequences* of the Internet/World Wide Web. Other *unintended consequences* might include such notions as: (1) global collaborative efforts to address the world's ever-growing energy and natural resources needs; (2) the increasing number of nations working together to fight diseases (such as efforts to eliminate AIDS and flu outbreaks around the world); (3) the movement toward more peaceful coexistence among nations that need each other economically; (4) the increased collaboration of *knowledge workers* around the world to engage in *new-age innovation* activities; and (5) the elevation of the world's current four billion *poor people*, who make less than $2,000 (U.S. dollars) annually, up a notch on the poverty and hunger-scale (Hutto, 2006). What do you think? Do we dare find hope in the midst of the *globalization* process and fight for competitive advantages for individuals, companies, and entire nations? To the extent possible, several chapters in this book shed light on these concepts and possibilities.

And now . . .

Before we get into these subjects, there's just one request I have for each of you as valued readers of this book. It is: imagine for a moment that there are very few borders or barriers in the world and that each of us has the opportunity to participate in a world-class game (many, for the first time in history). Also, imagine that each of us, as participants in the game, is equipped with an Internet connection to the world's data, video, and voice information resources. And finally, imagine that the prizes up for grabs are each of our jobs, products and services of all kinds, entire businesses, whole industries, and our beliefs and ideologies. While I might be overstating the case, I propose, for your consideration, that this *game scenario* is very close to where we are in today's world! Now, let's get started understanding the new global economy and how to survive and thrive in the present and the future!

"Globalization has altered the economic framework of both advanced and developing nations in ways that are difficult to comprehend."

Alan Greenspan, Ex-Chairman U.S. Federal Reserve System

PERSONAL THOUGHTS

Hopefully, the process of globalization can ultimately be defined by the *commonalities* and *interdependences* among individuals, businesses, and nations, rather than in terms of their *differences*.

Phil Watlington, Author "The World Is At Your Door!"

As an adjunct professor at a large university, teaching graduate and undergraduate courses in Finance, Accounting, and Strategy in the evening to *working adults*, I began joking several years ago with students that the world was becoming *flat* (Friedman, 2005). I would start and end each course, and still do today, with a PowerPoint slide that reads:

LATE BREAKING NEWS:
THE WORLD IS NOW FLAT

(from a business perspective!)

The heading on the slide also includes: "Leading with the Numbers," for courses in Finance and Accounting, and "Leading with Strategy," for courses in Strategic Planning. Whether you are an individual, a *for-profit* or *not-for-profit* organization, or an entire nation, *Leading* is, and will continue to be the key requirement for sustaining a competitive advantage in the new *flat world*. Little did I know that several authors would go on to discuss the *flat world* concept in some detail (namely Mr. Thomas Friedman, whom I have recognized several times in this book) (Friedman, 2005). Many students would respond to the *flat world* concept by saying they knew about it because some of their acquaintances lost jobs when their employers outsourced/offshored jobs to companies in China, India, and throughout Asia! The students would then go on to express concern that the U.S. economy and standard of living might be headed for a decline because China, India, and other developing nations are "taking jobs away from Americans." At the same time, I suspect students in Germany and Japan were remarking that Toyota, Honda, Volkswagen, and Mercedes Benz have built auto plants in the U.S. and throughout North America that are employing thousands of Americans, rather than workers in their home countries. To this point, Toyota—Asia's largest manufacturer—currently has 10 facilities and $13 billion (U.S. dollars) invested in the United States (Jobs Tomorrow, 2006; Toyota, 2006). This subject is covered in detail in Chapter 7: "The Standard of Living and Quality of Life Argument."

The concerns expressed above by students (as well as others) are, of course, too narrow a view of what is going on in the world. Herein lies one of the greatest problems: education and understanding the globalization process and its short and long-term economic, social, and political impacts on the world community! The importance of globally educated leaders and innovative thinkers is examined in this book in chapters titled: "Education—The Great Equalizer (Actually the Most Important Chapter!)" and "Artistic and Creative Visions for Innovative Organizations." I'll suggest strongly that it will be hard to become an innovative organization and leverage *globalization* and *new-age innovation* without a highly-educated workforce and leaders who focus their organizations on imaginative, creative, and customer-centered products and services.

I hope this book will help identify what is taking place, and broaden your view of how we are all interconnected in the new global economy and community. You can see examples of how this connectedness plays out in the chapters I have included on "Energy (Crisis?)—Globalization and Innovation at Their Best (or Worst)," and "The Cost of

Labor is Four Times Greater Than in China and India—Now What?"

I believe it is fair to say that *globalization* has touched everyone's lives in so many ways that we can't imagine or understand them all; certainly not enough to know what the right solutions might be in any given competitive situation. As a resident of Leawood, Kansas (a suburb of Kansas City on the edge of the great wheat, corn, and soybean fields of the Midwest), I am constantly reminded of *globalization* and that agricultural products are the second largest item China imports from the rest of the world. (Electronic components and aircraft are numbers one and three.) And, on many a warm fall day as I sat at my kitchen table writing this book, I could hear the distant hum of wheat combines as they crawled across nearby fields harvesting wheat for the world's bread and food supply. A major portion of this Kansas wheat was bound for China and India—the world's number one and two consumers of wheat. They are also major producers of wheat, but they still need imported wheat and flour products to sustain food supplies for their 1.3 (China) and 1.1 (India) billion people. As I sat writing and listening to the distant lullaby-like sound of these huge harvesting machines, I knew that *globalization* was at our community's doorstep, begging to be embraced and understood, rather than feared. Symbolically, these golden brown massive fields of freshly cut wheat reminded me of the "yellow brick road" which led to the "Emerald City" of abundance in the well-known Kansas classic, *The Wizard of Oz*. Only this time, the "yellow brick road" is a global connection that leads to the delivery of wheat and all sorts of products and services to distant communities around the world. One thing is clear: we're not just residents of Kansas anymore! We're all—no matter where we reside—connected and dependent on each other for our livelihood and existence. Are you ready for a ride on the yellow brick road of globalization and *new-age innovation*?

Finally, there seems to be a proliferation of doomsday scenarios regarding globalization's impact on economic, political, and social structures within and among many nations of the world community. Many of the scenarios are historically focused and some offer one-sided emotional points of view, rather than an objective look at this transitional period in history we are currently experiencing. Perhaps we should call it the *globalization and new-age innovation era*. When we're down the road a ways and look back, I believe we'll see that this era was a positive economic, political, and social transitional period in the history of many countries, perhaps even the world. In this regard, you'll want to read carefully the final chapter titled: "In Transition, It's Not a Pretty Sight, But. . .!" In many ways, this chapter is a discussion of the inherent short-term "bad news" part of the globalization process, as employees, employers, and entire nations struggle to survive and succeed in the new—and extremely competitive—global economy. You will see, however, that the evidence points to the fact that this long and winding transitional road will lead straight to a stronger global economy and more vibrant businesses, communities, and nations. What are desperately needed, I'll argue in this book, are innovative processes that foster new ways of thinking, working, and living in a world where each person's survival and well-being is dependent on another. *Innovation* has worked in the past. *New-age Innovation* will work today and in the future! The best is yet to come as China progresses toward becoming the world's largest economy, Toyota takes over the number one spot as the world's largest automaker, and a major shift in capital accumulation, power, and economic activity transitions to *the East*. In the long run, don't assume that as one country or company rises, others must therefore decline. *Globalization* can be a winner for all!

After reading this book and gaining an understanding of the concepts and recommended actions for leveraging *globalization* and *new-age innovation*, you may not like all

that you see but you will be better prepared to effectively participate in the new global economy. After all, *The World Is At Your Door! It is a door to the future!*

"Creativity and imagination when applied in a business context, lead to innovation."

Jeffery Immelt – Chairman and CEO, General Electric Company

Chapter 1

On the Road to the Airport, or On the Internet

"When it is possible to communicate and transact business around the world so conveniently, so economically, and so rapidly, the urge to do business is irresistible."

Paul A. Volcker, Ex-Chairman, U.S. Federal Reserve Bank

This morning, and for many to come, large numbers of business and pleasure travelers around the world are on the road to the airport, headed for a location outside their home country. For the rest of us, we're on the "*www.internet*," integrally linked with an ever-expanding global community of buyers, sellers, and information gatherers. Just what is driving this "phenomenon?" Answer: ***Globalization!*** *(Or, Globalisation!)*

Globalization–the basics.

To be successful in today's new global economy, leaders and individuals throughout an organization need a clear and concise understanding of what globalization is (and is not). More importantly, they must also understand that this process is constantly changing. Without this understanding, it will be impossible to effectively drive an organization to become creative, and use new-age innovation in a strategic manner to compete in the world's globalized markets and supply chains. It will be equally difficult for individuals, such as you and I, to live economically and socially rewarding lives without an understanding of the new global economy and community we now live in and the process that is driving it called "globalization."

The World Bank defines "globalization" as the "freedom and ability of individuals and firms to initiate voluntary economic transactions with residents of other countries" (N.O.W., 2005). The IMF (International Monetary Fund) defines "globalization" as the "growing economic interdependence of countries worldwide, brought about by an increasing volume and variety of cross-border transactions of goods and services, freer international capital flows, and more rapid and widespread diffusion of technology" (IMF, 1997).

In researching the current literature on globalization (of which there is an abundance), it was particularly interesting to note the number of times globalization was equated with "capitalism," "internationalism," and "democratic free-market driven economies." These terms, as well as globalization, are certainly not new terms. Many organizations have been doing business in what is called an "international" environment for decades. McDonalds, Coca Cola, Citibank, Motorola, Siemens, General Electric, Sony, Hewlett Packard, and Caterpillar are a few notable examples. Therefore, what is globalization? What does it mean to be a "global organization?" How does it differ from being an "international organization?" The following six distinguishing characteristics make the globalization process we are experiencing today far different from the "international activities" firms engaged in previously. These characteristics are:

(1) The activities, processes, and dynamic events that the term "globalization" conveys encompass the political, economic, technological, and cultural interdependencies and interrelationships among all nations comprising the "global

community." By the way, the new term for "world" is "global village," or "global community." The competitive playing field in this "global community" is becoming less dominated by "developed countries." Many "underdeveloped countries" are opening their borders, increasing trade relationships, and realizing improvements in their standard of living and economic wealth. Potentially, all nations can participate in globalization and take advantage of the world's global supply chains for raw materials, labor, finished goods, services, and natural resources.

(2) There are rapidly-growing, closer contacts among the nations of the world. These closer contacts, brought about by the opening of many borders, such as in China, India, Russia, and Eastern Europe, improve the potential for personal exchange, commercial transactions, and "friendship" among "world citizens." These closer contacts between people and nations also have the potential for negative results, such as the misuse of patents, copyrights, and intellectual property, as well as the abuse of human rights. Human rights issues are still visible today in many areas of the world, such as Africa, the Middle East, and parts of Asia. And, a widespread disregard for intellectual property rights and patents prevails across much of Asia.

In my view, the closer relationships and interdependencies brought about by globalization seem to drive individuals, businesses, and, often, entire nations in three different general directions. One is toward greater free trade and changes that foster the creation of a "world civilization" and "global economy." The second is just the opposite, and is called "protectionism," or "isolationism." Protectionism or isolationism seems to result from the fear of job, capital, culture, technology, political status, and standard of living losses. The third is a "neutral" position, or a stance of "wait and see; maybe globalization is really not going to last." I see the neutral approach to globalization, or lack of direction, as dangerous. I believe history tells us that the United States and all nations will benefit more from the pursuit of free trade rather than protectionism or isolationism. To this point, globalization needs to be viewed as an on-going process of finding better commercial and social uses of the interconnectedness that now exists among the world's people. Furthermore, these interconnected and closer relationships, specifically the economic relationships among nations, might lessen the number of aggressive military actions initiated among nations that are interdependent on each other for their survival and well being. Unfortunately, I could not find any specific data that would point to a trend in this direction, as the war on terrorism, the war in Iraq, military actions in Afghanistan, and unrest in the Middle East continue at an aggressive pace. However, globalization and the interdependence it fosters holds promise for change.

(3) Capitalism and "free-market" driven economies are spreading around the world, as is democracy, or at least modified forms of the "democratic process." Stated another way, communism and socialism are on the decline. Upon my wife's return from a month-long trip to The People's Republic of China in the spring of 2006, she remarked several times that Peking (called Beijing in Chinese) felt like an American city, with its restaurants, nightclubs, high rise office buildings, and shopping centers. For example, the central site of Chinese Communist authority, the "Great Hall of the People," which is located near Tiananmen Square (Beijing, China), when not in government use, is now rented out for trade shows, concerts, and corporate events. U.S. based firms, such as Ford Motor Company, Microsoft, General Motors, KFC (Kentucky Fried Chicken), and Motorola, have all used the hall for commercial events (A Hall That Beats All, 2006). Interestingly, this "great hall" was designed by the very first PhD graduate from Carnegie Mellon University (USA), Mao Yisheng, shortly after 1911 when he returned to his "native China" after graduation. Much of history has passed since this time, and likely, no

one envisioned the openness and exchange between the two countries that is occurring today (Dept., 2006).

(4) The following cross-border activities indicate an intensification of economic globalization as firms strive to become globally innovative organizations:

- The flow of goods and services in a "free-trade" manner;
- The flow of human capital (people and ideas). As I look out over each new group of students entering a course, it is evident by the diversity of cultures represented that globalization is at work, and advancing. The same is true of the work environments of many firms, particularly multinational organizations;
- The flow of many forms of capital investments, savings, and the accumulation of currencies;
- The flow of technology and the collaborative efforts by firms to develop new products and services.

(5) The leveraging, and sometimes exploitation of labor from unequally developed nations of the world with "cheap labor," continues at a fast pace. This aspect of globalization is quite often looked upon negatively, particularly by those individuals who might be out of work due to the offshoring and outsourcing of jobs by their employer. On the other hand, very positive results are being seen as a result of collaborative efforts among nations seeking to develop new products and services that help all of the world's peoples. And, consumers in all nations are enjoying the retail price advantages brought about by the free flow of goods and services from countries with low wage rates. However, prices will eventually be driven upward as consumption of products made from scarce natural resources, such as steel, copper, oil, and lumber, increases. The chapters that follow in this book deal with many of these issues, and provide insights into potential innovative solutions.

(6) The continuing rapid growth in communications and computer-based (digital) technologies, such as the Internet and World Wide Web, along with more affordable global travel, have compressed the world commercially, socially, and politically. This "demographic compression" gives everyone quick and easy access to people, products, services, education, ideas, and information. For example, members on a research and development team might reside in different countries, but work on common projects such as life-saving drugs and new software and hardware systems.

Globalization—rapid growth, roller coaster ride.

You simply cannot pick up a newspaper or magazine, or be on the Internet without seeing something about *globalization*. Just as the World Wars of the past defined several generations and guided their actions and beliefs, *"globalization"* is becoming one of this generation's defining moments. Why are we all on this global economic, social, and political roller coaster ride? Why is globalization growing rapidly and intensifying today rather than five to ten years ago? Is it here to stay, or will we soon forget about it, like we have Japan's run at the U.S. and world in the '70s with its cheap prices, innovative technologies, and productivity process improvements? More importantly, why is it imperative that all organizations recognize and modify their strategies to function in this new globally competitive world? Hopefully, in the brief summary that follows, I can tell you why as I look at history and anticipate the future.

First, one does not have to look too far back in history to see that today's world is much more conducive to cross-border activities and collaborative efforts than ever before. By the way, my wife, Nicki, who I promised to give some credit for assistance with this book, is a Master's level historian and also an English major. Historically, she can trace globalization back to the "Silk Road" trade route from Venice to China, trade with the Orient by the Netherlands's Dutch East and Dutch West India Companies, and Great Britain's empire that once extended around the globe. As a very brief snapshot, these three historical periods span a time line from approximately 1300 to 1914, when World War I ended "the first great age of globalization" (A Brief History, 2006).

As I promised in the "Introduction," this book is not meant to be a history of globalization. However, in order to bring the current day globalization process into perspective, the following major events seem to explain why we are where we are today, and, to an extent, why the globalization process will continue and in fact intensify. I'll make it brief.

- As indicated above, *World War I* brought the first great age of globalization to a halt—not to return again until after *World War II.* The industrial firms that grew up around the world after WWII faced little, if any, global competition. These firms, as well as the countries in which they resided, seemed to operate in a protectionist and isolationist mode. I surmise that the war years took its toll on the people and infrastructure of many countries and forced them to focus inwardly on survival, rather than on such notions as "global competition" and globalization. A few firms, such as Citigroup, Coca Cola, and The Singer Sewing Machine Company, did expand globally, but their primary focus was "business friendly" countries. This lackluster global expansion continued on through the Korean War, the Cold War, the Cuban Crisis, and the Vietnam War. If anything, these "crisis events" discouraged companies and countries from global expansion and collaboration. Slowly, however, the citizens of many countries began to experience and realize that there were products, services, and desirable interrelationships to be had outside their borders. For poor countries, I think that people were tired of being hungry. Incidentally, hunger is still a significant problem today. In fact, as of spring 2006, the United Nations World Food Programme faces the highest global food needs in its history (How Many, 2006). Globalization seems to be helping by spreading jobs, food, clothing, and other products and services around the world, but not fast enough. Approximately 800 million people in the developing nations of the world still go to bed hungry each night and "hunger and malnutrition remain the number one cause of death world wide" (How Many, 2006). At the same time, there have never been more individuals and entire nations that have amassed such huge sums of wealth and capital resources. Globalization is, in many ways, distributing some of this wealth, as discussed in later chapters in this book. And, globalization is also creating wealth that can then be spread around the world in the form of capital investments and commercial transactions for goods and services.

- As a result of the breakdown in monetary relations among the world's nations during the turmoil years of WWII, 29 countries formed the *International Monetary Fund (IMF)*. This organization, along with the International Bank of Reconstruction and Development (as discussed below), became the early drivers in collaborative efforts among nations to restore post-war monetary relations and global trade. The 1945 architects of the IMF are generally considered to be the well-known British Economist John Maynard Keynes and the Chief International Economist for the U.S. Treasury Department, Harry Dexter White. Today's IMF organization consists of a membership of 184 countries, most of whom are also members of the United Nations. The mission of the organization certainly coincides with globalization as it works to "foster global monetary cooperation, secure financial and currency stability, facilitate international trade, promote high employment, and reduce poverty in the world" (International Monetary Fund, 2006).

- Post WWII *1945* also saw the formation of the *United Nations (UN)* by the victorious world powers as a mechanism to prevent and deal with conflict in the world. The UN actually replaced the League of Nations formed following WWI. While we might wonder about the UN's power over the nations of the world, it clearly continues to provide a platform for "facilitating cooperation in international law, international security, economic development, and social equity" (United Nations, 2006). This organization, consisting of 191 member countries, has played and continues to play a major role in bringing countries together for discussion and collaborative efforts on such issues as trade efficiency, arms and disarmament, peacekeeping, human rights, poverty, and health. These issues occupy center stage in 2006 as globalization impacts each of them. Much of the literature on this subject points to the UN as a prime enabler of globalization and the effective functioning of today's new global economy. For all the criticism leveled at the UN over the years, we should not forget that it is a major world organization where issues can be brought for discussion—which is generally the starting point for the resolution of any issue.

- From the early years of a few large companies doing business in a small number of countries around the world, emerged the *multinational corporation (1950s and 60s)*. These multinational corporations, such as Ford and General Motors, began building cars in major countries. Eventually, automobiles and parts manufactured in these countries were shipped into other regions of the world and back to the home country of the multinational corporation. Now, all types of vehicles and replacement parts are produced and shipped among nations. Take at look at the fine print when you purchase that Ford or GM car, or others as well, and you might see that it was made in Mexico, Canada, China, or assembled in Ohio or Kansas City, with parts from around the world. Or, take a look at any of the electronic gear that we have available today and you will quickly see that there are many countries supplying parts that go into them. This was the early stage of (1) globalization as we know it today; (2) the early stage of global competition; and (3) the first recognition that "cheap labor" in business-friendly "developing nations" could be used to gain a competitive advantage. Today, these "developing nations" are becoming major players themselves in global markets and the new global economy.

In reality, this period set the stage for global sourcing models that are now in use by all of the world's multinational corporations. This included not only manufacturing companies like Motorola, IBM, and Caterpillar, but large retailers such as Wal-Mart, J.C. Penney, Sears, and K-Mart, who began nationally but quickly changed to sourcing goods from around the world (Palley, 2006).

- Then came *space exploration* and the race to put a "man on the moon." And, looking back, it is hard to believe that Russia and the U.S. actually worked in a cooperative manner on some aspects of space station development and operation.
- In the late *60s and early 70s*, *Japan* came on the scene with its cheap prices, innovative manufacturing processes, and advanced electronic technologies. For many years, the U.S. and other countries were trying

to leverage Japan's leadership in the areas of productivity, manufacturing process controls, and technological advancements.

- Then the *70s oil crisis* hit, and it became clear that we were, and still are today, all linked by many global economic dependencies and relationships.
- Next, the *Berlin Wall* fell in *1989*, and that same year, uprisings by protestors of China's government in *Tiananmen Square* gave a hint that people were looking beyond their borders at what was going on in the rest of the world. Freedom and a desire for the capitalistic standard of living, or some form of "better life," seemed to be on the minds of many.
- And then *Russia* failed as a unified nation in *1991*, virtually ending communism in Eastern Europe. Since this time, the newly-formed Russian Federation has been moving toward a democratic market economy and working toward becoming a member of the World Trade Organization. However, as of 2005, Cuba, the People's Republic of China, Vietnam, Laos, and North Korea were the only countries in the world that still professed adherence to communist ideology (Communist Party, 2006). There are many communist political parties operating in countries around the world, but they are generally in the minority. China, though, seems to be moving toward capitalism and a market driven society as globalization pulls much of the world together. Time will tell where this movement will go in China, or the other countries that still labor under Communism. I am left to wonder whether globalization is rendering communism obsolete—and to an extent, I think the answer is yes.
- As trade among the nations of the world continued to grow significantly in the *1990s*, it became clear to the leaders of many nations that some form of

organization was needed to bring nations together under a standardized set of fair trade practices. As a result of meetings among leaders around the world, the WTO *(World Trade Organization)* was formed in *1995*. It actually evolved from a prior 1948 arrangement by a group of nations known as GATT (General Agreement on Tariffs and Trade). The WTO, headquartered in Geneva, Switzerland has done much to foster "fair trade" among nations and, indirectly, globalization. It is currently the major global international organization dealing with the rules of trade between nations. Current membership includes 149 countries, which constitutes the bulk of the world's trading nations. The WTO's purpose is to help producers of goods and services, exporters, and importers conduct their business. Becoming a member is not a quick and easy process. Agreements must be reached between the WTO and the country applying for membership, regarding how "fair trade" practices and procedures will be implemented. And, in many cases, a country applying for membership must pass laws that show adherence to the agreements. This process for membership is known as accession and can take years before full membership is granted. The WTO has the potential to become an even greater catalyst for the globalization process and the new global economy. If nothing more, getting countries to agree on even minimal rules for conducting trade in the global economy is a significant step forward. Following is a representative sample of the 149 members of the WTO—many of whom were members of GATT (General Agreement on Tariffs and Trade) prior to the organization of the WTO—along with the year they became an official member: (WTO, 2005)

Australia	(1995)
Belgium	(1995)
Canada	(1995)
China	(2001)
India	(1995)
France	(1995)
Germany	(1995)
Japan	(1995)
Singapore	(1995)
United Kingdom	(1995)
Venezuela	(1995)
United Arab Emirates	(1996)
Pakistan	(1995)
Malaysia	(1995)
South Africa	(1995)
Spain	(1995)
Thailand	(1995)
Norway	(1995)
Greece	(1995)
Turkey	(1995)
United States	(1995)

Equally important, there are another 32 countries that are in various stages of their "accession" programs toward becoming official members. The Russian Federation, Iran, Iraq, Afghanistan, Viet Nam, Kazakhstan, Ethiopia, and Algeria are a few of the countries in this group. The Russian Federation began working on its requirements for becoming a member of the WTO in 1993 and continues today in 2006. While it may not seem like a giant step forward, the act of countries becoming a part of the World Trade Organization and the global community it supports is often the first step in resolving issues and conflicts among nations that otherwise may not ever communicate. Certainly, those countries applying for membership mentioned above are representative of volatile areas of the world that need help, not only with trade issues but with more peaceful means of resolving conflicts. The latest countries to be officially approved for membership are Tonga and Saudi Arabia in December 2005.

Since China is currently playing a major role in the global economy, here are the general commitments made by the Chinese government as part of their becoming an official member of the WTO in 2001 (WTO, 2005).

(1) China will provide non-discriminatory treatment to all WTO members. All foreign individuals and enterprises, including those not invested or registered in China, will be accorded treatment no less favorable than that accorded to enterprises in China, with respect to the right to trade;

(2) China will eliminate dual pricing practices as well as differences in treatment accorded to goods produced for sale in China in comparison to those produced for export;

(3) Price controls will not be used for purposes of affording protection to domestic industries or providers of services;

(4) The WTO Agreement will be implemented by China in an effective and uniform manner by revising its existing domestic laws and enacting new legislation fully in compliance with the WTO Agreement;

(5) Within three years of accession all enterprises will have the right to import and export all goods and trade them throughout the customs territory with limited exceptions;

(6) China will not maintain or introduce any export subsidies on agricultural products.

These agreements are very typical of those adopted by other countries that have joined the WTO. There currently exists some concern over China's ability to comply with the timeline required by the agreement with the WTO. However, the progress made to date represents a giant step forward in bringing China into the global economy with "fair-trade" practices.

- "If you want to play, then you have to pay," as the saying goes. Although globalization has enabled many of the developing and poor nations of the world to come on to the global economic playing field, they often run into difficulty in securing credit facilities. The *World Bank* (headquartered in Washington, D.C.), one of the specialized agencies of the United Nations, was formed to help alleviate this situation by assisting developing nations finance trade and economic growth. These low-income countries generally cannot borrow money in international markets or can only do so at high interest rates. One hundred nine offices located in major cities around the world and two operating units, the *International Bank of Reconstruction and Development (IBRD)* and *The International Development Association (IDA),* provide low-interest loans and often interest-free credit. In 2004, $20.1 billion U.S. dollars were provided to countries around the world in the form of grants, contributions, interest-free loans and technical assistance (World Bank—What Is, 2006).

  When we talk about globalization creating a level commercial playing field, the field is far from level when it comes to poverty. 2.8 billion people in the world live on less than $700 (U.S. dollars) per year. And, 1.2 billion of the 2.8 earn less than $1 per day. Yes, that's correct—less than one dollar per day! (World Bank—What Is, 2006) Although the focus of the World Bank is financial in nature, its underlying goal is to use its financial strength to foster sustainable poverty reduction around the world. To this end, the WB and its 189 country partnership is fighting poverty in the areas of health, child mortality, school enrollment, disease prevention, and access to clean water supplies.

And, you've probably been asking as you read this: "where does the World Bank and its operating units get all this money to loan and give out?" Well, globalization has created an ever-growing international bond market where China, the U.S., India, and other countries purchase the WB's AAA bonds ($13 billion worth in 2004). The proceeds from bond sales are then used for loans and grants to developing countries (World Bank—What Is, 2006).

- Next came the *information and communications age* which ushered in the rapid development of computer technology and the advent of the Internet and "www." These events, perhaps more than any, have enabled free trade to flourish, and information and ideas to be communicated in a "boundary-less" global environment.
- January, 1994 brought about *NAFTA* (North America Free Trade Agreement) between the U.S., Mexico, and Canada. This treaty eliminated duties on many categories of goods and services, removed restrictions on investments among the three countries, provided protection of intellectual property rights, and established worker and environmental protections. While the agreement applies to three countries in North America, it is being used as a model for other regional affiliations. Chief among these is *CAFTA* (Central America Free Trade Agreement), which is progressing as countries in Central America, one-by-one, sign the agreement. The major provisions of the treaty are similar to those of NAFTA. It is seen as an agreement that will level the trading field for U.S. exporters by doing away with many of the high tariffs that exist today. The

U.S. officially ratified the treaty in 2005. The agreement is also seen as a stepping stone to an agreement that will encompass South America and the Caribbean, except Cuba. Gradually, all Central American countries are ratifying the agreement and a majority are now (as of May 2006) officially members of CAFTA (Perez-Korinko, 2006).

- All of the above "*converging events*" are leading toward more open relationships among nations, and more open borders—the basis for globalization! (Friedman, 2005)

- Current update: Generally, war, terrorism, and other acts of aggression between and among nations would have the affect of causing the nations involved to resort to some form of protectionism, and even isolationism. This occurred during WWI and WWII and, to a degree, during the Korean and Vietnam Wars. The same does not seem to be occurring as the War in Iraq, the War on Terrorism, and unrest in the Middle East and Afghanistan continue.

  A question mark, however, remains regarding France and its labor law changes, and attempts at moving away from socialism, which have sparked a massive protest movement in that country. Due to the competitive pressures brought about by globalization, France is struggling to become more competitive in the world economy by changing its rigid labor laws that virtually guarantee employment. France's labor unions, whose members are used to guarantees and protections, are controlled by the Communist Workers' Party of France. Often, the Socialist Party, France's dominant political party, is at odds with the Communist Party in that country, and only occasionally finds some common ground on issues. So, the world watches to see if France will move toward a more capitalistic system and embrace globalization, or will it remain hostile toward global capitalism and less open to "fair trade?" (France, 2006) On a positive note, France was ranked number one this year on International Living's Global Quality of Life Index and many French companies do in fact compete successfully in free-trade markets. The future seems uncertain, though, as France struggles with globalization, just as the United States and other nations struggle to protect their high wages and standards of living, and to remain competitive in the new global economy.

While the above is not a complete chronology, these events exemplify the major forces leading up to what we now call globalization, and, to a greater extent, explain why we are all "on the road to the airport, or on the Internet." The world has simply become economically "flat" (Friedman, 2005). The globalization race is on! A race toward "capitalism;" a race toward various forms of capitalistic and free-market economies, which one might call "hybrid capitalism!" For example, China calls their form of capitalism "Socialism with Chinese Characteristics," as opposed to communism, which is commonly how outsiders describe China's governmental and economic structure. Remember that in China and many of Asia's developing countries, government and business are integrally linked by controls from a central governing regime. And, as more of China's State Owned Enterprises (SOE's) move toward private ownership, economists are saying that China is indeed becoming more capitalistic. I believe this to be a slow process that will take some time and I wouldn't look for China to be a capitalistic economy or democratic society in the near future.

When in doubt, do a little name calling!

Just who caused globalization anyway? Barry Lynn in his recent book "*End of the Line,*" attempts to trace globalization's roots back to outsourcing. And, he argues that we now have a new form of outsourcing. This new outsourcing was brought about by a "handful of visionary industrialists," who initiated purchase agreements with suppliers not just on the "far side of town or the far side of America, but on the far side of the earth" (Lynn, 2005). These "visionary industrialists" were the first to figure out that their companies could gain a tremendous competitive advantage by farming out work to companies located in countries with cheap and efficient labor. Lynn identifies these visionaries by name as the "computer maker Michael Dell, John Chambers of Cisco Systems, Jack Welch and Gary Wendt of the General Electric Company, Paul Galvin of Motorola, Fred Smith of FedEx, Jurgen Schrempp of DaimlerChrysler, Jose Ignacio Lopez de Arriortua of General Motors, and Sam Walton of Wal-Mart" (Lynn, 2005).

I would question whether we can give these individuals full credit for this new offshoring/outsourcing some now refer to as globalization. Rather, globalization is the result of several forces coming together, as discussed earlier in this chapter and briefly in the *Introduction*. The industrialists named above were certainly among the prime movers toward globalization, but, as Lynn points out, little did they know what the outcome would be. The list could probably be expanded with additional research. Other forces, as we have discussed earlier, such as the opening of borders, the fall of the Soviet Union, the fall of the Berlin Wall, the opening of China to the commercial world, the expansion of capitalism and democracy, Japan's competitive pressures in the '70s and '80s, and the information/internet revolution—all played (and continue to play) important roles. This is the broad view we need to take.

Put simply, we are left with the outcome—a new global economy that ties companies and nations together to compete economically for jobs, materials, and the world's natural resources. And, quite frankly, many individuals are fearful of this new global economy and scared about their well-being as their jobs are being outsourced or relocated to Asia. I'm not just talking about people in the United States. These same feelings are prevalent in other countries such as Britain, Germany, France, Canada, and Italy. On the other hand, many individuals in the developing nations of Asia are now able to escape from poverty because of these jobs coming to their countries. From a "Westerner's" perspective, this transition, which, in my view, is a balancing of the world's supply chains, means cheap labor, products, and services for businesses and consumers. However, the cost—at least in the short term—might also mean a loss of one's job. Learning how to deal with these types of issues and learning to survive and thrive in the age of globalization is, of course, the subject of this book. Many will say that globalization is too complex for anyone to understand, much less deal with effectively. When you get to the end of our journey through the book, you will understand what is going on and how to deal with it!

Outsourcing, Offshoring (and now Backshoring).

Now, here are a couple of terms that get thrown around a lot in any discussion regarding globalization. *Outsourcing* means farming out work to others, and the work outsourced is under the "control of others." *Offshoring* has two meanings. First, offshoring can be a form of outsourcing (called "offshore outsourcing") when work is moved to a country other than the one where the product or service will be sold or consumed—and, the work is under the control of others (Offshore Outsourcing, 2006). Second, offshoring can simply mean work is performed in a foreign country, either under the control of the company doing the offshoring, or under the control of a third party. Offshoring does not mean that there has to be a "shore" or a "body of water" involved; it simply means that a firm can do its work, or have it done, in another country (Heffes, 2004). Examples of *offshoring* include GM and Ford locating car and truck manufacturing plants under their ownership and control in India and other countries around the world. Examples of *outsourcing* include GM, Ford, and Honda having car seats and other major components made by "others," rather than making seats and components themselves. These purchases from "others" may be from "others" located domestically and/or in a foreign country. These are manufacturing examples, but business processes, such as engineering and call center operations, are also frequently outsourced and offshored.

To further clarify the *outsourcing* concept, note that Ford Motor Company at one time made steel, "only to determine that making steel was not a core function of their automotive business" (Heffes, 2004). So, they outsourced it and focused on making cars. Many companies are engaging in this same type activity, especially now that the outsourced cost of obtaining a needed product or service is almost always cheaper than the company's internal cost. And, you can be certain that *manufacturing costs* in China and *services costs* in India will be sufficiently "cheap" to lure most companies to "offshore/outsource." Likewise, the lure of "cheap" labor will encourage many companies to offshore and locate their own facilities in China, India, or wherever costs and quality will yield the greatest competitive advantage to the company. Have you been to Bangalore, India and seen all the major worldwide high-tech firms' facilities there? And, have you called for service on your computer, or to make an airline reservation, only to find that the service center you have reached is located in India or Malaysia? Just pick any business and there is a good chance that these same scenarios apply.

What we really hear <u>most</u> about with regard to *outsourcing* and *offshoring* is people losing their jobs to individuals in "cheap labor" countries. And, by the way, what we hear <u>least</u> about is "insourcing," such as Toyota and Honda (Japanese

Companies) locating operations in the U.S., Canada, and South America. Several chapters that follow discuss "insourcing" in detail.

However, if one looks at the numbers and reads the available literature carefully, there is much to gain from outsourcing and offshoring. Some of the gains include lower prices (we all love those), better standards of living for people, greater productivity, better quality products, and faster and more diversified research and development efforts. But, there will be "pain" in this global transition for those who lose their jobs, those who have to be retrained, or those who must settle for jobs of lesser status and pay. However, McKinsey's August 2003 study estimates that "every dollar of cost the U.S. moves out of the country brings the U.S. a net benefit of $1.12–$1.14." Furthermore, there is a benefit to the country receiving the outsourced or offshored work (Heffes, 2004). These findings might be of little consolation if you are the individual losing your job.

Currently, it doesn't happen that often, but there are a few organizations that have offshored labor requirements only to bring them back to their home site. This action is becoming known as "backshoring." Backshoring seems to be driven by the following conditions which are generally present when firms are not large enough to establish and control their own facilities/joint ventures at an offshore location:

- Intellectual property often ends up in the hands of individuals at an offshore location who pirate the property for their own personal gain;
- Turnover, especially among software and engineering personnel in India, is on the increase as competition grows for these skills in offshore locations. This often results in rework, poor quality, missed schedules, and a lack of continuity on projects in progress;
- In the case of software and development activities, some companies, such as KANA Software in Menlo

Park, California, feel that development is a collaborative process that works best when everybody involved—designers, programmers, project managers—are together under one roof (Fisher, 2006).

- Loyalty and teamwork are difficult to maintain, which can be critical components in developing vital software systems, and custom engineered hardware.

I believe it is fair to say that we will be seeing more *backshoring* as firms have time to figure out the most cost effective supply chain models for their businesses. Futhermore, backshoring will likely occur as labor prices increase in the "cheap labor" regions of China, India, Asia, and Eastern Europe. For example, software engineering salaries have grown at a rate of 11.5% in India over the past five years, and 7.5% in China (Software Engineer, 2006). If these high growth rates continue, or even if they moderate somewhat, then other countries will start to become competitive with India's and China's labor costs. On the other hand, the negative issues against offshoring listed above just may be signs of learning how to work in a global environment. At this time, the numbers don't show a slowdown in the outsourcing and offshoring of jobs. In fact, 2006 is currently projected to see a record one million U.S. jobs move out of the United States (Fisher, 2006).

This all points to the fact that we are, as a later chapter in this book suggests, "In Transition—It's Not a Pretty Sight, But…!" *Time Magazine's* Board of Economists states it more elegantly: "The future of U.S. competitiveness in a globalized economy depends on helping American workers through a period of historic transition" (Thottam, 2004). Although the reference is to "American workers" and "U.S. competitiveness," helping workers through this transition applies to many other countries facing the globalization transition as well. This subject is specifically addressed in Chapter 7: "The Standard of Living/Quality of Life Argument."

Leveraging Outsourcing.

At the risk of repeating myself, *outsourcing* means farming work out to "others," and the work farmed out is under the control of "others." Outsourced work can be done by another company in the same country or across the world. Outsourcing generally means that a company can focus on core functions in their business that are critical to maintaining a competitive advantage, while having others handle non-core functions. *GENPACT*, formerly GE Capital International Services, advertises that "our business is about making your business lighter, so you can soar and focus on what you do best" (GENPACT, 2006). For example, core functions might include project management for complex custom-engineered control systems, or capital investment management, or proprietary research projects. Non-core functions within a company might include call centers, financial services, data management, and routine human resource services (Global Outsourcing, 2006). The other major reason for outsourcing is cost savings. My experience tells me that significant savings can be achieved, ranging from 10%, all the way up to 60%+. As remarked earlier, India has become the "services" outsourcing center of the world, while China is the world's "manufacturing" center. And, Eastern European countries—Hungary, Bulgaria, Croatia, Czech Republic, Romania—are becoming known as locations to outsource IT (Information Technology) work. These countries have an increasing number of schools focusing on computer and digital technology.

The International Association of Outsourcing Professionals, which has 250 organizations around the world, says that there are many ways to leverage outsourcing to improve a company's cost structure and competitive advantage. The most common ways are to have outsourcing suppliers that: (Global Outsourcing, 2006)

- Provide products (manufacturing) and services (business processes) physically at the customer's site, such as on-site reproduction services by Xerox, or managing a computer center, or production unit;
- Provide products and services physically at a nearby facility, such as component parts manufacturers for Ford and GM, or payroll services by a nearby firm;
- Provide products and services physically in another state, province or country anywhere in the world. This includes a multitude of activities such as engineering and call center services in Bangalore and Hyderabad, India, to manufacturing in China, to service centers in major cities of a company's home country;
- Provide a combination of the above.

If you need to know where to look for outsourced products and services, *Fortune Magazine's* 2006 annual list of the top firms that provide outsourcing to companies around the world is a good place to start. Following are the top 10 global suppliers of outsourcing products and services: (IAOP, 2006) (Ranked in order of 1–10)

- **IBM (U.S.)** – information and communications technology management; customer relationship; human resources management.
- **Sodexho Alliance (France)** – real estate and capital asset management; facility services.
- **Accenture (U.S.)** – human resources management; information and communications technology management; financial services.
- **Hewlett-Packard (U.S.)** – information and communications technology management; financial services management; imaging and printing.

- **Capgemini (France)** – customer relationship management; information and communications technology management; financial services management.
- **ARAMARK (U.S.)** – facility services; uniform and career apparel.
- **Wipro Technologies (India)** – human resources management; information and communications technology management; transaction processing.
- **CGI Group (U.S.)** – human resources management; information and communications technology management; transaction processing.
- **Unisys (India)** – information and communications technology management; corporate services; transaction processing.
- **Cognizant Technology Solutions (U.S.)** – information and communications technology management.

Number one, IBM, long known for its computer equipment and software, has now turned into a "services" company. We'll be talking more about IBM in Chapter 5: "Global Strategy, Hedgehogs, Martha Stewart, and Others," and how they have leveraged globalization and new-age innovation to become the world's premier services (outsourcing) supplier. If the age-old culture of IBM can change, then there is hope for all of us. Number two on the list, Sodexho Alliance, exemplifies that, as some jobs are lost due to outsourcing, many are also created. This real estate and capital management company has 324,000 employees working at 26,700 sites in 76 countries (Global Outsourcing, 2006). Sixth ranked ARAMARK, with its home office in Chicago, Illinois, has 240,000 employees located around the world. The employment growth rate trend for the Top 100 companies on the list of outsourcing providers is 15% annually. Outsourcing is generally perceived as taking jobs away from employees, but these numbers indicate that outsourcing also creates and provides jobs.

As globalization continues, outsourcing will play a major role in a company's ability to compete globally. The trends above point to the fact that there will be jobs lost in many firms that utilize outsourcing, but, at the same time, many jobs will be created in the outsourcing industry. And, the cost savings and productivity gains by firms that leverage outsourcing as a strategic tactic will benefit consumers and businesses through lower prices on the goods and services purchased. Can we begin to view outsourcing and offshoring as positive business practices, rather than negatives? If you have just lost your job to one of these practices, it will likely be difficult. I've included a chapter on "Education—The Great Equalizer (Actually the Most Important Chapter)" later in this book which will be helpful in working through the transition.

<u>Observations by some of the world's best-known economic prognosticators.</u>

- ***Ben Bernanke,*** the new (2006) U.S. Federal Reserve Chairman, says: *Globalization* is upon us, but "to say that the U.S. economy benefits from trade is not to say that every individual American worker or family benefits, or that the structural changes induced by trade are not disruptive" (Bernanke, 2006).
- ***Alan Greenspan,*** Ex-U.S. Federal Reserve Chairman, says that "globalization and innovation, far more than in earlier years, appear to explain the events of the past ten years better than other conceptual constructs. Because of a lowering of trade barriers, deregulation and increased innovation, cross-border trade in recent years has been expanding at a far faster pace than GDP (Gross Domestic Product). As a result, domestic economies are increasingly exposed to the rigors of international

competition and comparative advantage. In the process, lower prices for some goods and services produced by trading partners have competitively suppressed domestic price pressures" (Greenspan, 2004). In speaking about the U.S. economy specifically, he advocates that a significant minority are suffering from globalization's effect on downward price pressures and a firm's ability to maintain a competitive advantage. "This is an issue that needs to be addressed if globalization is to sustain the necessary public support" (Greenspan, 2005).

- ***Thomas Friedman***, writer for the New York Times, and author of *"The World Is Flat"* and *"The Lexus and the Olive Tree,"* says that "globalization is the inexorable integration of markets, nation-states, and technologies to a degree never witnessed before, in a way that is enabling individuals, corporations, and nation-states to reach around the world faster, deeper and cheaper than ever before" (Lechner, 2001). He goes on to say that "globalization is made possible by its defining technologies, namely the internet." And, globalization's underlying economic basis is "free-market capitalism," which now has no serious rival (Lechner, 2001).

- ***Diana Farrell***, director of the McKinsey Global Institute's "economics think tank," says that we must understand that "we are all part of a global economy, from which there are real benefits to be derived." And, "such an understanding can help to move our models of fear, to models of: how do we channel globalization to productive uses and stave off the risks that exist?" (Heffes, 2004) Ms. Farrell also ties offshoring to the *globalization* process and argues that offshoring is part of a bigger process of global industry restructuring—or companies becoming global entities, so that their customer base is no longer primarily "national with a little bit of export sales on the side"(Heffes, 2004).

- ***Ed Hyman***, for 22 years in a row, has been voted the number one economist by Wall Streeters. He is Chairman and Chief Economist for International Strategy and Investment Group; an economics research firm he founded in 1991. Hyman advocates that "global liquidity and stronger foreign economies" could help prop up U.S. growth in coming years (Leeb, 2006). It appears that Hyman, like many, looks offshore for support of the U.S. economy. These comments by Mr. Hyman are indeed a theme that many individuals and firms echo as they flock to China and India to leverage globalization, and to maintain growth and profitability. Hyman also indicated that higher energy costs, interest rate hikes by the Federal Reserve, and a slow-down in mortgage financing might partially offset U.S. growth in coming years (Leeb, 2006).
- ***Jack Welch,*** Ex-Chairman and CEO of the General Electric Company, had four initiatives that he used to run the company. The first of the four, *globalization,* was initiated in 1987 and was often referred to as "Jack's Secret Weapon." Welch understood early on that "cheap labor" from India was an extremely powerful force in giving the company a competitive cost advantage. GE was one of the first companies to build a technology center in India—The John F. Welch Technology Center. The other three GE initiatives that came later were "Product Services (1995), Six-Sigma (1996), and Digitization (2000)" (Krames, 2005). **Jeffrey Immelt**, who took over the leadership of GE after Welch retired in 2001, has intensified the focus on globalization. Today, more than ⅓ of GE's leaders reside outside the United States and GE's non-U.S. revenues are growing at double-digit rates (Krames, 2005). Indeed, outsourcing and offshoring have played major roles in GE's growth strategy over the years. GE's leaders were among the world's first to leverage globalization to build sustainable shareholder value.

- ***Paul A. Samuelson***, 1970 Nobel Prize Winner in Economics, was skeptical about outsourcing and globalization benefiting the U.S. economy. He often remarked that "trade does not always work to all parties' advantage." He specifically argued that the "offshore outsourcing" of call-center and software programming jobs would hurt the U.S. economy. He did not adhere to the theory that, in the long term, all would gain from globalization (Teitelbaum, 2006).

- ***John Maynard Keynes***, who ranked number one in the 2006 *"Greatest Twentieth-Century Economists Poll,"* talked about globalization as far back as 1920 when he wrote *The Economic Consequences of Peace*. He reminded us that globalization, world trade, and interconnectedness among nations are not new processes. Until World War I brought globalization to a halt, Keynes describes life in 1914, "when a man in London could travel the world freely, invest wherever he wanted, and could order by telephone, while sipping his morning tea in bed, the various products of the whole earth, in such quantity as he might see fit, and reasonably expect their early delivery upon his doorstep" (Elliott, 2006). Globalization would not raise its head again until post WWII. Today, globalization is upon us as never before and many of the countries who were at war with each other are now intimately interconnected in a global economic network of dependency. Today, we could simply replace the word *"telephone"* in Keynes quote above with *"Internet,"* and the quote would be a good description of today's global economy.

The staying power of globalization.

The world's 40 largest multinational companies now employ an average of 55 percent of their work forces in "foreign countries and earn 59 percent of their revenues abroad"

(Breaking Links, 2006). In the United States alone, the "50 largest Standard and Poor's 500 companies earn approximately 40 percent of their revenues in offshore foreign countries" (Breaking Links, 2006). This dependency on other nations and the far-reaching effects of globalization are also quite evident by the growing volume of imports coming into the United States. Imports of foreign-made goods and services have doubled in the past 10 years and totaled $3.3 trillion dollars in 2005 (Cooper, 2006). These record imports have further widened the U.S. trade deficit to $726 billion at the end of 2005, which gives the U.S. the distinction of having the highest trade deficit among all the nations of the world. The next two nations behind the U.S. are the United Kingdom and Australia, with deficits in the $35 billion dollar range. This is a wide gap and really indicates how the U.S. and other nations as well, depend heavily on one another for their well-being and standard of living. Companies and countries are simply no longer tied to the economic conditions and policies of their domestic environment. They are free to move about and buy and sell goods and services anywhere in the "flat world."

It might be an over-simplification to explain the staying power of globalization by stating that China, India, other Asian nations, South America (namely Brazil and Argentina), and Eastern Europe have gotten a taste of prosperity and freedom, and there is no turning back. That is, there is no turning back from their growing demand for goods and services from around the world, a better standard of living and better wages. All of these "demands," I might add, can be traced in some form directly to the current globalization process and the rising cross-border import and export flows of goods, services, and capital investments. As one significant example, Chinese imports from all countries rose 40% in 2004, compared to 2003, and is expected to grow by a comparable amount in 2005 and 2006. And, according to the World Bank, foreign direct capital investments in China grew 13% in the same period, from $53 billion to $60 billion. These investments have totaled $560 billion in the period 1979 to 2004—which is one of those "never before in recorded history" events. I can't begin to imagine how much $560 billion is, but it's approximately two times Wal-Mart's annual sales. (Wal-Mart was the world's largest company until Exxon took that spot in 2006.) The United States alone imported $196.7 billion from China in 2004 and exported $34.7 billion to China, for a net import trade difference of $162 billion. According to Lee Scott, President and CEO of Wal-Mart Stores, Inc, speaking at their 2005 Annual Shareholders' Meeting, Wal-Mart (U.S.) alone purchased $18 billion (U.S. dollars) from Chinese vendors, compared to $150 billion purchased from U.S. vendors (Scott, 2005). On the export side, Australia, Brazil, the U.S., and Korea each increased their exports to China in excess of 40% in 2004.

Another significant example and indicator that globalization will be with us for the long-term lies in the fact that many countries, meaning many companies, are now starting to look to the developing countries (mainly in Asia) for not only standard products and services, but for research, development, and design services (knowledge-based, highly skilled services). As discussed above, General Electric was one of the first organizations to formally adopt "Globalization" as a major corporate strategic initiative in 1987, and subsequently established the John F. Welch Technology Center in Bangalore, India, to provide services to all six of the major industry groups that make up the General Electric Company. Today, Microsoft, Motorola, IBM, and many of the world's largest companies have centers in India. These centers play major roles in product development, software/hardware development, software support, and applications engineering services for these companies.

Microsoft opened shop in India in 1990, and then followed with a development center in 1998. Then in late 2005,

Microsoft, Intel, and CISCO Systems, three of the world's largest computer software and hardware firms, announced that they would invest additional amounts for research and development in India. Microsoft plans to invest $1.7 billion (U.S. dollars) over 4 years, Intel $1.0 billion over 5 years, and CISCO $1.1 billion over 3 years. In China, the same thing is going on, but to a lesser degree at the current time, in the city of Wuhan—the Bangalore of China.

Further reinforcement that "globalization" will be with us for the long term, and will likely be looked upon historically as a major economic, social, and political force in the 21st century, follows:

- Companies in countries with locally mature "served markets" will be required to look beyond homeland borders for top line (revenue) and bottom line (profit) growth, or perhaps to simply sustain profitability, or survive. For example, the market for automobiles in the United States, Canada, and Britain (and several other European countries as well) is mature. In other words, sales growth will be slow. Most families already have two vehicles, and, in many households, there are three or more. U.S., Canadian, and British auto manufacturers and parts suppliers are struggling for survival. And, as I began writing this book in the fall of 2005, both Ford Motor Company and General Motors announced that they would each be laying off 30,000 people over the next five years, and closing 12 to 14 manufacturing plants each. Both companies cited globalization and foreign competition as major drivers for their actions. Meanwhile, automobile sales in China are booming. About 6 million new cars annually (about 115 thousand per week) take to the roads as China becomes the world's number three automaker behind the U.S. and Japan (Green Car Congress, 2006). For another timely example, while U.S. airlines lined up in bankruptcy courts in 2004–2006, the need for airports, planes, and improved travel facilities in India, China, and many of the developing nations continues to soar. Firms in all of the "developed nations" are lining up for new business opportunities available due to an ever-increasing demand for products and services in the developing nations around the world. China alone is expected to purchase 500 new jet aircraft over the next five years and open 40–50 new major airports (Boeing, 2006). Can you name the last two major airports in the U.S. that were built from the ground up? Many other industry examples, such as water treatment, electrical, sewage systems, medical equipment, cosmetics, management consulting, training, railroads, and transportation systems—to name a few—fall into this same high-growth scenario. Most of these industries, however, are not facing the economic survival threat that U.S. auto manufacturers and airline carriers currently face. By the way, the last two major airports to be built in the United States from the ground up were Denver, Colorado (1995) and Dallas-Ft. Worth, Texas (1974).

- The globalization process going on around the world today has contributed significantly to the decrease in the number of "poor" people in many countries. For this reason alone, it is not likely that any nation will turn away or take a step back from globalization. The World Bank defines poverty as \$1.00 per person per day, or \$2.15 per day for people living in cold climates where heat and warm clothing are needed during the winter months of the year. For example, between 1998 and 2003, more than 40 million people in Eastern Europe and the former Soviet Union moved above the \$2.15 poverty level, but 60 million still remain below it (Growth–Poverty, 2004). Globalization is providing an increasing number of jobs and raising the standard of living in many countries. Two main elements of the globalization process seem to account for this improvement. One is a country's openness to foreign trade, which is strongly associated with economic growth. The second is a country's ability to make "capitalism" work (Growth–Poverty, 2004). On the other hand, globalization is also resulting in job losses in many countries, but it remains to be seen as to whether a corresponding decrease in the standard of living in these countries will occur. This subject will be explored in more detail in a later chapter titled "The Standard of Living/Quality of Life Argument."

- The generic strategy of "cost advantage" is a very powerful weapon for any company to have that operates in a competitive environment. In a later chapter in this book titled "Global Strategy, Hedgehogs, Martha Stewart, and Others," I will cover how organizations need to adapt their strategy to leverage cost advantages now available in the new global economy. For now, suffice it to say that the "cheap labor" found in China, India, Eastern Europe, and most Asian countries, will lure companies to take advantage of lowering their costs by offshoring/outsourcing labor to these countries. In fact, to remain competitive, many companies must take this action. Stated another way, if a firm's competitor is using engineering labor from India or China at one-third (often one-fourth) the cost of their homeland labor, then the firm will be forced to do the same or they will be unable to compete. It's important that companies not move too quickly since salaries and wages for jobs in high demand in these countries are growing at astonishing rates—20% and above per year. Now, many of you are saying that "cost" is not the only way to compete, and I agree. However, when quality, service, functionality, and delivery are approximately the same for offshore and on-shore products and services, then a firm most likely will not be able to compete profitably and win customer orders when their competitor is using the "cheap labor" found in the "flat world." We will walk through this scenario in detail in a later chapter titled "The Cost of Labor is Four Times Greater Than in China and India—Now What?" Therefore, I'll end here with the "cheap labor" scenario and offer that firms don't set out to "give" homeland jobs to under-developed countries. Nor do developing countries set out to take jobs from those in developed nations who are earning a "fair" wage and enjoying a higher standard of living. It's all about competition, cost-based pricing, and supply and demand.

- Don't forget that developing countries with "cheap labor," who are exporting products and services at cheaper prices than other countries, also have consumers who are very interested in purchasing goods and services not available in their local economy. These developing countries, namely China, India, and Eastern European nations, represent huge opportunities for firms to sell their goods and services. For example, China, with its 1.3 billion people (based on their 2004 census), is expected to become the world's largest economy by the middle of this century. And, India with its 1.1 billion people will not be far behind (Prestowitz, 2005). In fact, many companies who are facing mature markets in their homeland environment are looking to the "east" for survival, growth, and profitability. However, to take advantage of these opportunities, a firm might just have to follow the Microsoft, Intel, GE, and CISCO globalization models discussed earlier. That is, a firm will need to go there and establish a base of operations with a local cost structure that will allow the firm to sell its products and services competitively. For example, in the Microsoft investment case described above, Microsoft is establishing a research, development, and support services center in India to provide products and services to individual consumers and organizations in that country. This center will also provide services to other countries, including the U.S., which is the home base for Microsoft. In other words, Microsoft intends to be on-site in India and supply some of the 5 million PC's that consumers in India will purchase in 2006 (Semico, 2006). Consumers in India are projected to purchase 70 million wireless cell phones and 4 million DVD players. The numbers are even more staggering for China consumers. Finally, U.S. manufacturers simply can't produce PC's and other equipment solely in the U.S. and then expect to sell these products in India (China or elsewhere) when the average manufacturing job pays $20.00 per hour in the U.S, and about $1.00 per hour in India and China. It just won't work!

For companies to survive, they will need to create new products and services, and source labor and materials from the supply chains that provide the best competitive advantage. Perhaps you will recall in the "Introduction" section of this book, I remarked that: "at this point, it is a given that much of the world's manufacturing output has moved to China—perhaps unavoidably (perhaps even rightly) so." Much of the world has been converted to capitalism, and that's exactly what capitalism is all about—competition and balancing resources to drive prices to their lowest level of sustainability.

The "Big Three."

Since I have been and will continue to talk a lot about China, India, and the United States in this book, I believe some comparisons are in order to help get a perspective on the relationships among the three (Source: Pocket World in Figures, published 2006; in U.S. dollars; numbers are from 2004 and 2005 data).

	China	India	U.S.
Population	1.3 bil.	1.1 bil.	300 mil.
% population below poverty	12%	25%	n/a
World ranking – purchasing power	#2	#4	#1
Gross Domestic Product (GDP)	$1.4 trillion	$600 bil.	$11 tril.
GDP per capita	$1,090	$560	$37,240
GDP growth rate	9.0%	6.5%	3.3%
GDP coming from services	33%	51%	81%
GDP coming from agriculture	15%	22%	1%
GDP coming from manufacturing	39%	16%	13%
% people employed in services	29%	23%	76%
% people employed in agriculture	49%	60%	1%
% people employed in industry	22%	17%	23%
% unemployment	4.0%	11.6%	6.0%
Annual Salary – Programmer	$13,400	$10,300	$70,000
Education spending % of GDP	2.1%	4.1%	5.7%
Adult literacy	91%	62%	99%
Services output	$455 bil.	$285 bil.	$8.6 tril.
World ranking – energy usage	#2	#4	#1
Number cars per 1,000 people	6	7	481
World ranking – regular army	#1	#3	#2

The *"% of population below poverty"* data given above is based on the number of people in the country living on $1.00 per person or less per day. This is the global standard the World Bank uses to measure and track poverty levels in the world. China has about 150 million people and India about 275 million living on $1.00 or less per day. China's and India's economies are growing at 2½ to 3 times as fast as the United States, but they have a long way to go to reach the $11 trillion *GDP (Gross Domestic Product)* level the U.S. is currently experiencing. GDP is the total market value of all final goods and services produced in a country in a given year. Technically, it represents the sum of consumer spending plus business and residential investment, plus government spending, and plus or minus the trade excess or trade deficit for the country. Another significant indicator that is being impacted by globalization includes the percentages of *people employed in manufacturing and services.* Clearly, China has high percentages of their population working in manufacturing (39%) and agriculture (49%). India has a very high percentage of their population still on farms (60%). The U.S. has 76% of its work force in service jobs. India is growing significantly in service jobs, and is becoming known as a major service center, just as China is known as a major manufacturing center in the world. The statistic that really gets everyone's attention, though, is the sample of wages shown for a *programming* job, where the U.S. is about 5 times higher than China, and 7 times that of India. The *number of cars per 1,000 people*, which is also an interesting statistic, shows that India and China have the potential for significant growth. India and China have 7 and 6 cars per thousand people in their populations, respectively, while the U.S. has 481 cars for every 1,000 people. This is why automakers around the world are flocking to their doorsteps. We'll be discussing most of these statistics in this book, except the one about the *"world ranking—regular army,"* although I did find it "very interesting"—if that is the right word for it. If you include army reserves, the small country of North Korea is #1 in the world in terms of the size of its Army. South Korea is #2, China is #5, India is #7, and the U.S. is #6. It is interesting that some of the largest armies are in such small countries. These small countries are generally poor developing nations that reside on the fringes of globalization.

FedEx—A model for globalization.

FedEx is a great example of a company that embraces globalization and operates effectively in the new global economy. Its operations, headquartered in Memphis, Tennessee, U.S.A., span the world to deliver packages, freight, and mail. I know well the airport where its operations are based, having made the mistake on a business trip of staying at a hotel that bordered the runways used by FedEx to take off and land its aircraft. At about midnight, planes began taking off for all parts of the world. The flights continued all night and into the morning. It seems that globalization arrived at the Memphis airport some years ago when FedEx made it their home base. Today, the airport is the world's busiest in terms of "cargo," followed by Hong Kong and Tokyo (Infoplease, 2004).

FedEx has been doing business globally for 20+ years, including China and India which are the countries the firm now looks to for significant growth in coming years. In the past six months, FedEx has initiated direct flights between Shanghai and Japan, and opened a new central China headquarters in Wuhan, China. In addition, the Company has begun construction of a giant hub in Guangzhou, China, opened 5 branches in southern China, and started the first express delivery service between China and India. At the end of 2005, FedEx had a total of 26 air routes in China (Fisher, 2006). Fred Smith, Chairman and CEO, indicated in *Fortune Magazine* that the company had been in China for 22 years and had "developed deep relationships over the years" (Fisher, 2006). In fact, it is widely recognized that Chinese culture dictates the development of long-term relationships as a prerequisite to doing business successfully in China. (Helpful guidelines for building personal and commercial relationships in China can be found in the "Recommended Action Items" at the end of this chapter.) FedEx is currently the number one package and document transporter between the U.S. and China with a 39% market share for this type service. UPS (United Parcel Service) is number two with a 32% market share and DHL is number three with 27%. Globalization, along with Internet shopping around the world, has driven a booming business for these carriers' services.

In early 2004, FedEx took an innovative step into the printing business and bought Kinko's for $2.4 billion. This move provided FedEx with needed pickup and delivery points. With 1200 FedEx-Kinko's locations around the world in such places as Canada, China, Japan, Korea, Australia, Europe, Mexico, India, the U.K., the Middle East, and North America, FedEx has become a major player in printing services, in addition to its package, freight, and mail delivery services. The printing industry is the largest industry in the U.S. as measured by the number of production locations (39,000). Being apart of this industry gives FedEx-Kinko's greater access to local consumers and small and medium-sized business customers who need both printing and delivery services (Oppenheimer, 2006). As you are probably aware, the huge printing industry of the 21st century came about as a result of Johann Gutenberg's invention of the printing press in the 1450's (Oppenheimer, 2006). Today, the industry is being reshaped by such organizations as FedEx-Kinko's and The UPS Store—along with the Internet, of course. UPS Stores are a combination of UPS (United Parcel Service) and Mail Boxes Etc., much like FedEx and Kinko's. On a worldwide basis, the number of UPS Stores actually exceeds FedEx-Kinko's locations (UPS, 2006).

In addition, FedEx-Kinko's also offers Internet access and computer usage services, videoconferencing, and WiFi (wireless fidelity) services in its centers—many of which are open 24 hours a day, 7 days a week. Finally, FedEx and its Kinko's locations have agreements with the world's fourth largest employer, the U.S. Postal Service, for print and global delivery services (Oppenheimer, 2006).

FedEx is truly a global "new-age innovation" company!

UPS (United Parcel Service—great global company and barometer for globalization.

One needs only look at the investments global freight and "small package" carriers are making in facilities to handle higher volumes of global trade to know that globalization is upon us and here to stay. I could simply say that I believe FedEx, UPS, and DHL are among the best "barometers" of globalization's progress we have at our disposal. As Mike Eskew, UPS' chairman and CEO, states it: "We anticipate strong growth in global trade to continue for years to come. Expanding the centerpiece ("Louisville Worldport") of our worldwide infrastructure is absolutely necessary to support the long-term needs of our customers." (UPS Sets $1 Billion+, 2006.) UPS, the world's largest package delivery company and a global leader in supply chain services, is currently in the midst of a major expansion at its air shipping hub in Louisville, Kentucky (USA). This expansion will add 5,000 employees and create an "airline-based" shipping center the size of 113 football fields, with 197 miles of "new-age innovation" conveying systems (UPS Sets $1 Billion+, 2006). Since January of 2005, UPS has announced plans to begin operating an air hub in China by 2007, significantly expanded the capacity of its intra-Asia air hub in the Philippines, and completed the expansion of its European air hub in Cologne/Bonn, Germany—doubling that facility's sort capacity. By the way, UPS Airlines is currently the 9th largest airline in the world, with 2000 flights daily to over 200 countries and territories (UPS Sets $1 Billion+, 2006).

In addition to being an indicator and "barometer" of globalization's march across the world, UPS' actions also support two other points that I touch on again and again in this book. The first point is the fact that the globalization process is creating jobs around the world. It is not driving outsourcing/offshoring to eliminate jobs and create unemployment, as we read far too often in the media. This condition may, in fact, occur in isolated locations and within some industries, but, from a worldwide perspective, the globalization process we are in the midst of today is driving growth and development around the world. This growth, of course, is not limited to the package and freight delivery industry, but reaches all industries; many of which we'll discuss in this book.

The second point relates to education, which we'll be discussing in Chapter 4, "Education—The Great Equalizer (Actually the Most Important Chapter!)." Adding 5,000 people to UPS' "Worldport" to support their growth initiatives, will require a monumental employment, training, and coordination effort between the company and the communities from which employees will be drawn. We'll be discussing (in the "Education" chapter) the need for employers to take on a more collaborative posture with colleges, universities, technical schools, and specialized governmental educational programs in order to obtain and maintain an educated workforce. In this regard, many of the 5,000 new workers will be eligible for the Metropolitan College program. This program, which is jointly funded by UPS and the state of Kentucky, pays for the higher education of employees.

UPS certainly exemplifies a great global company and the many aspects of globalization at work in today's new global economy and community.

The Globalization of Stock Exchanges.

I know, this topic sounds more like a book title; maybe even a novel. On March 10, 2006, NASDAQ Stock Market Inc., which is the new name for the now publicly traded NASDAQ Stock Exchange, made an unsolicited $4.2 billion (U.S. dollars) bid to purchase the London Stock Exchange. Papers around the world reported it, but there was not much fanfare. The London Stock Exchange, of course, declined. I say "of course" because I'm guessing it was an insult—not just from a value standpoint but from a cultural perspective. I'm trying to visualize what it must have been like when the Exchange's board of directors opened the surprise bid. I'll bet they said: "Damn Yankees!" The London Stock Exchange is a 205 year old English institution, steeped in tradition and heritage, and tied integrally to the British Empire, where "the sun never sets on the London Stock Market" (Weber, 2006).

This event, I believe, marks the "opening pitch" for the "globalization games" for stock exchanges. Globalization has the world's stock exchanges in its sights as takeover targets! And, at this point, the "globalization games" seem to be off to a good start. Just as globalization has swept other industries into a global economic mode, it will do the same to the world's stock exchanges.

I was surprised to learn that there are in excess of 100 "Stock Exchanges" around the world (Stock Exchanges, 2006). I believe this means opportunities for globalization, combinations, consolidations, and interconnectedness. In the U.S., it's called "mergers and acquisitions." Can you envision the day of multinational stock exchanges? Or, stock exchanges functioning as conglomerates that operate all over the world? I wonder who the GE (General Electric) or Wal-Mart of stock exchanges will be. The U.S. NASDAQ and NYSE both have their sights set on the London Stock Exchange (LSE) as a potential takeover target. Wonder what's next? This is globalization at work in an open "boundary-less" world and global economy. I did not ever think that globalization would move this fast and reach the stock markets so quickly.

At last count (March, 2006), there were 102 exchanges around the globe distributed by region as follows: *(shown are region and number of exchanges)*

African Exchanges – 3

Asian Exchanges – 25

European Exchanges – 34

Middle Eastern Exchanges – 5

North American – 20

South American – 15

In Africa, perhaps the most well known is the Johannesburg Stock Exchange (South Africa). In the Asian region, there are the Australian, Hong Kong, Bombay, Tokyo, Indonesia, Korea, Singapore, Taiwan, and Thailand exchanges, to name a few. In Europe, the Paris, London, Frankfurt, Italian, Stockholm, Swiss, Barcelona, Warsaw, and EASDAQ (Belgium) exchanges stand out. In the Middle East, there are the well known Tel Aviv (Israel), Beirut (Lebanon), and Istanbul (Turkey) exchanges. In North America, Canada has the Toronto, Montreal, and Vancouver exchanges. The United States has the New York, American, NASDAQ, Chicago, and Philadelphia exchanges. Mexico has a stock exchange, as does Brazil, Venezuela, Jamaica, Ecuador, Colombia, and Trinidad. The tiny country of Croatia also has a stock exchange, as does Sri Lanka and the Cayman Islands (Stock Exchanges, 2006).

Actual merger and acquisition activity in the stock exchange arena has already started to show up in the U.S. The New York Stock Exchange (NYSE) and Archipelago Holdings,

Inc. (Arca) recently merged. Prior to merging with the NYSE, Archipelago purchased the Pacific Stock Exchange. Now, the merged organizations have their sights on Europe and other regions of the world as they make a run at being a global powerhouse for investments and stock trading. (Weber, 2006—March 6) Interestingly, the NASDQ, the Chicago Mercantile Exchange, and now the New York Stock Exchange have all gone public with an initial public offering (IPO) of their stock. Each now trades as a public company similar to the companies they list on their exchanges. I would suppose that they now have the cash to start looking globally for merger and acquisition activity. Other exchanges in North America that have successfully completed IPO's and are now trading as public companies, include the Toronto Exchange, the Chicago Board of Trade, and the International Securities Exchange (Weber, 2006). The International Securities Exchange (ISE) is the world's largest "options" trading exchange and calls the United States home. All ISE trades are executed electronically. All of these exchanges that have gone public seem to be doing quite well—at least at this point in their stock trading histories.

Looking ahead, it seems evident that we will soon be able to trade global stocks, bonds, futures, and other securities through a single multinational stock exchange conglomerate. When buying or selling a stock, it might even be transparent as to where the stock transaction is taking place and which exchange in the global network is involved. Today, for example, only a few foreign companies are traded on the New York Stock Exchange. These trades are accomplished under special trading rules and regulations. Investors can buy and sell these foreign stocks through the American Depository Receipts (ADR) system. Some examples of my favorite ADR traded foreign stocks are: Teva Pharmaceutical (Israel), Matsushita Electric (Japan), Taiwan Semiconductor (Taiwan), BHP Billiton (U.K.), WIPRO, Ltd (India), and Siemens (Germany). As globalization progresses with the stock exchanges, I would guess that we'll soon be able to buy stocks from around the world a lot easier than this outdated ADR system in use today. Finally, it appears that nearly all trades of the future will be digital (many already are), as new-age innovative electronic trading networks take over what people once did physically on a stock exchange floor.

Money makes the world go around, as the old saying goes. To this point, the globalization of stock exchanges means the further globalization of the world's capital (money) markets, which will drive global economies and new-age innovation. This is a positive trend for both developed <u>and</u> developing nations.

Wonder what kinds of global combinations we'll be seeing next in the world of securities trading? Wonder what else is lurking? If you haven't already figured it out, we're in for a ride! We're in the globalization and new-age innovation era! Whatever happens, I simply hope it will help us novices pick more winning stocks in the future than we've picked in the past.

****

I will close this chapter on the day I'm reading my tax return, which was in fact prepared in India. Yesterday, I had my car serviced and the diagnostics were translated at some offshore location and sent back digitally to the repair shop. And, I'm getting ready to call for online computer assistance which may come from southern Alabama, Hong Kong, Bangalore, or who knows where. Like some whisky lullaby in steamy Guangzhou, China, or Biloxi, Mississippi (USA), globalization and new-age innovation are moving at intoxicatingly fast paces!!! We're all on the road to the airport or on the Internet when it comes to globalization and "new-age innovation!"

Recommended Action Items:

1. Communicate clearly to all employees and stakeholders in your organization exactly what globalization means, and how it will impact your organization's ability to compete in the market and industry environment in which you operate.

2. Embrace and leverage globalization to maximize product and service profitability, even if it means the outsourcing/offshoring of jobs.

3. Look to the east (China, India, Eastern Europe) for major opportunities. See the developing nations around the world not only as suppliers of "cheap labor," but also as buyers of your products and services. According to the Department of Commerce, the following products and services are in greatest demand in these areas of the world. Do you see any your organization can supply?

   Airport and Ground Support Equipment
   Agro Chemicals
   Auto Components
   Aircraft Components
   Coal Mining Equipment
   Computers and peripherals
   Commodities such as Minerals, Agriculture, Scrap
   Construction Equipment
   Cosmetics and Toiletries
   Education and Training Products & Services
   Environmental Protection Equipment
   Pollution Control Equipment
   Financial Services
   Franchising – Food and Beverages
   Integrated Circuits & Semiconductors
   Machine Tools

Medical Equipment

Nuclear Power Equipment & Facilities

Oil and Gas Exploration & Processing Equipment

Retail Facilities

Software

Telecommunications Hardware & Software

If you are uncertain about which countries have the ability to buy, then here are the world's top twenty largest economies based on their "purchasing power" (Pocket World in Figures, 2006). Do you see countries that your organization can target for growth and profitability?

1) United States
2) China
3) Japan
4) India
5) Germany
6) France
7) United Kingdom
8) Italy
9) Brazil
10) Russia
11) Canada
12) Mexico
13) Spain
14) South Korea
15) Indonesia
16) Australia
17) Taiwan
18) Turkey
19) Netherlands
20) South Africa

4. Look to certain developing nations around the world as sources of collaborative research and development when introducing new products and services, or maintaining old ones. You might start with India, where many firms are today successfully sourcing these activities.

5. Know and understand the economy, markets, and business climate in the regions and countries targeted for global business. Don't lose sight of the fact that as the world seems to be growing smaller—at least in terms of our ability to communicate—the challenges of doing business in a global economy far surpass that of doing business

locally. The rule of "no pain, no gain" is quite applicable in this regard. I have personal experience that might lend some credibility to this statement. To this point, business is difficult to conduct in China, India, and the countries of Eastern Europe, but, at the same time, can be areas of great profitability. In reference to the table below, for example, China ranks number 126 out of 155 in the World Bank's rankings of "ease of starting business." In terms of "ease of doing business" China ranks 91 out of 155. India isn't much better and ranks 90 out of 155 countries in terms of "ease of starting business," and 116 out of 155 in terms of "ease of doing business."

The top ten countries, as ranked by the World Bank, in terms of "ease of starting business" and "ease of doing business" are as follows:

Ease of Starting Business		Ease of Doing Business	
#1	Canada	#1	New Zealand
#2	Australia	#2	Singapore
#3	United States	#3	United States
#4	New Zealand	#4	Canada
#5	Singapore	#5	Norway
#6	Hong Kong	#6	Australia
#7	Puerto Rico	#7	Hong Kong
#8	Romania	#8	Denmark
#9	United Kingdom	#9	United Kingdom
#10	Jamaica	#10	Japan

With regard to securing licenses and charters to do business in some of these countries, the word "nightmare" readily comes to mind. The same applies when it comes to the "enforcement of commercial contracts." According to the World Bank, India ranks 138 out of 155 countries, and China ranks 47. The western world's concept of binding commercial contracts is simply not the same as that of China and India. Quite often, the signing of a contract is merely the signal for additional negotiations to begin.

Check out these and other rankings on the World Bank's website. The link to this site can be found in the "*Notes and References*" section at the end of this book.

6. For organizations preparing to do business in China as well as other countries in the global economy, it is imperative to pay close attention to what is called the cultural aspects of doing business in a country. This is especially critical when it comes to China and is often an area that many companies overlook. Personal relationships, which are referred to in the Chinese language as "*Guanxi*," still rule the business environment today, although some practices are changing due to interaction and trade with others in the world. The "*Guanxi*" process is comprised of the following elements that must be adhered to when planning a successful business venture in China: (Graham & Lam, 2004)

    - *Personal connections* with potential customers and other business personnel require an intermediary. The intermediary is the one who makes contact with the potential customer on your behalf and plays the role of introducing and getting the parties together.

    - *Social status* is always adhered to in business relationships. Individuals of equal status must meet when negotiating business deals. For example, you would not send a 30-year-old salesperson to meet with senior bank or business executives.

    - *Interpersonal harmony* is always observed. That is, business cannot be conducted until the parties involved have reached a level of trust and familiarity with each other. This can be a long process, so don't be in a hurry.

- *Holistic thinking* dominates the negotiation style of Chinese business deals. Generally, the negotiation party representing a potential customer will want to cover all aspects of the business transaction at once; not in pieces and not in a sequential manner. "Nothing is settled until everything is settled" (Graham & Lam, 2004).
- *Thrift* is always on the minds of Chinese personnel negotiating for a business arrangement. Saving money personally or on goods and services purchased by a Chinese firm is always an important part of the negotiation process. This cultural aspect of doing business is thought to come from China's history of being a poor agricultural nation for many years.
- *Dignity, prestige, and respect* are always adhered to in the negotiation process and on-going business relationships, even in times of conflict. The use of questions is often the manner in which respectful disagreement takes place.
- *Work ethic* is very important in the Chinese culture and, often, negotiations can go on for weeks. Covering all aspects of a business deal in detail seems to be an expression of a good work ethic and desire to obtain the best products and services at the best price.

The bottom line is: be patient, don't think in terms of U.S. style, often high-energy and high-pressure negotiations. Signing a contract means more than a business deal. It is also a personal relationship.

7. When negotiating contracts in China, do some homework prior to the first negotiating session and know at least the

following three items about the leader of the Chinese negotiating team. First, know the age of the leader; second, know where he/she was born in China. Third, know when and where the leader went to school. This information will help you understand the frame of reference of the negotiator. Also, this information will help in the process of building a long-term personal relationship with a customer or potential customer, which is the cornerstone of doing business in China. Don't expect to be negotiating with someone who thinks like "westerners." No other culture places such high emphasis on personal relationships, patience, and respect for individuals and families as China, especially when it comes to working with others from around the world in a commercial environment.

8. Leverage globalization by taking a hard look at your organization's core competencies. Analyze the functions in your company that aren't directly involved in these competencies, and consider whether global outsourcing/offshoring and the Internet can enable you to spin off these tasks. Then, as Bill Gates of Microsoft says: "Let another company take over the responsibilities for this non-core work, and use modern communication technology to work closely with the people—now partners instead of employees—who are doing the work. In the 'Web work style,' employees can push the freedom the Web provides to its limits" (Gates, 1999).

Hopefully, the process of globalization can ultimately be defined by the commonalities and interdependences among individuals, businesses, and nations—rather than in terms of their differences.

Phil Watlington, Author "The World Is At Your Door!"
Lead Faculty and Area Chair, Financial Planning and Control,
University of Phoenix

Chapter 2

Artistic and Creative Visions for Innovative Organizations

"Creativity and imagination, applied in a business context, lead to innovation."

Jeffery Immelt—Chairman and CEO, General Electric Company

Chapter 1 dealt with *globalization.* This chapter deals with *innovation* and its rebirth into what I now call "*new-age innovation.*" For those who can embrace and competitively leverage (efficiently utilize) creativity, imagination, and innovation—astonishing new wealth can be realized.

A bit of history!

It is hard to look at creativity, innovation, and globalization without running into China and India as two of the world's greatest civilizations, greatest innovators, and largest economies. You might have forgotten—as I did—until my wife, whom I consider a rather astute historian, reminded me that, until the late 19th century, China and India were the world's largest economies and major centers for "inventiveness." The rest of the world was "emerging." Now, the tables have turned a bit. Today, China and India are considered two of the largest "emerging" nations, with about 2.4 billion people between them and economies that are growing at extraordinary yearly rates of 7%–10%. (The U.S. has just 300 million people.) Meanwhile, most of the so-called "developed nations" of the world are growing at 3%–4%, as measured in terms of annual GDP (Gross Domestic Product) growth (Pocket World In Figures, 2006). Many see part of the globalization process that is taking place today as India and China regaining their "historic place," once again, as the center of the world (Prestowitz, 2005).

There isn't time here to trace the history of how this role reversal happened, but the Industrial Revolution in Europe and America, the rise of communism, two world wars, and closed borders all played a role in the decline of these countries. If I recall history correctly, China's four great inventions which live on today are: (1) the compass; (2) gunpowder; (3) paper & ink, and (4) printing. Others include the cargo ship, iron castings, the blast furnace, kites, the wheelbarrow, fans, silk, bombs for war, the abacus, and acupuncture. India's contributions include the binary number system, planned cities, celestial calculations, and creation of the number "zero," to name just a few. Both China and India each played major roles in globalization long ago when Marco Polo opened trade with China and other regions along the "Silk Road" from Venice. At about the same time, India became a major trading partner with the East India Company from the Netherlands.

Today, the march of technology and knowledge continues as the information age gives rise to creative economies and "new-age innovation." Many believe, as I do, that history will reflect the late 19th and first half of the 20th century as an industrial period where men and women functioned as machines of production (the age of assembly lines). Since that period, and continuing today, the process has reversed and the search is on for how to make machines function like people; with thought processes and decision-making abilities. This is really what "new-age innovation" is all about. Have you talked to a computer today? I have, several times, as I made some reservations and got information to fix my computer.

Renaissance: twenty-first century style.

Before we place history in our rear view mirror, I'd like to bring to light some interesting similarities (as I see them) between the Renaissance period of the 14th through 16th centuries and today's globalization and innovation of the 21st century. No other periods in history reveal such similarities. I almost missed them in my research since I associate, as many do, the Renaissance period in history with art and architecture. The "tools" that helped usher in the Renaissance period were the magnetic compass, more accurate maps by Portuguese cartographers, the printing press to produce books, and the astrolabe (a navigational aid that uses the stars to help sailors find their way on the seas for trade with other nations) (Annenberg, 2006). The main "tools" that ushered in and continue to enable globalization and new-age innovation in today's world are the Internet and "www."

The free online encyclopedia, Wikipedia, describes the Renaissance period as the "reconnection of the west with classical antiquity, the absorption of knowledge—particularly mathematics—from Arabic, the return of experimentalism, a focus on the importance of living well in the present (e.g. Renaissance humanism), and an explosion in the dissemination of knowledge brought on by printing and the creation of new techniques in art, poetry, and architecture. This period represents Europe emerging from a long period as a backwater, and the rise of commerce and exploration" (Wikipedia, 2006). Can you spot some similarities between then and now? For example: the "explosion in the dissemination of knowledge"—then by printing from Gutenberg's invention of the printing press in 1445 and today by the Internet and "www." Another similarity might be found in the "rise of commerce," which then included searches for trade routes to the East, while today's search is for world trade opportunities in the new Internet driven global economy. Lastly, a connection can be seen in the "return of experimentalism"—then with new ways of thinking that laid the foundation for modern science, and today with "new-age innovation" that encompasses the development of products, services, processes, and knowledge.

You might be asking: where do the "new techniques in art, poetry and architecture" of the Renaissance period fit in with today's globalization and innovation? I believe the quote at the beginning of this chapter answers the question: "creativity and imagination, applied in a business context, lead to innovation" (Immelt, 2005). Today, we are moving beyond, but not abandoning, traditional research and development methodologies. Previously, the focus was on laboratory-based research and development, while today's focus is on creative and imaginative new products and services and innovative supply chains for their delivery. Two companies, U.S.-based Proctor & Gamble and The General Electric Company, exemplify new-age innovators and likenesses to the artistic, creative, and scientific collaboration of the Renaissance period. We'll talk in more detail about these companies and their creativity and imagination later in this chapter.

New-age Innovation.

"Innovation" is the creation, development, and implementation of a new product, service, or process, with the aim of improving efficiency, effectiveness, or competitive advantage. Innovation may apply to products, services, manufacturing processes, managerial processes, or the design of an organization. It is most often viewed at a product or process level, where product innovation satisfies a customer's needs and process innovation improves efficiency and effectiveness" (Digital Strategy, 2005). Put simply, "new-age innovation" is the renewed interest and expansion of globally-focused applications of human intellectual capital (knowledge) to create, develop, and implement new products, services and processes. Globalization is demanding (driving) this innovation, and the Internet and World Wide Web are the great enablers of the process. One need only sign on to the Internet and perform a simple "Google Search" to confirm that the world's information is at your fingertips. We're all close neighbors, in the new "global village," competing for the world's scarce resources and becoming ever-more dependent on others we may or may not ever see. How we use and misuse these tools remains to be seen. On some days, this "flat world" is just plain scary to me. What about you? Today, as I worked at my job with one of the world's largest and most admired companies, The General Electric Company, someone somewhere in the world had somehow gotten a "virus" past our firewalls and security and brought most of the company's global PC-based communications network to a crawl. Scary stuff!

The 21st century Renaissance of inventiveness and creativity.

The worldwide rebirth of innovation that we are seeing today is, to a large extent, in response to globalization and the leveling of the world's economic competitive playing fields. Here are a few of the recent "new-age innovations" that exemplify this response, as many individuals, organizations, and entire nations struggle to survive and gain a competitive advantage in the new global economy:

YESTERDAY	TODAY / TOMORROW
Routine Periodic Maintenance on aircraft engines	Real-time continuous monitoring of engines to detect problems and initiate corrected action as quickly as possible *(Rolls Royce, PLC – United Kingdom)*
Battery operated hearing aids	Implanted "hearing devices" that transmit sound waves to the human brain for translation *(Cochleur, LTD – Australia)*
Watching a prime time TV show at home on TV	Watching the same show on your Apple Video iPod (anywhere) on a pay per view basis *(Apple Computers – U.S.)*
Studying about China and Chinese culture from a "World History" textbook	Learning the Chinese language and preparing teachers to teach these subjects through the University of Kansas' *Confucius Institute*. The Institute is being established as a collaborative effort between the *University of Kansas and China's Ministry of Education*. China is the third largest buyer of Kansas products. The State of Kansas also has a trade office in Beijing.
Front & Side Auto Airbags	Air bags, radar, night vision, automatic braking to assist drivers in avoiding accidents *(Honda and Toyota Motor Co.'s – Japan)*
Paper highway maps for auto travelers	Portable electronic navigational units covering all of North America, in 30 languages *(Garmin, Inc.)*

YESTERDAY	**TODAY / TOMORROW**
Software licensed for each personal computer	Software Live, where anyone can access and use software free; paid for by advertising
Building elevators, raised and lowered by cables	Elevators raised and lowered by magnetic levitational force *(Japan)*
Disneyland: Orlando, Fla.; Hong Kong; Los Angeles	Disney online theme park, where children can visit a park online
Local centralized manufacturing/service organization	Global, functionally distributed *virtual organization* with a cost-effective and efficient supply chain
Filling up your auto with *gasoline* refined from oil from the *Mideast*, (*Saudi Arabia*)	Filling up your auto with *Ethanol* refined from "bio farm products" such as corn and soybeans from the *Midwest* *(United States)*
On-site "order taking" at drive-thru window at fast food restaurant	Outsourced "order taking" from distant location.
Study of China on-site at University of Missouri, Kansas City	University opens office in Beijing, China for collaborative learning, and real life communication of Chinese Culture and business
Hard copy books	On-line "E-Books" and "Digital Books" that can be to read on an Apple iPod or Sony Reader
Conservatism	Risk taking
Owning a car and finding a parking place	Car sharing—using a car only when needed (*Zip-Car & Flexcar Services*); Using your cell phone to find, locate, and reserve a parking space ahead of time. *(SpotScout, Inc.)*

YESTERDAY	TODAY / TOMORROW
Conventional fuel vehicles	Flex-fuel vehicles that can burn any mixture of ethanol or conventional fuels
Wheeled trains on tracks	Magnetic levitation train. (*China* is currently building a second one)
Tailored accident insurance policies	Terrorism death insurance policies (*Iraq*)
Selling via direct mail, telemarketing, E-Mail	Selling via eBay online store. Entrepreneurial web-based auctions for all kinds of personal and business products and services
Teleconferencing or direct telephone calls	Internet phone links
Home radio	Sirius 24/7 Satellite Radio. Do you listen to Martha Stewart on Channel 112?
Ford or GM automobiles and SUV's (Sport Utility Vehicles)	Advanced fuel technology; Micro Cars & Vehicles; Smart Cars; Electric City Cars (*DaimlerChrysler; ZAP Co.)*
Standalone health care; medical clinics	*RediClinics* in *Wal-Mart Superstores* staffed with nurse practitioners. Could this be the answer to the delivery of healthcare to a large number of people who otherwise might not have access to care? Other firms will, no doubt, also adopt this delivery method.

YESTERDAY	TODAY / TOMORROW
Personal Computers and software for the masses	PC's and software for seniors and others with specific needs (*SSPDirect.Com)*
Robotic equipment that builds cars	Robots that reside with and assist people with disabilities, or assist the elderly. *(MIT's Media Lab)*
Military delivery vehicle driven by a person	Driverless vehicle (not remote controlled) with computer "brain" and sensors." Under development by *Defense Advanced Research Projects Agency* and *Stanford University*. Test model already operating in a simulated military supply mission environment. Civilian uses also under review. Remember our discussions on computers that simulate human thought processes? This is an example of a computer driven vehicle. Next tests will be in a city environment. Computers may be better drivers than humans!
Separate high school and junior college	Combined high school and junior college program allowing junior and senior high school students to graduate simultaneously from high school and junior college with an Associate of Arts degree. (See Chapter 4; "Education—The Great Equalizer.")

YESTERDAY	TODAY / TOMORROW
Large technology items	Small "nanotechnology" inventions. This is technology that deals with combining and realigning particles in nanometers (one-billionith of a meter) to produce new and exotic materials, chemicals, and mini-machines. The global spread of nanotechnology "will make the computer revolution look like small change" (Kahn, 2006). And, with regard to the engineering of new materials, "Nano's going to be like the invention of plastic" (Kahn, 2006). The National Science Foundation predicts the global market for nanotechnology products to reach one trillion dollars by 2015. Examples of uses of nanotechnology include identifying and fighting cancer cells, cheaper solar panels, reattaching veins after surgery, fire-resistant glass, computer storage devices, filtering devices, and windows that never need washing. (Kahn, 2006)
Driver parallel parking	Computer that parallel parks your car for you. Volvo and Toyota now have cars that will parallel park themselves. Four ultra sonic sensors scan the desired space and a computer calculates if parking is feasible. The computer, after directing the driver to release the steering wheel, then parks the car. *(AutoBlog, 2006)*

This "short" list of "new-age innovations" certainly reveals that creativity, imagination, and visionary thinking have pushed innovation well beyond traditional research and development. I find it hard to look at the list and come up with any conclusion other than a bright future for individuals, organizations, and nations who embrace "new-age innovation." Economically, there are fortunes to be made—fortunes sufficient to sustain the global economy and community. Who makes them depends on you and how you leverage (efficiently and effectively utilize) globalization and "new-age innovation."

More importantly, as I gathered the information for this "short list," my purpose was to find more than just new innovative products and services. It was to zero in on "new-age" innovative processes that encompass creative business models, technologies, strategies, and just plain common sense approaches for the development and delivery of products and services. I believe that this new way of thinking about innovation was exactly what IBM's CEO, Samuel J. Palmisano, had in mind when he told the attendees at one of IBM's 2006 leadership forums: "the way you will thrive in this environment is by innovating—innovating in technologies, innovating in strategies, innovating in business models. And, today's innovation is about a lot more than just new products and services. It is about reinventing business processes and building entirely new markets that meet untapped customer needs" (Worlds Most Innovative, 2006). This sounds like a good description of "new-age innovation," which will surely play a crucial role in dealing with globalization and the new "world" economy. By the way, IBM is one of the world's most innovative computer technology and business process services companies. According to the U.S. Patent Office, it currently holds 40,000 patented new ideas, which is more than any other company, individual or organization in the world.

Bruce Nussbaum, in his August 2005 *Business Week* Special Report, "How To Build Innovative Companies," says that this new wave of innovation is starting to drive many countries with a "Knowledge Based Economy," toward a "Creativity Economy" (Nussbaum, 2005). Proctor & Gambles' CEO, A.G. Lafley, describes the new form of innovation as "trying to identify consumer-product needs that consumers haven't identified themselves" (Nussbaum, 2005). This new-age of innovation and its nomenclature of creativity and imagination are more than "buzzwords" of our day. Creativity and imagination have substance and reality in creating value out of new ideas. They offer many opportunities to participate successfully and gain competitive advantages in the new globalized world economy. We must continue to push innovation beyond its laboratory style R&D (research and development) modality and into the processes, strategies, and business models that can drive an organization's success in the new intensely competitive global economy. So I say to you, don't just think laboratory style R&D innovation; think in terms of broad-based "new-age innovation" that encompasses every aspect of an organization's operations and processes. And, don't just think locally—which has been the conventional wisdom far too long. Think globally. *The World Is At Your Door*! It is a door to your future.

Beware of "romantic notions."

When I speak of globalization as a "driver" for individuals, organizations, and nations to become more creative and innovative, I am not advocating that, by doing so, success and a secure future will therefore follow. In fact, the "Western World" does not have a "corner" on innovation and creativity. There are plenty of new ideas waiting to be explored by anyone who will venture into the land of imagination and creativity. The rewards from these ventures will be sufficient for everyone to share. One will not have to win at the expense of another! Creativity, imagination, and innovation will secure many of the future needs for us all (Rieke, 2005). I believe that Mr. Roger Martin, Dean of the School of Management at the University of Toronto, has stated the issue much better than I. In *Business Week's* January 2006 "Ideas & Viewpoint" column, Mr. Martin says "there is a romantic notion among North American businesses that their futures lie in design and innovation, while India and China will be the home of less skilled, lower-paying operations churning out the products and services the U.S. (and other developed countries) come up with" (Martin, 2006). He goes on to state that innovation and creativity will become universally accepted "tools" for use in gaining competitive advantages. This approach indeed ties with the central theme of this book, which is: individuals, businesses (all types of organizations), and entire nations, wherever located, must use innovation and creativity to survive and thrive in the new global economy. While some will be better than others at this process, expect to begin seeing an ever-increasing number of collaborative efforts among organizations around the world. On the other hand, don't expect to see North America's strengths go away, but others may learn the strengths as well. And, new strengths will be discovered by those who embrace globalization, innovation, and collaborative development methodologies. North America, specifically the U.S., will just simply have to strive to be the "best of the best" by using innovation, creativity, entrepreneurship and other tools as required. For example, providing engineering services and equipment for infrastructure needs, such as nuclear and non-nuclear power generating plants, are significant U.S. strengths. They won't go away because of globalization as long as the U.S. continues to support its educational and research and development programs, which are so desperately required to support these "high-tech" industries. The same can be said for U.S. computer and software technology, genetic research, medical research programs, legal/accounting/financial systems and services, management training, advanced education programs, agricultural products, capital market management, transportation systems, and entrepreneurship. China alone will need 25–35 new power generating plants over the next 20 years, and 40–50 new airports and 500 new airplanes—just in the next 5 years (Boeing, 2006). India, Eastern Europe, South American nations (Brazil, Argentina, etc), and other emerging Asian countries will also need these products, services, and infrastructure capabilities. More importantly, the large numbers of people in emerging countries such as India, China, Indonesia and Eastern Europe, will begin to earn enough money to purchase goods beyond subsistence levels, and will demand a growing volume of every type product and service imaginable. I propose, for your consideration, that this global demand will drive a frenzy of innovation as never before seen, as firms compete for growing numbers of consumer and commercial purchases. Mr. Clyde Prestowitz, in his recent book, *Three Billion New Capitalists,* traces this revolutionary growth in consumerism (and the number of consumers) back to the fact that over the past 20 years, India, China, and the former Soviet Union have abandoned many of their socialist and communist doctrines and taken the "once despised" capitalistic road towards consumerism (Prestowitz, 2005). While many of the people in these countries remain poor, vast numbers are gaining enough income—mainly from jobs as a result of globalization and innovation, I might add—to demand an increasing volume of non-subsistence goods and services. For example, I noticed this week that the U.S. Department of Commerce's list of goods and services needed by other countries included cosmetics and skin care products for China in quantities that will stretch the capacities of many suppliers around the world.

Snapshot—World View of Innovation.

To get grounded, sometimes one simply has to "fly over" the landscape (environment) and get a broad view of countries, companies, key leaders, and support groups who are driving new-age innovation and globalization. Following are the top *20 countries*, ranked according to global patent application filings in 2005: (World Intellectual Property Organization, 2005)

1. United States
2. Japan
3. Germany
4. France
5. United Kingdom
6. Netherlands
7. Republic of Korea
8. Switzerland
9. Sweden
10. Canada
11. Italy
12. China
13. Australia
14. Finland
15. Israel
16. Spain
17. Denmark
18. Belgium
19. Austria
20. Russian Federation

It is interesting to note that 92% of all reported inventions in 2005 came from 14 countries. These 14 innovative countries are as follows: (WIPO, 2005)

1. United States
2. Japan
3. Germany
4. France
5. United Kingdom
6. Netherlands
7. Republic of Korea
8. Switzerland
9. Sweden
10. Canada
11. Italy
12. China
13. Australia
14. Finland

The emerging countries from the Soviet empire collapse in 1990 are missing from the top 14; whereas the once powerful Soviet Union was one of the "big three" innovators in the 20th Century. The U.S. and Japan were the other two. From 1900 to approximately 1958, the U.S. led the world's inventiveness. Then, from 1958 to 1990, Japan and the Soviet Union, with about an equal number of inventions each, moved ahead of the U.S. (Vedres, 2005). Many of us perhaps remember, or have read about, the "*Cold War*" and the "*race to space*" that was so intense when the Soviet Union moved ahead of the U.S. as an innovator. The United States has remained the clear leader since 1990.

However, one has to look at the entire list to get a picture of "new-age innovators." By doing so, it is clear that emerging nations are moving up the ladder. For example, China and South Korea are moving rapidly, and now account for a significant number of global inventions. Many smaller countries, such as Croatia, Hungary, and Czech Republic, are participating and contributing to the world's inventiveness. I believe we can trace this rise in part to the Internet and

World Wide Web ("www"), which have become the "great enablers" for all countries to access information and work with others in a collaborative team environment. Other enablers are, of course, the increase in capital and wealth, and the lowering of national political barriers and borders in many of the emerging countries. Indeed, the rebirth of innovation, and its spread globally, just might be an "*unintended consequence*" of the Internet and "www!"

It will be interesting to see how this openness and collaboration plays out, since China still maintains a communist posture (since 1949 when Communist organizers seized the country) and censors all communications. India, on the other hand, is a democracy based on English Common Law similar to the U.S. *Business Week* reported in its January 23, 2006 issue, "The Great Firewall of China," that the Chinese government has approximately 30,000 employees working in censorship capacities in their country to screen and monitor communications, which include the Internet and World Wide Web (Einhorn, 2006). This is about two times the number of people employed by the CIA (Central Intelligence Authority) organization in the United States. In addition, the pirating and copying of products and services is a major issue in China and much of Asia. China's intellectual property protection laws are weak and enforcement is even weaker. This is a major consideration for global companies, and even a more critical issue when it comes to protecting intellectual property and engaging in global collaborative innovation projects. However, I could not find any evidence that these issues are stifling globalization, or collaborative innovative efforts among businesses and nations. To the contrary, firms are flocking to China (and Asia) in record numbers to take advantage of buying labor and materials at bargain prices, and, at the same time, selling their products and services to the fast-growing consumer and industrial markets in that part of the world. Precautions are required, and the WTO (World Trade Organization) is bringing pressure to bear on the Chinese government to step up enforcement efforts against those who pirate intellectual property. As I write this book in 2006, I believe it is fair to say that the problem has reached epidemic levels. Have you seen the new Harley bike that wasn't made by Harley Davidson, U.S.A.? Can't tell the difference!!!

Global new-age "innovative" and "creative" companies.

The *Top 20 Innovative Companies in the World*, according to surveys of senior executives in 63+ countries, by *BusinessWeek* and the Boston Consulting Group (2005 and 2006) are: (World's Most Innovative, 2005 & 2006)

2005 Ranking	2006 Ranking
1. Apple Computers	1. Apple Computers
2. 3M	2. Google
3. Microsoft	3. 3M
4. GE (General Electric)	4. Toyota
5. Sony	5. Microsoft
6. Dell Computers	6. GE (General Electric)
7. IBM	7. Procter & Gamble
8. Google	8. Nokia
9. Procter & Gamble	9. Starbucks
10. Nokia	10. IBM
11. Virgin Air	11. Virgin Group
12. Samsung	12. Samsung
13. Wal-Mart	13. Sony
14. Toyota	14. Dell
15. eBay	15. IDEO Consultants
16. Intel	16. BMW Automotive
17. Amazon	17. Intel
18. IDEO Consultants	18. eBay
19. Starbucks Coffee	19. IKEA
20. BMW Automotive	20. Wal-Mart

Many of the companies discussed in this book are on the list, which indicates that innovation is taking a front seat when it comes to driving competitive strategies in the age of globalization and "new-age innovation." In fact, 72% of the executives surveyed said that innovation was one of their top three initiatives (World's Most Innovative, 2006). I do not know if the other two initiatives were reported, but I would guess that one of them would be globalization. Interestingly, the most recent GE (General Electric Company) annual report I am reading has individual sections in the "Chairman's letter to shareholders" on "Innovation" and "Globalization." These are definitely major initiatives at GE and have been for years. I am sure we will be seeing more annual reports focus on these initiatives.

Global new-age "innovative" and "creative" leaders.

Listed below are the names most frequently mentioned in the literature with regard to the progression of "western world" nations from *Knowledge Based* to *Creativity Based Economies*. These individuals certainly stand at the top when it comes to creativity and innovation, but the list is not meant to be a ranking. I am sure there are many others around the world, such as the leaders at Samsung, eBay, Nokia, Sony Electronics, Honda, Starbucks, Google, IBM, and Siemens, to name a few.

Steve Jobs – Apple Computer
Bill Gates – Microsoft
A.G. Lafley – Proctor & Gamble
Jeffrey R. Immelt – GE
David Kelly – IDEO Consulting
Roger Martin – University of Toronto
Larry Keeley – Doblin Group
Bill Ford – Ford Motor Company

Steve Jobs, of course, needs no introduction as it is well known that he has turned Apple Computers into one of the most creative companies in the world with a multitude of innovative and creative music, video, and information processing products. In fact, the Apple iPod/PMPs, as of 2006, are selling like gangbusters, with new products on the horizon. Bill Gates, of Microsoft fame and fortune, continues to direct that organization as another of the world's most creative companies. It goes without saying that the Microsoft suite of products (e.g. "Windows") has become the world's standard for personal and business computer users. The next two individuals on the list, A.G. Lafley and Jeffrey R. Immelt, seem to be partners in the "creativity movement," and are leading their companies on a global path of innovative products and services. Lafley's organization, Proctor & Gamble, continually pursues new products and the improvement of existing ones. P&G's new "Swiffer" product is an electrostatic dry mop that is destined to be its next billion dollar seller. Immelt, who has followed the legendary Jack Welch (former Chairman and CEO of the General Electric Company) is credited with being a major leader of the "creativity movement." Windmill gear boxes for wind energy farms, fuel efficient aircraft and locomotive engines, medical imaging equipment, customer focused capital financing programs, freight tracking devices, and new energy-saving conversion packages for locomotives, are but a few of the current GE innovations. David Kelly, Roger Martin, and Larry Keeley are the leading consultants and "thinkers" on the list. Each specializes in guiding firms toward designing innovative products and services that will improve their competitive advantage and add value for stakeholders. Bill Ford, a well recognized name in the auto industry and leader of the Ford Motor Company, has made innovation Ford's new mission. While Ford Motor, as well as GM (General Motors), struggles under the weight of high payrolls, increasing benefits costs, and global competition, each is committed to innovative strategies designed around reinventing these companies and their offerings of products and services. With Chinese auto assembly workers earning wages and benefits of $2.00 an hour, Korean workers earning $22, and U.S. workers earning $58–$60, Ford's and GM's challenge to remain global automotive leaders will no doubt be a daunting one. Yet, their plans call for success as they reignite their creativity and innovative engines. The world needs these organizations. They have been a major enabler for families around the world to achieve a better standard of living. And, capital investments in property, plant, and equipment in many countries have helped pull communities and nations out of poverty.

Support for Innovation & Globalization.

Michael Porter, Professor at the Harvard Business School, and Scott Stern, Professor at MIT's Sloan School, in one of their early works on innovation concluded that there are nine factors that drive and determine a country's ability to support organizations that can produce and commercialize innovative products, services, and processes. The nine factors are as follows: (Porter, M & Stern, S, 1999)

1. Investment in basic research
2. Tax policy impact on R&D and investment spending
3. Supply of risk capital
4. Aggregate level of education in the population
5. Pool of talent in science and technology
6. Information and communications infrastructure
7. Protection of Intellectual Property
8. Openness to international trade and investment
9. Overall sophistication and demand for innovation

As you read this chapter from your corner of the world, take a moment and think about how your homeland stacks up against these factors. I know that here in the United States, there are looming challenges to be faced. That's why I have included chapters in this book on innovation, globalization, education, energy, standards of living, and strategy.

The following is a ranking of countries based on their ability to meet the above nine criteria in support of organizations that can produce and commercialize innovative products, services, and processes: (Porter, M & Stern, S, 1999); (Schwab, 2005)

	1995	2005
(1)	United States	Finland
(2)	Switzerland	United States
(3)	Japan	Sweden
(4)	Sweden	Denmark
(5)	Germany	Taiwan
(6)	Finland	Singapore
(7)	Denmark	Iceland
(8)	France	Switzerland
(9)	Norway	Norway
(10)	Netherlands	Australia
(11)	Australia	Netherlands
(12)	Austria	Japan
(13)	United Kingdom	United Kingdom
(14)	New Zealand	Canada
(15)	Italy	Germany
(16)	Spain	New Zealand

So, the next time you start thinking that the world is "*going to hell in a hand basket,*" which was one of my father's favorite sayings, think positively about how globalization has driven innovation and creativity in a manner that will certainly benefit many peoples and nations. Perhaps the benefits will be more for some than others, especially in the case of poor and developing nations. Each will have opportunities to find their own niche. Think about the strength and leadership capabilities of the companies and leaders discussed earlier in this chapter, and you will certainly come away inspired to face the new frontiers of globalization and "new-age innovation." Or, as Mr. Jimmy Carter, ex-president of the United States so often puts it: "I have total confidence in this nation (U.S.) and its peoples' ability to use technology, innovation, and creative thinking to solve the world's problems" (Jimmy Carter's Town Hall, 2005). Britain's Prime Minister, Mr. Tony Blair, also likes to quote this statement by Mr. Carter. One need only look at history to see that the Industrial Revolution, the Information Age/Internet Revolutions, and now the "New-Age Innovation and Creativity Revolution" (at least that's what I'm calling it these days) have improved the well-being of the masses—especially those in the "West." It's now time to stop "whining" about globalization! It's time to take action, be creative, and look to the East! The new revolution has just begun, and the best is yet to come. By now, you should know what I mean!

The fast pace of change—every day is tomorrow.

The pace of innovation and technological change in many of the world's nations continues to intensify. The U.S. provides an excellent historical and current day perspective on this change. "It took 55 years for the passenger automobile to spread to one-quarter of Americans; 35 years for the telephone; 22 years for the radio; 16 years for the personal computer and only 7 for the Internet" (Clinton, 2005). All these U.S. driven innovations and technologies have now spread around the world. And, the globalization process is enabling more and more of the world's population to participate and make use of these innovations and technologies—especially the personal computer and Internet. Together, these two innovations are major drivers and enablers of globalization and the fast pace of change we are experiencing in today's global economy and world community. Exactly what technology will bring tomorrow I will leave to your imagination. But, one thing is very clear: Innovation and technological change, combined with globalization, will make the world a better place to live if we can channel these efforts toward improving the human condition, rather than war machinery. As Senator Hillary Rodham Clinton remarks in many of her speeches: We all need to "spend some time thinking about these issues, because they will have a profound impact on what our future holds" (Clinton, 2005).

Research (Innovation and Inventiveness) grows globally.

The Kansas City based Ewing Marion Kauffman Foundation, the world's premier foundation dedicated to creating entrepreneurial companies around the world, sponsored a survey of more than 200 multinational corporations in the United States and Western Europe. The survey asked how these corporations would be spending their money on research and development in the future. The results: 38% said they planned to reorganize their research and development efforts to take advantage of global resources. India and China were reported by almost all the companies surveyed as being the two countries from which top-notch scientific and engineering work would be purchased. The study results were loud and clear: "Multinational firms will send research work to China and India primarily because of their top-notch scientists and strong education systems, not lower labor costs" (Lohr, 2006).

There were several other findings from this study that I believe dispel the belief many have that the globalization of research investments is just another step in offshoring jobs *from* developed countries *to* developing nations where cheap labor is available (Lohr, 2006).

- First, when companies think about research and development, "cheap labor" is not the first consideration in the investment decision. Achieving results is first and foremost;
- Second, companies generally look for the best qualified scientists and researchers they can find, irrespective of their location. However, having research and development in close proximity to users and markets often helps gear efforts toward local targeted markets;
- Third, companies generally favor locations where strong educational systems exist and there are opportunities for collaboration with universities and other educational and research organizations;
- Fourth, the offshoring of research and development activities does not always mean reduced efforts in a company's home country.

This study is a key indicator that we will be seeing more and more research and development, and innovative type activities in developing nations where educational levels are rapidly improving, and where there is an emphasis on educational systems. This is especially true when a country such as China or India can supply top quality scientists, and others who are highly skilled in mathematics, engineering, and the sciences. Hyderabad and Bangalore are two such innovation centers now very active in India.

****

New-age innovation uses imagination and creativity to design innovative new products, services, and processes that enable individuals, companies, and nations to compete successfully in the new global economy. So, we have now come full circle from the first Renaissance period, when China and India "ruled" the world of innovation, to a new twenty-first century Renaissance. This new Renaissance in inventiveness is best exemplified in what Starbuck's CEO, Jim Donald and others, call "ideation," which is the ability to convert imaginative, inventive, and creative visions (ideas) into the satisfaction of consumer (and commercial) needs and wants (Donald, 2006).

Recommended Action Items:

1. Create a culture of innovation and creativity in which idea generation can flourish. Focus on "creativity" and "imagination" to move beyond basic R&D (Research and Development) methodologies. Keep up to date with technological changes of all kinds to identify those that are beneficial to your firm; e.g. nanotechnology, wireless and digital technologies.

2. Determine what you do best and establish programs for continuous improvement and new innovations in these areas.

3. As Tom Kelly and Jonathan Littman propose in their book, *The Ten Faces of Innovation*, make innovation a team sport, and the team must be made up of a diverse group of talented people who bring the right disciplines to the "idea generating table" (Kelly, 2005).

4. Establish a physical place conducive to "new ways of thinking." For example, Starbucks has a facility at their corporate offices where new ideas can be generated and tested. Proctor and Gamble, Mattel Toys, and Eastman Kodak do also.

5. If you are an organization with a board of directors, make globalization and innovation an agenda item for board meetings, where program funding and direction-setting can take place.

6. Include innovation as a major initiative in the long-term strategic planning process for your organization. Details will follow in Chapter 5: "Global Strategy, Hedgehogs, Martha Stewart, and Others." Planning will help you live and work in the current era of globalization and innovation, as well as prepare you for the next wave of worldwide economic, social, and political changes that are sure to come.

7. Take precautionary measures to protect intellectual property rights, especially in China and all of Asia.

8. Lobby your political representatives for increased governmental funding for research and development in the biological sciences, the physical sciences, alternative energy sources, educational excellence programs, and information technology. An example of the importance of governmental support can be seen in the fact that "virtually every aspect of information technology that we rely on today, from the single-use workstation to the modern microprocessor to the Internet, is descended from federally funded research" (Clinton, 2005).

9. Consider adding an individual to your organization who is skilled in "new-age innovation design disciplines," such as product, graphic, process, environmental, transportation, communication, illustration, advertising, textile, furniture, automotive, fashion, home products, architectural, technology, or industrial design—to name a few. Following are several of the top schools in the U.S. that have embraced innovation and these new "design disciplines," to prepare graduates for work in the new global economy: (Jana, 2006)

    - *The Institute of Design* – Illinois Institute of Technology, Chicago, Ill.
    - *Rhode Island School of Design*, Providence, RI.

- *Parsons The New School of Design*, New York, NY.
- *Carnegie Mellon University's School of Design*, Pittsburgh, PA.
- *The Kansas City Art Institute*, Kansas City, Missouri (KCAI, 2006)
- *Art Center College of Design*, Pasadena, CA.

These schools are turning out graduates who are being employed by such companies as GM, Colgate Palmolive, GE, Michelin, Microsoft, Target, SAP, and others around the world. These companies are applying "new-age innovation" and "design strategies" to successfully compete in the new global economy. Incorporating "design theory and practices" into an organization's strategy can be the difference between success and failure, so don't overlook it. It is here today, and it is the way of the future!

10. Embrace "digital technology," such as document storage and exchange, communications/telephony, graphics, video/photography, books/procedures manuals, in all areas of your organization. And, make "digital information" regarding products and services available to customers and employees, using not only personal computers, but wireless devices such as "E-Book Readers" and digital information download services. Sony (Japan), Apple (USA), Google (USA), Jinke (China), and such well-known book publishers as Random House (USA) and McGraw Hill (USA), are rapidly making information available in "digital medium," which was previously available only in "hard copy form." And Amazon, the world's largest online book distributor, is moving quickly to make digital versions of books available for purchase to download immediately. This is a booming technology area that

promises not only to make information available to people anytime and anywhere, but make it available in a useful format that can improve efficiency, delight customers, and save costs. It's great to be living in this "new-age of innovation!" I'm reading a book now on my Palm Pilot device and considering making this book available to my readers in "digital" format.

"Innovation is our mission.
The guiding compass of everything we do."

Bill Ford, Chairman and CEO, Ford Motor Company

"U.S. technological leadership, innovation, and jobs of tomorrow require a commitment to basic research funding today."

Craig Barrett, Chairman and CEO, Intel

"Like most overnight success,
it was about twenty years in the making."

Sam Walton, founder of WalMart

Chapter 3

The Cost of Labor is Four Times Greater Than In China & India—Now What?

"There is no job that is America's God-given right anymore"

Carly Fiorina, Ex-CEO Hewlett-Packard

Electronic Design Engineers in the United States and Europe earn about $7,000–$8,000 per month (U.S. dollars), while engineers in India and China earn $2,000–$3,000. Apparel workers in the U.S. earn about $10.00 per hour (U.S. dollars), while workers in South America earn $1.65, and workers in China earn $.85. And, Wal-Mart hourly workers in the U.S. earn on average about $10.11 per hour (Wal-Mart Fact Sheets, 2005). No! It's not a "typo"—it is eighty-five cents per hour in China. In 2005, Americans purchased about $12 billion (U.S. dollars) worth of apparel and clothing that carried the label: "Made In China" (Elliott, 2005). In addition, products such as furniture, circuit boards, cell phones, machine tools, household furnishings, and computer hardware that make use of "cheap labor" from China, India, and the rest of Southeast Asia, cost 30–75% less than if manufactured in the U.S. or Western Europe. The result is a loss of 2.7 million manufacturing jobs in the U.S. alone since 2000, and about one-half this number in services and related jobs (Engardio, 2004).

You have heard all the stories about cheap labor and cheap products and services from China and India. And, you've no doubt seen the comparative numbers far too many times. So, the question remains: *Now What?* How can businesses in the U.S. and other "developed countries" compete effectively with the "cheap labor" currently available from many of the "developing countries" around the world? The answer is: on the basis of "cheap labor," many businesses within "developed countries" cannot compete! The advice to managers and leaders in these countries and businesses must be: don't waste your time and other resources trying—"the gap is simply too wide!" (Shenkar, 2005) For companies that still "make things" and are labor intensive, Oded Shenkar, in his recent book titled *The Chinese Century,* recommends that they begin thinking about getting out of manufacturing or leveraging outsourcing to meet their manufacturing needs (Shenkar, 2005).

As a result (and as I will be discussing later in this book in a chapter titled "Global Strategy, Hedgehogs, Martha Stewart, and Others"), organizations will need to drastically revise, or perhaps completely redo, their business model (strategic plan) to be able to compete in the new globally-competitive environment. And, with regard to competing on a labor cost basis, the environment (or "playing field" as Ex-GE Chairman & CEO Jack Welch calls it in his book titled *Winning*), continues to be flat but not equal (Welch, 2004). "Flat" in the sense that all can participate. "Not equal" in the sense that on a country by country, and business by business basis, strengths and weaknesses will vary. Labor cost, the subject of this chapter, is one example of the flat but unequal nature of globalization thus far in the 21st century. Any strategy for competing and succeeding must take this reality into consideration.

Protecting workers and wages.

You'll hear it over and over again, and not just in the United States: Why doesn't the government step in and protect workers (employees) and their wages in this transitional period of globalization (outsourcing/offshoring/insourcing)? Unions and entire industries lobby for tariffs and job protections to stem the flow of jobs to "cheap labor" countries. The conventional wisdom that focuses on job losses tends to overlook the fact that "outsourcing benefits people because it lowers prices"—not just at worldwide Wal-Mart stores, but worldwide companies such as Siemens, GE, Motorola, Sony, GM, Citicorp, Microsoft, etc. Therefore, it is unlikely that any significant protectionist measures will be enacted, at least in the near term. Further, protecting employees too much in industries, such as automotive and airline, has proven disastrous for many of the companies in those industries. Over the years, unions have tended to force wages and benefits up to unsustainable levels. Now companies such as Ford, GM, Daimler/Chrysler, and nearly all major airlines, are in cash flow trouble when it comes to paying these wages, health care costs, and pension benefits, while at the same time trying to remain competitive in the markets they serve. Diana Farrrell, director of the McKinsey Global Institute, says "the way to protect people is <u>not</u> by <u>not</u> allowing them to lose their jobs. The way to protect them, she says, is to educate and retrain them and make sure they are not exposed to periods where they are not covered for healthcare and benefits. It's in the interest of the global economy in terms of migrating to higher value-added work to let some jobs go and create better ones" (Heffes, 2004). However, I'll let you try to explain this "benefit" to someone who just lost their job due to globalization.

My research for this book tells me that the "free market forces" of capitalism will be left to determine wages, and that work will migrate to where it is most economical to perform. This is an example of "balancing the world's global supply chains." And, another example of capitalism and competition at work.

Who will be the cheapest workers in the world?

I might as well go ahead and spring it on you now so we can stop laying all the blame on China, India, and Asia for taking manufacturing and service jobs away from the U.S. and the rest of the developed countries of the world. When it comes to producing "cheap" goods and providing basic services, there are a couple of other culprits at work, although I should not call them culprits. They are—productivity improvements and technology! I think I defined it earlier, but improving productivity means getting more output with less input or the same input. In other words, many production and service jobs haven't just been shipped to China and India; they have been eliminated due to productivity gains. It is no secret that "productivity" has grown tremendously and resulted in the elimination of jobs in the United States and other countries who have invested heavily in technology. In fact, from 1995 to 2002, productivity gains averaged 4 to 4.5 percent per year in the world's twenty largest economies, and eliminated millions of manufacturing jobs (Carson, 2003). The driver for these gains has been (and continues to be) technology. In other words, software and hardware systems, and "intelligent" machines are doing the work that people once did. So, one person can now do the work of two or more (mostly more) when equipped with these new-age innovation tools. And now that we are squarely in the middle of the new-age innovation and information revolutions, "intelligent machines, in the form of computer software, robotics, nanotechnology, and biotechnology are increasingly replacing human labor in the services, manufacturing, and agricultural sectors" of the global economy (Rifkin, 2004). Just step inside any manufacturing or service center, at least in what is called the "developed nations" of the world, and the automation will amaze you. Jeremy Rifkin, who has written numerous books that touch on this theme, says in his updated book, *The End of Work,* "more and more physical and mental labor, from menial repetitive tasks to highly conceptual professional work, will be done by cheaper and more efficient 'thinking machines' in the twenty-first century. The cheapest workers in the world will likely not be as cheap as the technology coming online to replace them" (Rifkin, 2004). And this leads us to ask what will those who are displaced with "intelligent machines" do for a living? We might just as well ask, what are they doing today?—because technology and intelligent machines are already upon us. The chapters in this book titled "Artistic and Creative Visions for Innovative Organizations" and "Energy (Crisis?)—Globalization and Innovation at Their Best (or Worst)," clearly point out the businesses, industries, and markets that are producing new jobs to employ these individuals. Their work already is, and will become more so, knowledge and technology based. By the way, automation is starting to eliminate jobs in China and India as well. And, the cheapest workers in the world are not in China and India. They are intelligent machines! And they are everywhere. Are you tracking your teenage children with a GPS (Global Positioning System)? Have you seen the new heart defibrillator that gives voice instructions to its user during a rescue emergency?

Pay rates increasing in China and India—when good news can also be bad news.

I first started hearing about it back in early 2005, when Dan Krouse, Operations Vice President—Global Procurement for Kansas City based Hallmark Cards, Inc., mentioned it at an International Trade Council Meeting in Kansas City, Missouri (USA). "Labor shortages are starting to show up in many countries in Asia, primarily China and India," he remarked. "These shortages are driving wages upward, which will in turn eventually drive prices up on products and services coming from that part of the world" (International Trade Council, 2005). Well, I'm sure you know where this story is going. If wages go up, procurement (purchase) prices go up, and then, ultimately, selling prices to consumers go up. When I say that selling prices to consumers will go up, I mean selling prices to consumers around the world. This includes consumers in China as well, since they now embrace consumerism just as the Western World has for many years. For example, when you go to Wal-Mart, Target, Kmart, Sears, J.C. Penney's, Nike, Ikea, Best Buy, or Timberland, expect some price increases in the future. This is the "*bad news*" part of the story. Consumers get to pay more for products and services at a time when prices for such necessities as gasoline and heating are soaring. For now, some of the increases are being held back, but eventually it will have to happen.

The "*good news*" part of this story is that factory workers in Asia (China) are now starting to earn more than the 85 cents per hour I mentioned at the beginning of this chapter. For example, factories in Dongguan, China, that make lamps and furniture for many of the world's large retailers are now paying 40% more for hourly wages than last year (Roberts, 2006). In U.S. dollars, this means about $160 to $180 per month, or $1.00 to $1.12 per hour. These rates don't sound like much in terms of the Western World's standards, but the increases are significant to China's economic base, which is founded on this level of pay rates.

There is another shortage in China and India that is worth noting here. Demand is outstripping the supply of managers and highly-skilled workers. This is especially true in the well established coastal manufacturing centers in China and the service centers in India (Deloitte, 2005). In the managerial ranks where demand is high, wages have been escalating at a rate of 25% per year for 2004 and 2005. Universities in China and India are responding, and many employers are taking on the task of training and educating managers themselves. One company, InfoSys (India) is discussed in Chapter 4, "Education—The Great Equalizer (Actually the Most Important Chapter!)." This company, a $1.6 billion dollar software technology firm, is serving as a model for employee education by employers. Motorola University in Beijing, China, is another example of employee training to bridge the management shortage gap. In addition, Intel has supported the Chinese government's initiatives over the years, resulting in 600,000 teachers being trained in all disciplines (Roberts, 2006). I believe we can say that the supply and demand forces of capitalism are taking hold in China and gaining momentum in India, where capitalism and democracy have flourished for many years. (India is the largest democracy in the world.)

From a competitive point of view, there might be even more "*bad news*." As wages rise in China, the products and services that China sells to the rest of the world may become less competitive. Companies will start to look elsewhere, such as Vietnam and Indonesia, for cheaper products to sustain their competitive advantage. This same scenario applies to India, the services capital of the world, as well. Similar worker shortages and wage increases are on the rise. What does this mean to the rest of the world? Why must we care and be concerned?

The simple answer to these questions is that the future of China and India is linked to that of the U.S., and the rest of the world. Remember back to chapter 1—the chapter with the weird title—"On The Road To The Airport, or On The Internet." It is hard to find a company that is not dependent upon a significant portion of its growth and profitability coming from Asia—primarily China and India. If these huge economies stumble, then so might the rest of the world. Specifically in the case of the U.S., these countries hold billions of dollars of U.S. debt and have thousands of companies' investments embedded in their economies (Elliott, 2005). And, these countries—along with other foreign countries—have recently been investing an average of $100 billion dollars a month in U.S. stocks and bonds (George, 2006). Now you know the real meaning of globalization and "interconnectedness" (a word Ex-Federal Reserve Chairman Alan Greenspan was so fond of using) (Woodard, 2000). When I said earlier in this book that we are all integrally linked in a global economy, and dependent on each other for our well being, I meant just that—"integrally"!

What each does best, leveraging global supply chains.

Smart strategists (business leaders, entrepreneurs, managers, small business owners) find ways to leverage (efficiently and effectively utilize) their weaknesses into strengths. Chapter 5, "Global Strategy, Hedgehogs, Martha Stewart, and Others," discusses two excellent techniques: *SWOT* and *TOWS* analysis. Don't worry about their meanings just yet; we'll get to them. These techniques can be used to establish winning strategies based on a firm's strengths as well as its weaknesses. If a firm's internal supply chain of labor costs is competitively too high, then an alternative is to leverage a global supply chain where labor costs allow a firm to be competitive. A supply chain, as I use it here, refers to sources of materials, labor, and other resources needed to produce a product or provide a service. Many examples abound where firms are leveraging "cheap labor" supplies from China, India, Eastern Europe and Southeast Asia by off-shoring (and outsourcing if you prefer) their labor requirements. Most are seeking a competitive advantage, but many are simply trying to survive or maintain their market position until they can figure out their place in the new global market environment.

It's not as easy as it sounds, though, to leverage a firm's capability to survive and succeed. This point was illustrated at the *U.S.–China Economic and Security Review*

Commission's meeting where "economists, union officials, and small business owners and manufacturers took to the microphone to describe the devastation Chinese competitors are inflicting on such U.S. industries as furniture, kitchenware, car tires, and electronic circuit boards" (Engardio, 2004). On top of these conditions, a new round of very high quality products and services are now available from China and India at selling prices that are often below a U.S. or Western European firm's costs. For example, two top-quality auto firms, Honda and Nissan, will begin exporting their cars from factories in China in late 2006 or early 2007. And, it is expected that others will follow. Toyota's first car, the "Camry," rolled off the production line in May of 2006 at its new $470 million state-of-the-art manufacturing facility in China. Exports will follow.

There is more to the equation than just "cheap labor." At this point, we have talked about extremely low hourly and monthly wage rates, and good (and improving) quality products and services coming from China, India, and other developing nations around the world. But there is also another factor at play. If you are a business, economics, or management graduate, you might recall that dreaded accounting or finance course that covered "cost-volume-profit" relationships in a business. But in case you don't recall—as volume goes up, per unit costs come down. And, China and India both have the volume that it takes to drive costs and selling prices down (way down), right in their own countries where consumerism and industrial goods' requirements drive their country's economic growth at two to three times that of the U.S. and most other nations of the world. Low hourly labor rates, workers who are willing to put in 12-hour days, good quality products and services, and high volumes make for an absolute winning combination. And, if you look at the additional volumes achieved by Chinese and Indian suppliers exporting vast quantities of goods and services, then there can be but one conclusion: It will be impossible for the "developed" countries and economies of the Western World to compete on the basis of low costs. Another strategy is definitely in order.

But, aren't we all benefiting from the low prices resulting from the combinations of factors described above? I think the answer has to be yes—but it is hard to see if you are the individual who just lost your job and haven't found employment in an alternate profession yet. Have you been to Wal-Mart, Target, Home Depot, Circuit City, J.C. Penney, or Best Buy lately and taken advantage of low-priced merchandise? China's increasing middle class is also reaping the benefits of low prices, since they, too, are now able to shop at Wal-Mart and many of the same stores that others do. Depending on which source one is reading, Wal-Mart now buys 70%–80% of what it sells from China. Finally, inflation in many parts of the world, especially the U.S. and Western Europe, has been held down due to never-ending supplies of low cost goods and services (primarily from China, India, and the rest of the countries in Asia). The restraint of inflation, which eats away at the buying power of the dollar, has sustained and, in many cases, improved the standard of living for many.

****

We've arrived at the "**Now What**?" question in this chapter's title. I know that I keep bringing up this question; and for good reason. My answer is: The world is going through a transition to a globally-based economic union that ties us all even closer together and allows each to do what they do best. In business and economic terms, we're experiencing a balancing of the world's supply chains for goods and services, and natural resources. For example, the evidence suggests that if China's strengths lie in being the world's manufacturing location of "competitive choice" for the global economy, and India's strengths lie in providing services, then that's where these economic events will, and should, occur. Likewise, if the strengths of the U.S. are in "new-age innovation," technology, design, entrepreneurship, capital management, and bioscience, then these are the disciplines the U.S. will provide in the global supply chain. We must not forget, however, that strengths and weaknesses will continue to shift, just as they have in the past when Japan, Britain, Germany, France, the U.S. and others have made their run at being world super powers. In many ways, this is capitalism at its best. Hasn't the U.S. been trying to convert the world to capitalism and democracy? Well, much of the world has now been converted to capitalism. With *The World At Your Door,* how will you, personally, and your organization respond? Here is what I suggest:

Recommended Action Items:

1. Stop hoping for some economic or political fix that will come along and do away with the competitiveness of low cost (cheap) labor and globalization. The evidence indicates it will not happen.

2. Get your best leaders around the table and figure out how your organization is going to leverage (efficiently and effectively utilize) the world's supply chains for the continued growth and profitability of your firm. For example, if you are a full service engineering firm and find that you need to have engineering done where it is competitively feasible, then outsource or offshore engineering and become a project management/ consulting firm. Or, if you are a manufacturer and find that the manufacturing component of your business cannot compete with another global location, then offshore manufacturing to that location and become a distributor. If you are in any type of labor intensive business, begin immediately looking at how to leverage "cheap labor" from the developing nations of the world. If you can't leverage global supply chains profitably,

then it is time to move to another business, or simply move out. Wal-Mart has gotten its share of bad publicity lately, but I believe that it will reside in history as a classic example of leveraging supply chains. We can learn from its model. It does not manufacture or assemble anything. It sources goods and services from whatever supply chains that provide the best competitive value, which spells low prices for customers around the world. Currently, Wal-Mart is China's sixth largest export market (Elliott, 2005).

3. If you or your organization participates in a market or industry—such as bioscience, medical services, natural resources, or capital management services—that has not seen much impact from globalization, modify your strategic plan immediately. Proceed as though competitive world economic pressures are at you door step. It may/probably will happen.

4. Whether you are an individual, a small-medium-large business, for profit or not-for-profit, begin immediately to think globally in every action taken—from accounting to product development, sales, and manufacturing.

"The cheapest workers in the world will likely not be as cheap as the technology coming online to replace them."

Jeremy Rifkin, Fellow at the University of Pennsylvania's Wharton Business School and CEO, The Foundation of Economic Trends, Washington, D.C.

Chapter 4

Education—The Great Equalizer (Actually the Most Important Chapter!)

"One of the most important needs individuals, especially our children, face today is 'to learn how to learn'. Jobs will come and go rapidly. Competing for jobs in the global economy will require the constant modification of job skills and learning new jobs."

Thomas Friedman, New York Times Writer and Author of "The World is Flat," Speech at the 2005 National Book Fair, Washington, D.C.

"Education is the only commodity that some consumers don't want what they pay for." This is a comment I heard one day from my sister-in-law, Rebecca (Becki) Williams, Professor of Chemistry at Richland College (Dallas, Texas, USA) during one of our many discussions on the state of education in America. I found this to be an interesting comment and, unfortunately, I think it has some truth to it. Becki provided anecdotal evidence when she cited statements frequently made by students: "Do I need to learn this? Can we get out of class early today? Do I really need to read the chapters for the assignment?" And, it didn't take long until someone tried to prove it out. David Weale, of Canada's University of Prince Edward Island, actually set out to prove that some students don't want what they pay for. He offered "B–" grades to any students in his large history course who wanted to skip the classes and course work. Twenty (20) students out of ninety-five (95), or 21%, took him up on it. You can probably guess the rest of the story. The university eventually found out about it and fired Mr. Weale (Weird News, 2006). Is this an isolated incident or does it exemplify some apathy that might exist toward education today?

Before we move on, be sure to read this entire chapter, which includes some very interesting information about the community college (Richland) I mentioned at the start of this chapter. Richland College is the first community college to ever win the Malcolm Baldrige National Quality Award, which is the nation's highest presidential honor for quality and organizational excellence. It is uplifting testimony that there continues to be extremely talented and dedicated leaders, as well as front-line teachers, who are making a difference in the most important endeavor of one's life—education! This is also evidence that organizations do not have to be huge multinational entities in order to make a difference.

Now, what I believe Becki was really saying in our conversations mentioned above was that there seems to be a growing lack of importance placed on education, when we live in a world and time where learning and knowledge are more important than ever. In fact, the phrase "knowledge economy" resonates throughout many of the "developed countries" of the world. And, how can a "knowledge economy" exist without a continuing stream of highly educated workers—primarily educated in the technical sciences of research, development, engineering, chemistry, biomedicine, and physics? Jobs for people in the "knowledge economy," who have higher educational skills—beyond high school—are growing. Conversely, jobs for people without higher educational skills are declining. Anthony Carnevale, Senior Fellow at the National Center on Education and the Economy in Washington, D.C., says "there are still opportunities for those without higher education, but they're shrinking every year" (Carnevale, 2004) (Welch, D. 2006).

What does this mean? Are Americans and Europeans, for example, losing interest in education and knowledge, while developing nations are hungry and grasping for it?

The National Academy of Sciences indicates that U.S. high school students test well below Asian students in science and math. Have students in the "developed" nations of the world come to believe that they are entitled to a degree and a job, by virtue of their status of growing up in countries where educational opportunities and well paying jobs are plentiful? With regard to this "entitlement issue," Thomas Friedman, author of *The World is Flat*, writes about his interview with David Baltimore, Nobel Prize-winning president of Caltech (one of the leading scientific universities in the world). Friedman reports that the amazing thing Mr. Baltimore sees about students who make it to Caltech is that they almost all "come from public schools and not from private schools that sometimes nurture a sense that just because you are there, you are special and entitled" (Friedman, 2005).

If this lack of interest and complacency does exist, then where will we find the increased numbers of knowledge workers required to sustain and grow creative and innovative organizations, countries, and cultures? While I'm generalizing, I'll offer that the current answer seems to be drifting toward the increase in supply coming from "the East," primarily China, India, Japan, and Eastern Europe. Increasingly, "children in the U.S. will be competing head-to-head against Chinese, Indian, and Asian kids" for jobs of all kinds, including primarily knowledge-based work in the global economy (Friedman, 2005). At Caltech, for example, about one-third of the students have an Asian background and a large portion of the faculty comes from outside the U.S., primarily China and India (Friedman, 2005). At Johns Hopkins University, one of the best medical and scientific research schools in the world, about sixty percent of the graduate students are from outside the U.S. Nearly all graduate students in math are from Asia, primarily China.

China graduated approximately 2.5 million technicians and engineers in 2005, and the number is expected to keep growing over the next few years at a very rapid pace of 20%–30% per year (Lieberthal, 2005). India is experiencing much the same situation, and Japan has long been known for its technical education. With respect to the engineering disciplines, China and India will each graduate approximately 300,000 engineers per year compared to 100,000 in the U.S. (Finder, 2006). South Korea is also a country hungry for education. And, there are pockets of educational emphasis in Eastern Europe and the Middle East as well. Does it follow, then, that America and other "developed countries" are losing their leadership positions as the world's suppliers of knowledge workers and innovators? While I do not think the answer is a resounding "yes," the U.S., Japan, and Europe are starting to share the leadership role with China, India, and other countries that are spending heavily and have high enrollments in "tertiary" education. "Tertiary" level educational spending and enrollment includes all levels of post-secondary education. This includes courses leading to awards not equivalent to a university degree, courses leading to a first university degree, and postgraduate courses (Pocket World in Figures, 2006). The following are the top 20 countries with regard to "tertiary" education enrollments. Look for them to begin, or continue, to contribute more and more of the world's need for knowledge workers.

Rank	Country	% Enrollment** In Relevant Age Group
1	Finland	86%
2	South Korea	85%
3	United States	81%
4	Sweden	76%
5	Australia	74%
6	New Zealand	74%
7	Norway	74%

Rank	Country	% Enrollment** In Relevant Age Group
8	Russia	70%
9	Latvia	69%
10	Greece	68%
11	Macau	66%
12	Slovenia	66%
13	Estonia	64%
14	Lithuania	64%
15	United Kingdom	64%
16	Denmark	63%
17	Bermuda	62%
18	Belarus	60%
19	Belgium	60%
20	Poland	60%

** "% Enrollment" = number enrolled in the relevant age group, expressed as a percentage of the total number of people in the relevant age group.

These "tertiary" level educated students will be the graduates who drive globalization and "new-age innovation" in the new global community and economy.

Signs of Enlightenment.

It is well known that the United States has been ranked number one in the world for its "standard of living" and "quality of life" due to innovation and the rapid development of technology by its highly educated and productive workforce. As discussed in Chapter 7, "The Standard of Living and Quality of Life Argument," this number one ranking dropped for the first time ever in 2006, and sank all the way down to number seven. Concern is now growing, even faster than before, that education is not keeping pace with the need for science, math, engineering, and technology graduates, who are the drivers of inventiveness, technology, and a high standard of living/quality of life (Broder, 2005). These concerns could also be those of other "developed" countries, or the "developing" nations around the world. The concerns are indeed founded in fact. A Blue Ribbon panel at the National Academy of Sciences, headed by Norman Augustine, retired CEO of Lockheed Martin, found that there have been declines in math, science, and engineering graduates in the U.S., as well as government and private investments that underpin innovation and technology growth. To end these declines, both the U.S. House of Representatives and the Senate have proposed the following: (Broder, 2005)

1. Increase Federal Spending investment in basic research by 10%;
2. Recruit 10,000 new science and math teachers each year, and award them four-year scholarships and financial rewards for teaching in disciplines with shortages;
3. Provide additional training for 250,000 current math and science teachers;
4. Provide grants to 200 promising young researchers;
5. Establish an Advanced Research Projects Agency within the Department of Energy;
6. Give 25,000 competitive scholarships each year to undergraduates in math, science, and engineering;
7. Provide 5,000 new graduate fellowship grants to students in math, science, and engineering;
8. Expand immigration opportunities for people with math, science, and engineering skills; ease visa restrictions for studying and remaining to work in the U.S.;
9. Provide tax incentives for U.S.-based innovations;

10. Expand access to broadband communications.

These ten initiatives, which will be moved through the U.S. legislative process in 2006, could also serve as a blueprint for any country in the global economy that wants to improve their competitive position by leveraging education.

I was reminded, as I studied these initiatives, that, in 1978, China had its own set of initiatives, which constituted an emergency education effort. This effort included, among other things, sending hundreds of thousands of students to the United States and other countries around the world to be educated; educated primarily in science, math, and engineering. Following the departure of the British in 1947, India also established educational initiatives which led to the founding of the seven campus Indian Institute of Technology. This Institute's world-class engineering programs are all on par with MIT, Oxford, and Caltech (Prestowitz, 2005).

There is simply no greater need than education when it comes to making the world a better place for all to live.

Educational excellence.

I'd like to return for a moment to Richland College, where my sister-in-law has taught chemistry for many years. It's not a huge internationally known school, or a richly endowed organization, but it is making a difference and is on the cutting edge of educational excellence and relevant learning programs for the 21st century. As remarked earlier, it is the first ever U.S. community college to win the *Malcolm Baldrige National Quality Award*. I believe its innovative methodologies in education and learning programs exemplify the needs required to live and successfully participate in the new global economy and community. Richland's mission is "to offer programs and services that enable its 14,500 students to achieve their educational goals and become life-long learners, community builders, and global citizens" (Award Winner, 2005). The school is also a learning ground for educational leaders and 22 of its former employees have been named as presidents of other colleges and universities. In discussions with several faculty members, the school's success seems to be rooted in its caring people, its innovative and entrepreneurial culture, its use of business processes, such as strategic planning and data-based decision making, and its collaborative working relationships with the communities and students it serves. Take a look below at a few of the key programs the school has initiated and you will see why the college won the award. Do you recognize initiatives that address the need for improvements in math, science, and engineering, which are the bases for innovation and technological advancements? Do you recognize programs that link learning experiences in communications and cultural diversity back to the modern day global workplace where we're all interconnected and interdependent on each other for our economic, social, and political well-being? Richland's programs inextricably prepare students for global collaborative work experiences in what Thomas Friedman, well known New York Times writer and author, has labeled the "flat world." The following is a sample of these programs:

- Richland Collegiate High School of Mathematics, Science, and Engineering. To open fall 2006. This High School will enable up to 400 students to graduate simultaneously from High School and Junior College with an Associates Degree. Tuition will be free—including books and a laptop computer. This is an example of "new-age innovation" that we discussed back in chapter two—applied to the educational process;
- Richland's African American/Black Studies Program;

- Richland's three new Associate Degrees in Mass Communication: Print Journalism, Broadcast Journalism and Advertising/Public Relations;
- Richland's Mexican American/Latino Studies Program;
- Richland's Health Professions Programs. Ten healthcare certificate programs prepare job-ready individuals to fulfill the needs of healthcare employers;
- Global Studies, including study abroad;
- Peace Studies, which includes an in-depth look at violence, non-violence, and conflict resolution;
- Richland's Rising Star program that provides scholarships to students at risk of not succeeding in school;
- Outdoor horticulture program where Richland has created the nation's largest urban tree farm on its campus.

Interestingly, Richland's amazing accomplishments have come at a time when its state funding has been reduced from 70 percent to 30 percent of its total budget. The funding reductions have required the college to find innovative ways to maintain reasonable tuition rates and, at the same time, maintain and improve educational quality and services. I am sure there are many other examples of great schools in the U.S. and other nations of the world that are fostering student competencies in global studies, math, science, engineering, and health and social issues. Richland is an exemplary example that stands ahead of others at this time.

Other excellent colleges and universities around the world are highlighted each year in several periodicals, but I follow *BusinessWeek's* rankings for worldwide "Executive Education Programs." Their four primary ranking criteria include: Global Business, Innovation, Leadership, and

Strategy Programs. The first two criteria, Global Business and Innovation, which are also main subjects of this book, are the reasons I follow *BusinessWeek's* rankings. I propose, for your consideration, that how an organization uses these four criteria in its business, determines the difference between succeeding and failing in the new global economy, where everyone gets to participate and compete. The following top 20 schools for 2005, as ranked by *BusinessWeek*, have recognized that more than ever before, students must be able to function effectively in the global economy, and respond with strategies that leverage innovation and leadership.

Rank	School	Location
1	Harvard	USA, Boston, MA
2	INSEAD	France/Singapore
3	IMD	Switzerland
4	Stanford	USA, Stanford, CA
5	London Business School	U.K., London
6	Michigan	USA, Ann Arbor, MI
7	Columbia	USA, New York, NY
8	Pennsylvania (Wharton)	USA, Philadelphia, PA
9	Northwestern (Kellogg)	USA, Evanston, Il
10	Queen's University	Canada, Ontario
11	IESE	Spain, Barcelona
12	Virginia (Darden)	USA, Charlottesville, Va.
13	Duke (Fuqua)	USA, Durham, NC
14	Western Ontario	Canada, Ontario
15	MIT (Sloan)	USA, Cambridge, MA
16	Thunderbird	USA, Glendale, AZ
17	York (Schulich)	Canada, Toronto
18	Chicago	USA, Chicago, Il
19	UNC (Kenan)	USA, Chapel Hill, NC
20	Toronto (Rotman)	Canada, Toronto

Twelve of the twenty schools are located in the USA. Four are located in Canada, while France, Switzerland, The United Kingdom, and Spain each have one. As I read these rankings, I couldn't help but wonder why we keep reading every day that the educational system in the United States is declining. Additionally, last year, the number of graduate students coming to the United States increased by 11%, with significant increases from China and India (Finder, 2006).

If the U.S. educational system is showing signs of decline, then I believe that the pressures of globalization will certainly bring it back. Perhaps the decline we continually hear about is limited to math, science, and engineering.

The Confucius Institute Project.

Recognition of the need for students to have global competencies in today's interconnected and interdependent world was the driving force that led to the establishment of *The Confucius Institute Project* by The People's Republic of China in 2004. Additionally, the Institute is a part of China's national plan which calls for expanding its economy by assisting people worldwide in understanding the language and culture to increase both trade and tourism. The Confucius Institute program was developed in Beijing by China's "National Office for Teaching Chinese as a Foreign Language." Its basic mission is to promote friendly and collaborative relationships with other countries and enhance understanding of the Chinese language and culture through facilitating instruction. Key goals of the Institute include: (Intro, 2005)

- Providing cross-cultural communication seminars and workshops for the business community and all levels of government in order to promote Chinese culture and trade internationally;

- Enhancing the teaching and learning skills of Chinese language teachers outside of China;
- Offering innovative and flexible Chinese language learning courses;
- Forging strategic alliances with business, industry, government, and other institutions with an interest in closer and more productive ties with China;
- Promoting an awareness of Chinese language and culture amongst the wider community in which the institute operates;
- Providing multimedia and web-based Mandarin language and Chinese culture courses;
- Providing and enhancing existing professional training for university, secondary, and elementary school Chinese teachers;
- Hosting scholars, researchers, and teachers from China.

China intends to establish at least 100 institutes around the world by 2010 and currently has 55 operating in 30 different countries (Backgrounder, 2006). Portugal, Scotland, and Sweden were among the first countries to establish an institute and there are currently four in the United States located at: (Bessier, 2006)

- The University of Maryland
- The Chicago Public School System
- New York's China Institute
- The University of Kansas' Edwards Campus, Overland Park, Kansas—the latest to be inaugurated.

I had the pleasure of attending the opening ceremonies of the latest U.S. location—Overland Park, Kansas—and seeing China's vice minister for education, Wu Qidi, and Kansas Governor, Kathleen Sebelius, officially recognize the new location. It was, in a sense, an emotional sight as we stood in a large assembly room on the Edwards Campus of the University of Kansas and witnessed two peoples who are physically miles apart shake hands and agree to better understand one another in a world of differences—a world where the global economic superpower, The People's Republic of China, and the tiny state of Kansas are linked by dependency on each other. On my way home, as I drove past acres of land being prepared to grow wheat and soybeans that would be bound for China, the strong but gentle breeze of globalization and cooperation that moved across the great plains of Kansas that day in May, 2006 replaced ages of distance. The world was at our door and we were trying to let it in.

These *Confucius Institutes* around the world promise to help with internationalizing educational institutions for the purpose of developing students with global competencies in the new world economy and community.

The boom in "working adult" educational programs.

Job skill needs are rapidly shifting in the new global economy. Since a significant portion of the world's manufacturing needs are being met by China, Malaysia, and other regions in Southeast Asia, there is less demand for production skills in other countries and regions of the world. Companies that have shifted their manufacturing to these developing ("cheap labor") countries are left with a tremendous employee retraining effort or, in many cases, a reduction in local employment needs. At the same time, companies are focusing more on knowledge-based activities. This is certainly true for the United States, Canada, France, Germany, Britain, and many of the nations in Eastern Europe.

The same scenario exists in the services sectors of many economies. India is fast becoming the world's center for all types of services—from reservations to engineering, to report writing. As companies shift their service jobs to India, and other countries of Malaysia and Southeast Asia, employees are displaced locally. These workers need retraining and an updating of skill levels in order to maintain gainful employment. In the short term, this scenario can become a crisis for the displaced workers. In the long term, evidence points to the fact that most of the workers move on to more "value added" and "knowledge based" work.

As discussed earlier, countries become centers for manufacturing (China), while others become centers for services (India). Other countries become specialized centers for science, engineering, capital management, training, biomedicine, technology, research, development, and design (United States, Britain, France, Germany, etc). This is the great transition that is occurring, and the subject of the last chapter of this book – "In Transition, It's Not a Pretty Sight, but….!"

This transition is driving a boom in educational programs and retraining efforts aimed at a growing number of working adults. As I look at my local community, the Kansas City Metropolitan area (population 1.9 million), I am amazed at the number of institutions that are in the business of educating "working adults." I tried to list them all, and may have overlooked a few. Here is my list and you will likely recognize a few of the names in your local area. If you perform a search of any metropolitan area, I suspect you will find a large number of programs.

University of Phoenix – Kansas City
DeVry University
Webster University
University of Kansas – Kansas City Campus
University of Missouri – Kansas City Campus
Washburn University – Kansas City Campus

Park College
American University
Missouri State College – Kansas City Campus
Northwest Missouri State – Kansas City Campus
Pittsburg State University of Kansas – Kansas City Campus
Concorde Career Academy
Rockhurst College
Johnson County Community College
Penn Valley Community College
Maple Woods Community College
Longview Community College
Blue River Community College
Benedictine College
University of St. Mary
Baker University – Kansas City Campus
Central Missouri State University – Kansas City Campus
Ottawa University
Avila University
Keller Graduate School of Management
Brown Mackie College
Central Michigan University – Kansas City Campus
Columbia College – Kansas City Caampus
Kansas State University – Kansas City Campus
Graceland University – Kansas City Campus
Friends University
Kansas City Kansas Community College
Mid American Nazarene University
National American University
William Jewel College
Colorado Technical University

I believe the indication is clear. There is a huge demand for educational services as many individuals struggle to find their place in the ever-changing globally competitive job markets. And, it is the driving forces of globalization and "new-age innovation" that are behind these changes. They are demanding new skills from all who wish to participate. Or, to put it in more practical terms, the globalization process underway today is requiring new skills from workers around the world who want to prosper and make a decent standard of living, and enjoy a better quality of life in the new global community. Mr. Ron Heim, Assistant Director Academic Affairs, University of Phoenix (Kansas City Campuses), says that "historically, difficult economic conditions have driven working adults back to school. Currently, though, there is more to the picture. Working adults are going to school as a result of new job skill requirements in the global economy and to better compete for higher paying/higher quality jobs. 80% of the fastest growing jobs in the U.S. now require some level of post secondary education." Mr. Heim goes on to say that "the University of Phoenix (the largest private for-profit university in the world) expects to see a continuation of growth in working adults attending college as a result of (1) globalization and the need to compete in a global job market for knowledge based jobs; (2) rising educational costs which require larger numbers of students to work to pay for their education, and (3) the increasing number of high school graduates (expected to peak in 2008)—many of whom will desire to work and attend college at the same time."

Employer Training Programs—Bridging the Education Gap.

Employers, who have the resources, are realizing that they must play a major role in employee training as the global shortage of knowledge workers approaches. Many employers already have educational reimbursement programs, but, by and large, I believe these programs have been ineffective (See "Recommended Action Items" at the end of this chapter). To bridge the educational and training gap, there is a growing number of employers who are finding it to be in their best interests to take on more of the responsibility for educating employees and training them in specific skills related to their businesses. Be it GE, GM, Motorola, or Proctor and Gamble, none stands taller for its employee training programs than Infosys in Mysore, India. Infosys is a $1.6 billion dollar software firm that provides outsourcing services for Cisco, Nordstrom, Microsoft, and other major companies around the world (Schlosser, 2006). The company has about 50,000 employees and is growing so rapidly that it averages 30–40 new hires per day. The company launched its own training facility, Infosys U., to keep up with its training needs for software and hardware systems engineering personnel. At any given time, there are 4,000 employees on campus engaged in computer-based and instructor led courses. The company expects to be training 10,000 employees by 2007. Salaries for employees being trained in engineering start at $5,000 (U.S. dollars) per year, which is about 1/10th of what beginning salaries are in the U.S. and Western Europe. The company has locations in 18 countries around the world, and is making a major push in the Chinese markets. This commitment to training, coupled with low salaries, will certainly draw more outsourcing from companies around the world. Infosys is an excellent case study in leveraging internal training and educational programs to gain a competitive advantage in the markets it serves.

Education breaks down barriers and fosters globalization.

Each week, it seems that another U.S. college or university opens a campus in another country, creates an affiliate relationship with a school in another country, or provides its Internet based educational programs to students around the world. This is fast becoming a trend. Countries and educational institutions are especially targeting China, India, the Middle East, Indonesia, and Eastern European nations as areas for establishing programs and relationships. As globalization and the enabling force of the Internet make the world smaller and more interconnected, educational instruction and facilitation—just like business services—can now be made available to individuals located anywhere in the world. More importantly, education is often viewed as a vehicle by which people come to understand each other in a world of differences. Educational institutions often choose to physically locate their facilities in a country—in addition to having Internet capabilities—simply for the purpose of direct contact with students and the culture of a country. For example, we talked about China's Confucius Institute program earlier in this chapter and how its 100 locations around the world will seek to use education to break down barriers and foster collaboration and cooperation between China and other countries around the world.

For many years, international students have come to the U.S. in record numbers and, today, there are over 500,000 foreign students studying in U.S. colleges and universities. The U.S. is, by far, the country with the largest number of foreign students. For example, India has about 80,000 students studying in the U.S., Japan has 75,000, China 65,000, and Taiwan 29,000 (Study in U.S., 2006). Within the U.S., The University of Southern California has about 6,000 foreign students and New York University and Columbia have 5,000 each. Many other institutions, such as Cornell, Princeton, Northwestern, Yale, the University of California-Berkeley, Harvard, the University of Buffalo, MIT, and the Julliard School of Music, have significant numbers of foreign students studying primarily science, engineering, medicine, and advanced technology. While there is a significant number of U.S. students abroad, their fields of study emphasize culture, international business, and government. In recognition of the fact that we now live and work in a new global economy and community, many Business Schools (primarily graduate programs) now require study abroad as part of their educational programs. China and India are currently experiencing a growing number of foreign students attending educational facilities in their countries. In addition, many colleges and universities from elsewhere are locating facilities within the borders of China and India. There are other examples around the world, as well. A case in point is the tiny Arab nation of Qatar, which now hosts campuses from Cornell University, Texas A&M, Carnegie Mellon, Virginia Commonwealth, and Georgetown University on its 2,500 acre Education City campus near the capital city of Doha (MU Considered, 2006). And, right here in the Midwest, where I call home, the University of Missouri School of Journalism, one of the world's most respected journalism schools and the oldest journalism school in the U.S. (established in 1908), is vying to open a branch campus in Qatar (MU Considered, 2006). My how the world has become small!

The idea of cross-border educational offerings is not new, but today's recognition that all students need global competencies is driving a significant increase in cooperation and collaboration among many nations of the global community and economy. What is new today is that the Internet and the globalization process are new tools for changing the world—one student at a time!

Recommended Action Items:

1. Include education as a core strategic program in your organization's overall strategic planning process. For many organizations, the program will need to consist of both internal (in-house employee education, training, and personal development) and external (college, university, technical schools, specialized training) learning opportunities and experiences.

2. If your organization pays for all, or a portion, of an employee's education, recognize and celebrate the

employee's achievement of a degree or milestone in their program. Take an active role in coordinating student needs with the organization's needs, to ensure that the organization maintains its needed supply of innovative, global thinking employees at all levels of the organization. Business organizations, especially, will need to assume additional educational and expanded employee development responsibilities to fill shortages in science, math, and engineering positions.

3. Many firms have adopted an employee benefit program that calls for paying an employee's educational expenses if they achieve a "satisfactory" grade for an educational experience. In many grading systems, this "satisfactory grade" would equate to a letter grade of "C," which generally means passing with a satisfactory understanding of the subject matter. Too often, these payments for employees' educations are taken for granted by employees, and with little involvement by the employer who pays the bill. I would suggest that what might be needed is an incentive scale that allows payments to be made for educational expenses based on levels of achievement. For example, a passing grade ("C") would command a lesser payment than an excellent grade ("A"). Perhaps this would provide some incentive for a student to do better than just getting by. Another version of the incentive scale might call for bonus payments to be made when grades greater than "passing" are achieved. For example, an excellent grade ("A") might call for a 10% bonus payment above what would normally be paid by the employer. Yet another payment program might allow for bonus payments when employees take courses that are deemed to be in "critical need" by the employer. In conclusion, educational payment programs must be utilized to improve knowledge and productivity rather than serve as another "entitlement program." Whatever the algorithm, changes are in order.

4. Make "learning" and "education" life-long activities. This applies to individuals, organizations, and entire nations.

5. Initiate and maintain a collaborative process with local educational institutions to ensure that learning experiences match the needs of your organization.

6. Support local, state, and national educational initiatives to ensure the availability of "knowledge workers" who are trained in global business, innovation, leadership, and strategic planning.

7. Provide cultural exchanges with other countries to promote an understanding of the global community and economy in which we all live. For example, China is celebrating the "Year of Russia" during 2006, and Russia will celebrate the "Year of China" in 2007.

8. Educational institutions need to build key programs that address the same issues faced by businesses today with regard to new technology, new organizational structures, a highly skilled and autonomous work force, new management techniques, and labor-management collaboration (Carnevale, 2004).

9. There is just no getting around it; students need global competencies in today's world. Whether you are an individual or organization, push for and support initiatives that bring the study of global languages, cultures, and business practices into all levels of your school systems. To this point, kindergarten students in China's larger cities now study English and "western world" history. This is why most Chinese citizens speak good English and can more effectively do business with the English speaking nations of the world. India is also an example of a nation that has vast numbers of English speaking citizens. Understanding language and culture

will enhance working relationships with others in all countries, and perhaps even reduce conflict in the global economy and community in which we all reside.

10. It is important enough that I would like to repeat a portion of "Recommended Action Item #9" from Chapter 2. Consider adding an individual to your organization who is educated and skilled in "new-age innovation design disciplines," such as product, graphic, process, environmental, transportation, communication, illustration, advertising, textile, furniture, automotive, fashion, home products, architectural, technology, or industrial design—to name a few. Utilize this individual to lead your organization's awareness and actions to incorporate education in these disciplines into your operations, as well as perform hands-on training for others. Take a look back at Chapter 2 and you will see a sampling of some of the top schools, such as Carnegie Mellon University's School of Design, Pittsburgh, PA., that are turning out students skilled in these "new-age innovation methodologies."

11. To learn more about educational excellence and innovative leadership processes that can be applied to any learning process or program, see Richland College's website at *www.richlandcollege.edu*.

12. Apply the disciplines of "data-driven" decision-making and strategic planning to running a college or university. The Dallas, Texas, college discussed in this chapter, Richland College—the first community college in the U.S. to win the *Malcolm Baldrige National Quality Award*—uses data in all decision-making activities, and then uses data to monitor and track progress. The leadership team for the college also uses strategic planning, similar to that used to run a business, to focus the organization on its mission of "teaching, learning, and community building."

"The emergence of the global knowledge economy has put a premium on learning throughout the world. Without investment in education, there is virtually no way for a country to move to the head of the class."

World Bank Report, 2004. As found in "Measuring Globalization," KeepMedia, May 1, 2005

"Permanent education is going to be the name of the game in the world of 3 billion new capitalists." (In reference to China's population of 1.3 billion, India's population of 1.1 billion, and the former Soviet Union's population of 600 million—which totals 3.0 billion new capitalists.)

Clyde Prestowitz, President Economic Strategy Institute, Washington, D.C.

"Learn as if you are going to live forever. Live as if you were going to die tomorrow."

Mahatma Gandhi

Chapter 5

Global Strategy, Hedgehogs, Martha Stewart and Others

"Strategy is simply finding the 'big aha' and setting a broad direction, putting the right people behind it, and then executing with an unyielding emphasis on continual improvement."

Jack Welch, Retired GE Chairman and CEO

"A business plan is only a piece of paper, and even the greatest business plan of all will prove worthless unless the people of the company buy into it."

Howard Schultz, STARBUCKS Chairman and CEO

What does "Strategic Planning" have to do with globalization and new-age innovation? To be successful and gain a competitive advantage, many organizations will need to change their current strategic planning process. Their strategy will have to be modified, perhaps even reformulated entirely, to successfully compete in today's economically flattened world, where everyone can more equally participate. As the Internet and globalization whittle away at many companies' competitive advantage, it will be even more important to move beyond traditional strategic planning and focus on innovative and creative ways to build new products and services that sustain customer loyalty.

In this chapter, we will discuss some of the traditional and classical strategic planning methodologies that have been with us for a while, and introduce new strategic planning models that embrace and leverage globalization and "new-age innovation." Starbucks, Apple Computer, and Microsoft, to name a few, exemplify this new focus with their continuing stream of new products and services that keep us coming back for more. The new strategic planning methodologies that follow take into account the use of new-age innovation and the leveraging of globalization as tools and tactics for winning in the new global economy—quite often in the face of overwhelming competitive odds and constraints. More on this later!

Traditional and classical strategic planning processes.

IBM's chairman, Samuel J. Palmisano, stated one of the most classic views of strategy, when he remarked in an interview with *BusinessWeek* that "the holy grail of strategic thinking is: how do you come up with a business model that differentiates you and creates value for your customers and stakeholders and, by doing so, puts you in a unique position in your industry?" (Hamm, 2006) However, this discussion of classic strategic thinking only serves to lay the groundwork and understanding required for organizations to be able to move forward and incorporate globalization and "new-age innovation" into an expanded strategic planning model. To achieve and maintain a competitive position today, and in the future, companies must also rethink leadership and people strategies. Leaders with an understanding of "business architecture," globalization, and "new-age innovation" seem to be scarce, but are critical and key to the process of developing and executing global innovative strategies. Be prepared to learn that many individuals, and sometimes entire organizations, don't yet fully recognize globalization's impact, much less have an understanding of how to begin dealing effectively with it. Unfortunately, many are simply in denial.

As an MBA program instructor in "Strategy Formulation and Implementation," I have observed and used various outlines for effective strategic planning. Suffice it to say, I have not yet seen (though I hear a lot of talk about it) many specific line items in plans that deal with globalization, or the use of "new-age innovation" as a strategic tool (tactic) for addressing the impact globalization is having on organizations around the world.

Here is an outline of a typical traditional "strategic planning process map" that I believe is "representative" of what is <u>currently</u> in use by many organizations today:

<u>ROAD MAP FOR STRATEGIC PLANNING PROCESS (OUTLINE)</u>

I. Company/Organization's background
II. Vision Statement
III. Mission (Purpose) Statement
IV. Values/Ethics/Social Responsibility Statement
V. Environmental Analysis—Internal & External
VI. Long Term Objectives
VII. Strategic Directions/Guidance—Generic and Grand strategies
VIII. Implementation Tactics
IX. Financial Analysis and Projections
X. Determination of Key/Critical Success Factors
XI. Evaluation, Control, Feedback Methods, and Metrics

If you recognize this "map" and already consider globalization and "new-age innovation" in your planning process, that's great! But, stay with me, let's continue.

Makeover for your strategic planning process.

Each step in the above traditional "Strategic Planning Outline" must be expanded to include the impact of globalization on an organization, and how innovation, creativity, and imagination will be used by the organization to achieve and sustain its competitive global advantage. For example, a "Mission (Purpose) Statement" (Step III in the above outline) must include a precise description of what an organization does. It must describe the business the organization is in. It must define "why" the organization currently exists and must incorporate "socially meaningful and measurable criteria addressing concepts such as the moral/ethical position of the enterprise, public image, the target market, products/services, the geographic domain and expectations of growth and profitability" (Mission Statement, 2006). And today, more than ever before, Mission Statements need to focus on the global reach of the organization, and how its people will use "new-age innovation" to achieve a winning position in the markets and industry in which the organization participates and competes. Ideally, each member of an organization should understand and be able to verbally express the mission (purpose) of the organization (Healthfield, 2006). I tested this out on several Starbucks' employees and they could recite it word for word!

Listed below are some examples of good, and not so good, complete and one-liner "Mission Statements." At the end of each "statement," I have rated it Good (G) or Not So Good (NSG).

Saturn. "Our mission is to earn the loyalty of Saturn owners and grow our family by developing and marketing U.S. manufactured vehicles that are world leaders in quality, cost, and customer enthusiasm through the integration of people, technology, and business systems." (G)

Federal Express. "FedEx is committed to our People-Service-Profit Philosophy. We will produce outstanding financial returns by providing totally reliable, competitively superior, global, air-ground transportation of high-priority goods and documents that require rapid, time-certain delivery." (G)

Starbucks. "To establish Starbucks as the premier purveyor of the finest coffee in the world, while maintaining our uncompromising principles as we grow." (G)

IBM. "Our goal is simply stated. We want to be the best service organization in the world." (NSG)

Wal-Mart. "To give ordinary folk the chance to buy the same things as rich people."(NSG)

Mary Kay Cosmetics. "To give unlimited opportunity to women." (G)/(NSG) (Mission Statement, 2006)

Richland College. (First Community College in the U.S. to win the *Malcolm Baldrige National Quality Award.)* "To offer programs and services that enable students to achieve their educational goals and become life-long learners, community builders, and global citizens" (Award Winner, 2005). Their "short" statement, which is posted on all 275 external doors at the college in Dallas, Texas, is: "Teaching, Learning, Community Building." (G)

Boeing (1950). "Become the dominant player in commercial aircraft and bring the world into the jet age." This is an example that shows how statements change with the times. (G—back then) ((Mission Statement, 2006)

Those I ranked as "Good" (G) include such terms in their mission statements as "world" and "global," which recognize the globalization process that is prevalent today in all markets and industries. They also included the elements of technology and recognition of the people side of the strategic equation. I suspect we'll be seeing more emphasis on "new-age innovation," creativity, customer focus, and leadership in updated "Mission Statements" as globalization continues to put competitive pressures on all organizations.

For those that I ranked "Not So Good" (NSG), I don't see that they really convey what the organization's mission or purpose is. Employees, customers, and other stakeholders inside or outside of a company must be able to relate to a mission statement. Those statements marked "NSG" do not provide sufficient detail(s) and clarity in describing the company's mission. The statements from IBM and Wal-Mart could apply to a number of organizations. It is true, however, that IBM has reengineered the company with an intense focus on providing services. For years, IBM has been known primarily for its equipment. I believe globalization helped move IBM in this direction, even though they have been doing business around the world for years. For example, making PC's is no longer one of their focuses. Someone else; China-based Lenovo, can produce a low cost, great quality computer much better, so IBM has leveraged these capabilities and moved toward what it does best—services, integrated computer based systems, and applications of digital technology. IBM sold approximately 80% of its PC business to Lenovo in 2004. My how times have changed! IBM and the once closed communist country of China (through Lenovo) are now linked to sell PC's and related equipment, totaling $12 billion dollars per year through their operations in New York, Beijing, and Raleigh, North Carolina (Kanellos & Spooner, 2004). Globalization works in mysterious ways. There are a thousand other stories just like this one! This is another example of how we're all dependent on one another, but the IBM "one-liner" mission statement does not seem to relate this message.

Regarding the Wal-Mart one-liner mission statement, I'm not sure what it means. Is it really their mission and purpose in life "to give ordinary folk the chance to buy the same things as rich people?" I don't think so, but that's my opinion. Have you heard about the new Wal-Mart "test store" that opened in the Spring of 2006 in Plano, Texas? It caters to "rich people" (whatever "rich" means). It has high-end flat-screen TV's and expensive wines. You can take it from here.

An analysis, such as the one performed on the mission statements, must be conducted on each of the remaining steps in the strategic planning process. "Appendix A," located at the back of this book, gives a detailed "how to" reconstruction of all steps in the planning process. I hope you will use it. I also hope that you will execute your organization's strategy in a manner that leverages globalization and "new-age innovation" to gain a competitive advantage in the new global economy.

Leadership, management, and people capital.

As indicated at the beginning of this chapter, a firm's ability to leverage globalization and "new-age innovation" will require an ever-increasing number of leaders who can think strategically and act globally. Unfortunately, the literature on this subject says that there is an approaching shortage (critical) of people who have these skills, and who can effectively drive "new-age innovation" and globalization throughout an organization. In general, this shortage is the result of: (1) educational systems that are playing catch-up in establishing courses that address globalization, innovation and customer-centered business architectures; (2) management shortages in nearly all of the developing countries such as China, India, and Eastern Europe; and (3) the existence of a culture in the commercial world where many industries did not need to focus on global competitive factors. In other words, in many businesses, competition only extended to the borders of the country or region in which the organization was located. Now, the competitive playing field has changed, and the "team players" are from around the globe. For example, both the machine tool manufacturer in the small U.S. Midwestern town of Peoria, Illinois, and the apparel manufacturer near the eastern industrial coast of

China, know that global competition and the world is knocking at their doors.

<u>Be a great company and the rest will follow—if you are strategically focused.</u>

We have discussed briefly the "need" and the "how" to make globalization and innovation integral parts of an organization's strategic planning process. But, where does the rest of this chapter's title, "...Hedgehogs, Martha Stewart, and Others," fit in? (If you are thinking it, I am not referring to Martha Stewart as a Hedgehog.) Read further and you'll understand its meaning.

Martha Stewart, in her 2004 book, *THE Martha Rules*, focuses on finding that "big idea" upon which a business can be founded, and the strategic "rules" by which success can then be achieved (Stewart, 2005). Jim Collins, in his 2001 study and book entitled *Good To Great,* discovered (among other things) that success is founded in strategies that are "fueled by creativity, imagination, bold moves into uncharted waters, and visionary zeal" (Collins, 2001). Howard Schultz in his 1997 book, *Pour Your Heart Into It—how STARBUCKS built a Company, One Cup at a Time,* says that, by having a strategy with a "strong commitment to reinvention and self-renewal and by keeping the entrepreneurial spirit alive, an organization can foster an atmosphere that encourages innovation." Schultz also says: "I believe we can defy conventional wisdom by maintaining our passion, style, entrepreneurial drive, and personal connection—even as we become a larger global company" (Schultz, 1997). Jack Welch, retired GE Chairman and CEO, in his 2005 book *Winning*, says that "strategy is finding the 'big aha', but in real life strategy is actually very straightforward. You pick a general direction and implement like hell" (Welch, 2005). General Electric, under the leadership of Jack Welch in the 1980s and 1990s, was among the first major companies in the world to formally adopt "globalization" as one of its key strategic initiatives. As part of this strategy, the Company constructed a large technology center, The John F. Welch Technology Center, in Bangalore, India, and it is still very active today. In addition to Bangalore, during the 1990s, GE established additional service centers in Gurgaon, Hyderabad, and Jaipur, India, to handle work for 30 other GE businesses located around the world. These service centers were established in accordance with Jack Welch's "70-70-70 strategy," which required 70% of GE's work to be outsourced. Out of this, 70% of that work would be completed from offshore service centers. And out of this, 70% would be sent to India. This comes out to about 30% of GE's work being outsourced to India (Offshore, 2006). GE also constructed The GE China Technology Center in Shanghai, and most recently established The GE China Learning Center in the same facility. The firm is also known for two other major strategic initiatives: "digitization" (the use of computer technology) and the "Six Sigma Process" (a quality management and decision-making program). GE's new leader, Jeffery Immelt, continues to embrace these initiatives and has now refocused the organization's direction on "innovation" and "growth" as strategies for making sure GE continues to be a global growth leader in each industry in which it participates.

Even though these individuals represent a wide spectrum of thoughts on strategy, innovation, and globalization, a common theme emerges as one reads their books. To be great, organizations have to learn how to: 1) "simplify a complex world into a single organizing idea—a basic principle or concept that unifies and guides everything, and 2) build strategies around this single organizing idea that drives the organization to achieve greatness" (Collins, 2001). Jim Collins has attached a name to this theme of "simplicity" and "unification of direction." It is called being a "***hedgehog***" (Collins, 2005). Organizations that act like a "hedgehog" create focused strategies, essential to their single organizing purpose, that confront the often brutal challenges of survival and competition. All non-essential ideas are ignored. I suppose this is how a "hedgehog" acts as he looks for food and fights for survival.

Regarding another "hedgehog" company, *Starbucks* says that their simple and single organizing concept that guides all actions in the organization is: "to bring a great cup of coffee to everyone everywhere, in stores that provide a rewarding experience that enriches peoples' lives in communities around the world, one cup at a time" (Schultz, 1997). Did you ever think a cup of coffee and a coffee shop could turn into a billion dollar business? I sure didn't! Certainly, Starbucks has embraced globalization and new-age innovation and is winning around the world. As of May 2006, there were 11,377 Starbucks locations around the globe, employing 112,833 partners (which is how everyone in the company refers to each other). By the time you are reading this, these numbers will be much larger. Starbucks sales in 2005 were $6.7 billion (U.S. dollars), up 20% from 2004. I've often wondered, just how many cups of coffee this might be? Even more admirable is the fact that the company has realized 14 consecutive years of comparable store sales growth of 5% or more, which earned it a rank of #24 on *BusinessWeek's* 2006 "Top Performers" list (The Ranking, 2006). Net income of $524 million in 2005 was up 26% over 2004, with a steady growth rate over the past three years that has averaged 34%. Starbucks' innovative expansion programs into new product offerings, drive-through service, and rural locations—which are all 2005-6 initiatives driven by new CEO Jim Donald—promise to enable the continuation of excellent sales and profitability trends (The Ranking, 2006). Three year projections call for a greater number of Starbucks' locations in China than in the United States. By the way, I recently visited my local Starbucks (yes! there are Starbucks in Leawood, Kansas) and spoke with the manager, a young lady in her twenties named Christy Sue. She told me that Starbucks was more than a coffee shop serving the best coffee products. "Starbucks is a people business serving coffee," she remarked. She emphasized that Starbucks focuses on providing a community location for bringing people together in a comfortable atmosphere, "over a cup of coffee!" When asked how she saw Starbucks connected globally, she remarked that the company's diversity and community involvement programs keep everyone connected to people and communities around the world. She went on to say that she would be visiting a coffee farm in Central America (Costa Rica) next year as part of Starbucks program to keep connected within the company and with global communities that are an integral part of the Company's success. Not only do employees (partners) visit coffee farms, but Starbucks awards the communities in which these farms reside with cash awards for use in improving healthcare, community needs, school support, computers, water supplies, etc. Starbucks is certainly an excellent example of how a company can leverage globalization and "new-age innovation" to gain a competitive advantage in the new global economy. Have you tried the new Rwanda Blue Bourbon or Brazilian Ipanema Bourbon coffees yet? "They" tell me they're great!

Now, I would like to turn our attention to Martha Stewart's "hedgehog" organization, Martha Stewart Living Omnimedia, Inc. Martha's company (she owns 92% of the voting stock) is the world's leading integrated content (information) company devoted to enriching the changing lives of today's women and their families. With regard to strategy, Martha says, "simple ideas are the most compelling and the easiest to sell. To be successful, it is essential to start with one 'big idea' and then leverage it into something bigger. It is not good business to launch your big idea when it is too complex or has too many diverse parts" (Stewart, 2005). In terms of specific strategic initiatives, Martha Stewart Living is a global organization with "how to" experts who are "committed to teaching, innovating, designing, and inspiring with ideas and products that make every day more meaningful, more functional, and *more beautiful*" (Stewart, 2005). This is certainly a great example of taking one big idea—providing information and help about the familiar elements of daily life (cooking, cleaning, decorating, gardening, entertaining, etc)—and turning them into a billion dollar business. *Martha Stewart Living Magazine* reaches 14 million people globally each month and her television shows reach 30 million. *Everyday Food*, another of Martha's popular magazines, reaches 850,000 readers each month. And, she now has a Sirius Satellite radio channel to communicate and promote these and other products and services. The "Martha Stewart" name can also be found on all kinds of home merchandise at Kmart stores worldwide, and next year, her name will be associated with an upscale line of home products ("The Martha Stewart Collection") for Macy's department stores. As an aside, Martha Stewart bought the magazine, *Martha Stewart Living,* from Time Warner, Inc. in 1997 for $85 million with borrowed funds collateralized by her personal assets. With her entrepreneurial and innovative style, she formulated a global strategy that grew the company into a highly visible and successful media business, which is still growing today. (2005 sales revenues were $209 million, which was a 12% growth rate over 2004.) In 1999, she took the company public and raised enough money to completely pay off the $85 million she borrowed from her bank and all other debts. Along the way, Martha spent 5 months in prison and 5 months under home confinement for being involved with the use of insider stock trading information, which was unrelated to her *Martha Stewart Living Omnimedia* business.

Martha Stewart Living Omnimedia, Starbucks, and the General Electric Company (GE) certainly exemplify how companies that act like "hedgehogs," and passionately focus on single unifying ideas above all else, can move from a "good company" to a "great company" (Collins, 2005).

More about Martha's strategy.

In *THE Martha's Rules, 10 Essentials for Achieving Success as You Start, Build, and Manage a Business*, Martha Stewart discusses ten strategic rules to follow in order to achieve success in the new global economy. The assumption that innovation, new ideas, and change are the cornerstones to success in the globalized world runs throughout the book. The rules seem to have application to many of the issues that might be encountered by any organization—competitive pricing, quality, personnel, new products and services, and supply chain management—to name a few. Does Ms. Stewart see globalization as a negative force on her business? As a threat? *No* seems to be the answer. She spends her time and energy innovating new products and services, and focusing on strategies that make for a winning competitive advantage. Leveraging the benefits brought about by globalization, rather than fearing it, seems to work at Martha Stewart Living Omnimedia, Inc. More organizations need to take this approach. Martha's rules are: (Stewart, 2005)

1. "Build your business success around something that you love—something that is inherently and endlessly interesting to you."
2. "Focus your attention and creativity on basic things, things that people need and want. Then look for ways to enlarge, improve, and enhance your big idea."
3. "Create a business plan that allows you to stay true to your big idea but helps you focus on the details. Then, remain flexible enough to zoom in and out on the vital aspects of your enterprise as your business grows."
4. "By sharing your knowledge about your product or service with your customers, you create a deep connection that will help you learn how best to build and manage your business."

5. "Use smart, cost effective promotional techniques that will arrest the eye, tug at your heart, and convey what is unique and special about your business or service."
6. "Quality should be placed at the top of your list of priorities, and it must remain there. Quality is something you should strive for in every decision, every day."
7. "Seek out and hire employees who are brimming with talent, energy, integrity, optimism, and generosity. Search for advisors and partners who complement your skills and understand your ideals."
8. "When faced with a business challenge, evaluate and assess the situation, gather the good things in sight, abandon the bad, clear your mind, and move on. Focus on the positive. Stay in control, and never panic."
9. "In business, there is a difference between a risk and a chance. A well-calculated risk may very well end up as an investment in your business. A careless chance can cause it to crumble. And, when an opportunity presents itself, never assume it will be your last."
10. "Listen intently, learn new things every day, be willing to innovate, and become an authority your customers will trust. As an entrepreneur, you will find great joy and satisfaction in making your customers' lives easier, more meaningful, and more beautiful."

The above is simply a list of Martha's Rules. You can learn more detail by reading the chapters in her book devoted to each of these "rules."

More about strategies for becoming a great company.

I would like to conclude and summarize this chapter by using what I call Jack Welch's "Five Slide Approach to Setting, Testing, and Continually Improving an Organization's Strategy." Use of this "five slide" approach does not mean that the revised detailed formal strategic planning process, previously outlined, can be skipped. These supporting details are necessary when using the following summarized "five slide" approach to strategic planning:

Slide One – "What does the global playing field look like today?"

Slide Two – "What has the competition been up to?"

Slide Three – "What have you been up to?"

Slide Four – "What is around the corner?"

Slide Five – "What is your winning move?"

I suggest, in a general sense, short answers to the above questions might be: (1) The playing field is global and continues to be economically leveled, as many of the developing nations of the world come on to the playing field. Capitalism and consumerism will continue to characterize the field; (2) The competition is global, innovative, and continues to grow in numbers and strength. Companies in "developed countries" will have a difficult time competing on price in areas where labor costs are extremely low; (3) Whatever your organization has been up to, some changes will probably be in order. As outlined in this chapter, an excellent way to start is by revamping your strategic planning process to encompass globalization and the use of "new-age innovation" to achieve and maintain a competitive advantage; (4) Intensified global competition, innovation, and the globalization of markets will continue as more manufacturing, services, and capital continues to move to Asia and Eastern Europe; (5) Winning will require the strategic rebirth of innovation, and organizations will need to work together in a global collaborative manner to develop new and improved products and services. Instead of fearing globalization, individuals who lead organizations will need to look at "cheap labor" developing nations around the world not just as suppliers of products and services, but as new markets for their organization's products and services.

Recommended Action Items.

1. Incorporate the leveraging of globalization and "new-age innovation" techniques into your strategic planning process. Senior managers must take the daily leadership role in driving and supporting the process. The board of directors must lend support for the process and conduct an overview of the plan to ensure that the organization has a direction that includes the effective use of globalization and "new-age innovation." More importantly, everyone in an organization, from top to bottom, must understand the organization's direction with regard to globalization and innovation. It has been my experience that you cannot over-communicate the strategic direction for an organization. The trend in the new global economy is to empower all in an organization who play a part in carrying out a strategic plan. I guess one might say that this includes everyone! "Old" thinking that a strategic plan is for the use and understanding of "top management" is not valid today, and probably never was. You will be amazed at the results you can achieve by including functional and lower level leaders in the strategic planning process. Open lines of communication with all stakeholders will facilitate understanding of the strategic direction of the company. For example, employees will be better informed and prepared for the outsourcing and offshoring of jobs should this be required in carrying out the plan. All stakeholders in the organization will understand their role in innovation, globalization, and change management.

2. Incorporate "SWOT" and "TOWS" techniques when performing an environmental marketing analysis for your organization. Do you remember that basic marketing class you might have taken in college? Well, two important analytical techniques included in that course will prove beneficial in establishing an effective global

strategic plan. These techniques are discussed below. Both require a global perspective!

SWOT (**S**trengths-**W**eaknesses; **O**pportunities-**T**hreats) analysis results in the identification, analysis, and establishment of long-term objectives that can minimize weaknesses and capitalize on a firm's strengths. SWOT analysis requires the identification and evaluation of a firm's internal strengths and weaknesses, as well as its external competitive opportunities and threats. The most important element of the SWOT analysis process, though, is that it requires an organization to evaluate where it stands in relation to competitors, and the global markets and industry in which it competes. This process can often be difficult because it requires recognition of weaknesses. Admitting one's weaknesses doesn't seem to come easy, but is a requirement in order to sort out the brutal hard facts of the competitive business world and the new global economy.

The ***"TOWS"*** process (**T**hreats-**O**pportunities; **W**eaknesses-**S**trengths) takes the SWOT technique one step further. It requires the deliberate development and use of opportunities to offset threats And, it requires a look at strengths that might offset weaknesses.

These techniques can help an organization develop an effective competitive strategic plan that leverages strengths and mitigates weaknesses.

3. Include a review of the supply chains your organization utilizes for labor, materials, and services. Make sure the review ends with a strategic choice of the most cost and quality effective supply chains available globally. And, become integrally involved with your supply chains and focus on helping suppliers improve their cost structures, productivity, and financial health.

4. Establish flexible strategies that allow for change so that focus can be placed on what your organization does best. If you find that printing is cheaper in China than in the U.S., then buy printing from China and leverage that supply chain's cost advantage. Then, focus your attention on selling and innovating new products and services, rather than managing a labor and capital intensive printing operation. To this point, strive to be a less capital and labor intensive company by managing supply chains for your business. For example, Wal-Mart is the world's best at being a supply chain based company. In other words, it does not manufacture anything—it only sells what is supplied by others. And, it seeks out "others" who excel (in terms of quality and price) at providing products and services needed for the thousands of Wal-Mart stores around the world.

5. Try out your strategic plans by running them through key scenarios. ***Scenario planning*** is a "what if" technique that uses possible events in the future to simulate the impacts on an organization, if such events were to occur. Today's heightened interest and use of scenario planning is the result of the 9/11 attacks on the United States and rising global competition. This type of analysis allows an organization to be better prepared for the future as changes occur—such as significant interest rate spikes for a mortgage company.

6. Become a "***hedgehog***" company; one that focuses on a single and unifying idea (product and/or service line).

7. Be willing to step outside the box and rethink business architecture (organizational structure). Sometimes, the best strategic plan in the world can't work when implemented in an incorrect or inefficient organizational model.

8. Use the Jack Welch strategic planning model discussed in this chapter. This model is an abbreviated "5-slide" (referring to PowerPoint slides) approach to establishing, monitoring, and changing strategies. But, don't forget to do the detail backup work required in order to realistically understand strengths, weaknesses, and alternative courses of action that will maximize strengths and minimize, or mitigate, weaknesses. The two techniques presented in "Action Item #2"—*SWOT* and *TOWS*—are excellent processes for this analysis.

9. Hire leaders with a global perspective who are skilled at dealing with the many aspects of globalization, "new-age innovation," business architecture, and competitive analysis. They are often in short supply. In some cases, you might have to train your own.

10. When it comes to tactics and the implementation of strategic plans, always consider the use of new technologies: Internet based marketing, web applications for use by customers, and wireless applications that unhook customers and employees from being tied to a location.

11. Communicate, communicate, communicate—all stakeholders must know and understand a company's strategic direction in order to effectively help achieve its objectives.

12. Above all, use the Martha Helen (her middle name) Stewart "rules" and strategies, especially if you plan on starting a business, which requires a "great idea, a unique vision, and a lot of stamina" (Welcome Home, 2005).

13. Include in your strategic planning process a review and hard look at your organization's core competencies. Analyze the areas in your company that aren't directly involved in these competencies, and consider whether

global outsourcing/offshoring and the Internet can enable you to spin off these tasks. Then, as Bill Gates of Microsoft says, "Consider letting another company take over the responsibilities for the non-core work, and use modern communication technology to work closely with the people—now partners instead of employees—who are doing the work. In the 'Web work style,' employees can push the freedom the Web provides to its limits" (Gates, 1999). This is an example of using strategic planning to leverage globalization and "new age innovation" for the purpose of achieving and maintaining a competitive advantage in the new global economy. (This action item is also included as an action item in Chapter 1, since "strategic plans" for today's organization's often require the outsourcing/offshoring of "non-core functions" as a means of achieving a competitive advantage.)

"We changed our strategy to focus more on developing markets and low-income consumers, and today we're reaching three-fifths of the world's consumers."

Bob McDonald, Vice Chairman of Global Operations, Proctor & Gamble

---

Chapter 6

Governance, Accountability, and Ethics in the New Global Economy: Whose Standards Apply?

Wednesday February 15, 2006, Associated Press Reports: "Four U.S. high-tech companies were branded collaborators with the Chinese government in suppressing dissent in return for access to a booming Internet market."

Foster Klug, Associated Press Writer

There it was, tucked away on page three of the *Kansas City Star*: "Internet firms criticized as allies of Chinese censorship!" (Klug, 2006) With regard to globalization and conducting business in an international environment—censorship, governance, accountability and ethics are all topics we'll be hearing more about in the future. Frankly, I don't believe these are subjects anyone is looking forward to tackling, much less dealing with their resolutions. Why? The task of finding "common ground" among even a few of the nations of the world will be daunting. Secondly, for firms that are competing in the new world economy (which includes almost all—a few just don't know it yet) there is too much at stake in terms of profitability, economic survival, and competitive positioning. However, there will be no choice. Inaction is not an option! The world cannot be economically “flat,” and ethically “round!” But whose standards of conduct will apply when it comes to ethics, governance, and accountability for actions that impact people? It’s almost like asking, whose religion is “right?” Can the profit motive of capitalism, that is taking hold in many of the developing nations of the world today, find adaptation and collaboration with social responsibility? We are at the tip of this iceberg.

This chapter will attempt to discuss these “fuzzy” issues. And, yes, there are right and wrong standards that apply—at least from my uncensored and freedom of speech perspective!

Wink-Wink; Turn your head; Look the other way!

The world has become economically flat, but it is not flat in terms of ethics, governance, and accountability. We have all been haunted over the years by the sweatshops and abuses of people across Asia and the developing nations of the world. Globalization seems to be helping these situations on the one hand but hurting them on the other. First, help comes in the form of large companies and organizations locating within many of the economically developing nations and bringing with them their environmental and human rights polices. Second, many of the world’s businesses have refused to carry on cross-border commercial transactions with countries (governments and businesses) that do not have responsible environmental and human rights programs in place, or do not enforce the ones they have.

General Electric, Motorola, Proctor & Gamble, Ford, General Motors, Airbus, Boeing, McDonalds, Patagonia, Sony, and Coca Cola are but a few of the well-known companies who adhere to a set of high standards for all operations, wherever located. These standards respect individual’s rights and well-being, and the environment in which they live and work. In addition, these companies have well established and enforced high standards of ethical business, human rights, and legal practices.

On the other hand, some companies have been lured into questionable practices in order to take advantage of two irresistible general economic conditions:

1. To gain a ***supply*** of products and services at significantly decreased prices due to cheap labor found in many of the world's developing countries;
2. To tap into large and ever-expanding markets within these developing countries to ***sell*** products and services and invest capital for the achievement of top-line revenue sales growth and/or bottom line profitability growth.

In both cases, companies can often achieve tremendous wealth, profitability, and growth that are significantly beyond levels obtained in the past. Or, in some cases, these markets may simply provide sufficient profitability for a firm's survival.

For example, the above conditions may indicate why many companies are looking to China, India, and all of Southeast Asia for their growth, profitability, and economic survival. It is well known that everyone is looking to the "East" for prosperity. I often wonder if the Chinese and Indian people realize that much of the rest of the world is depending on their economies for survival and growth. Yet, everyday we hear and read about another company's expansion strategy that calls for their growth to be driven by the purchase of low cost labor from China, India, Eastern Europe, and Southeast Asia. In addition, many of these expansion strategies also include establishing markets for the sale of products and services in these countries and regions. In fact, as I recently drove past the large Kansas City Harley Davidson motorcycle manufacturing facility on my way to the airport for a business trip, I was reminded that just this month (May,

2006) the company announced that it would expand sales into India and Vietnam. Expansion into China is already underway. Do you recall when we were all looking to Mexico and South America for cheap labor and resources to power economic growth? It seems to change over the years, doesn't it? These expansion strategies, for the most part, have been beneficial for both "developing" and "developed" countries. We now call it globalization. Back then, it was simply called international trade.

Globalization, though, is different. It is powerful and driven by growth in countries that will amass and control large amounts of the world's capital and resources of production. This is the irresistible lure—a powerful economic force—that might cause companies to adjust, or ignore their value systems in order to take advantage of the huge opportunities for growth and profitability.

For example, in order to do business in the communist controlled country of China, officially known as the People's Republic of China (PRC), companies must abide by Chinese laws and programs for censorship. As mentioned earlier in this book, China has approximately 30,000 personnel throughout the country engaged in censorship activities and enforcement of their restrictions on free speech. Several of the key Chinese censorship requirements include: (Klug, 2006)

1. The screening of personnel and organizations who might be dissident towards the Chinese government and its policies. This includes screening and censorship of both Chinese citizens, as well as visitors and others from outside the country;
2. The screening and blocking of Web sites that the Chinese government considers objectionable;
3. The banning of what the Chinese government considers subversive and pornographic;

4. The requirement that Internet service providers enforce government censorship, and include self-censorship procedures in their communications over the Internet;
5. The screening out of certain words that might denote subversive activities, or words that the government deems inappropriate for viewing.

Item number four on the list above has brought several U.S. companies under critical scrutiny by the U.S. government. Microsoft, Yahoo, Cisco Systems, and Google were "criticized" for being allies of Chinese censorship by members of the U.S. House of Representatives in February 2006 (Klug, 2006). Tom Lantos, of the House International Relations Committee, stated "these companies' actions in China are a disgrace." And, Jim Leach of the same committee, stated that "Google seemingly had acted as a functionary of the Chinese government" (Klug, 2006). These companies stand to gain a large share of the 110 million Internet user's market in China, which will result in significant profitability for each company. So, the dilemma intensifies as each company tries to find a solution to doing business in China in a manner considered ethical by differing world standards. At this point, the choices seem to be: comply with Chinese law, or leave the country and substantial profits behind. I believe it is fair to say that these companies would never think of engaging in any form of censorship in the United States. Actually, it is against U.S. law and the free speech provisions found in the *Constitution of the United States.* Britain, France, Canada, and Germany as well as others have much the same protections against governmental censorship and human rights.

I did find an interesting perspective on the Congressional hearings as I read a well-known personal investment newsletter. Neil George and Roger Conrad in their monthly "Personal Finance" newsletter remarked: "Hearings such as these are primarily for show, for both the politicians asking the questions and the people answering them. As a result, don't expect any significant changes for these 'tech companies' or China's economic and political situation" (Conrad, 2006). You be the judge!

In the end, we are basically left with the fact that social norms, and business standards and practices vary widely from country to country. What is considered "right" and "acceptable," or "wrong" and "unacceptable" in one country may be just the opposite in another. In many of the developing countries, business and legal practices are often poorly developed and enforced. And, "corruption is rife" (Volcker, 2001). Furthermore, there is a tendency for companies to simply comply with the wishes of a particular country, in the name of *obeying the rules* established by that country. This is where compliance becomes a grey issue. Is the need to accept a country's rules in order to do business in that country sufficient enough to ignore certain human rights and freedom of speech issues? Is it okay to limit search results through the internet, block certain websites from use, and screen out certain words in order to get a piece of the profits in China? Where does a company draw the line? Is it okay to go along with a limited program of censorship or some small "under the table" payments to officials to achieve one's goals? I believe "No" is the answer to these questions. Others, depending on their country and value system, will perhaps see it differently. How far does a company go? Should a company use its country's accepted laws and standards to guide its ethical and socially responsible behaviors? It would, of course, be easy if there was a set of globally acceptable standards. However, I doubt a set of agreed upon world standards will be available any time soon—perhaps never.

Other examples of this "*Wink-Wink; Turn your head; Look the other way*" modus operandi can also be seen in other parts of the world. For example, the strained relationship that exists between China and Taiwan regarding Chinese Communist Party control over Taiwan, seems to be fading in importance. Fading in the sense that China now buys 40% of Taiwan's exports, and, according to the January 2006 *Economist*, most Taiwanese see the Chinese-Taiwan economic relationship "far too important to disrupt" (No Questions Asked, 2006). The more politically correct observation might be that "economic dependence is breaking down barriers and restoring peaceful relationships" (Taiwan, 2006). On the other hand, it will be insightful to keep asking: Is it okay to accept a little communistic censorship and control for the sake of economic gain, or do ethical actions, human rights, and freedom of speech rule? And, as the title of this chapter states: "whose standards apply?"

It's not just about doing business in China and maintaining some sense of effective governance, accountability, and ethical principles while doing so. It is also about China doing business in the rest of the world. The January 2006 issue of the *Economist* reported in an article titled "No Questions Asked—Human Rights are No Bar to China's Hunt for Resources," that "China has long been an advocate of keeping human rights and other pesky political issues separate from business. And, in Africa it is practicing what it preaches" ("No Questions Asked," 2006). China's significant focus on Africa appears to be another part of its shopping spree around the world to secure oil and other resources it needs to sustain its growing economy and population of 1.3 billion people. China now gets 30% of its oil from Africa; mainly Sudan, Angola, and parts of Congo. China's total trade with Africa for all products and services is estimated at $40+ billion (U.S. dollars). Many of China's trading partners in Africa are countries that don't get high marks for human rights. To name a few, these include Nigeria, Equatorial Guinea, Somalia, Zimbabwe, Ethiopia, Sudan, Angola, and Libya; all countries in which the Chinese government is beginning to have significant financial and trading relationships. Most Western World countries have been reluctant to do any type of business in many of these nations. The United States and several major European countries have shown an "increasing concern with China's involvement in Africa, because it undermines their own efforts to tie trade and aid to human rights, and to help Africa overcome corruption. These countries fear that many Chinese companies show scant regard for either consideration" (No Questions Asked, 2006). Two of the more recent significant transactions have been a $2.0 billion (U.S. dollars) loan to Angola from China in return for oil, and an agreement with Nigeria to supply 30,000 barrels of oil per day to the PRC (People's Republic of China). Since 2004, China's president, Hu Jintao, and foreign minister, Li Zhaoxing, have both made personal visits to several of these countries to discuss and arrange trade deals (No Questions Asked, 2006).

So, what are we to think about countries that do business with nations whose humanitarian standards are severely lacking and where political corruption is widespread? What are we to think about companies who adhere to human rights standards in their home country, but turn their heads and look away when doing business in a censored environment in another country? There can be but one answer—the lure of profits (money)! Or, to state it in the conventional jargon: "the power of the almighty dollar, peso, yuan, franc, yen, rupee . . .!" And, more importantly, whose standards will be the measuring stick?

Back in the USA—wiretapping, data mining, Patriot Act.

Globalization is making the world smaller in terms of the free flow of communications and commercial transactions among nations. It also binds us together economically. Travel and the movement of goods and services among all nations are freer than ever before. With these increased cross-border activities and open communications in the new digital world comes the possibility of abuses by those who take advantage of such opportunities. This was the case on

9/11/2001, when terrorists toppled the World Trade Center in New York City. This event ushered in the war on terrorism, which continues today and will for many years to come. In fact, many contend that the world has changed permanently. This reminds me of the stories I often heard my mother and father tell that went something like: "I can remember when we didn't have to lock our houses, and you could leave the keys in your car on Main Street." I often wondered what "Main Street" they were talking about. Well, those days are gone. We now need heightened security measures and far-reaching governmental controls to protect us from terrorism and harm. This is new to citizens in the United States and a few other countries. It is <u>not</u> new to much of the rest of the world—the volatile Middle East, Africa, and Asia. This is yet another indicator that we live in a global community; none of us can escape the realities of diverse beliefs, religions, political persuasions, and social norms. The world is simply becoming "flat" (Friedman, 2005). But, "whose standards will apply" in determining what is good or bad; right or wrong? Or, can we reach a global middle ground? Many of us long for a return of the "good 'ole days." We'll need to get over it; it's not going to happen!

Countries around the world, specifically, the United States, have increased security measures and given lawmakers and intelligence agencies expanded powers to combat terrorism in many areas. As a result, The U.S. Patriot Act of 2001, under certain conditions, now allows limited domestic wiretapping, access to personal data, and surveillance of citizen's actions (E.F.F., 2006). Specifically, in the United States, we are wrestling with the question of how many of our civil liberties and rights to free speech, privacy, and dissent we are willing to give up in the name of combating terrorism and maintaining security. To monitor this issue and provide some control over lawmakers and intelligence agencies and their use of these new powers, the U.S. Congress has established the Civil Liberties Oversight Board. To date, there has been little action from the 5-

member Board, but they expect to start with a look at Pentagon data mining, the President's domestic wiretapping program, and the Patriot Act (Isikoff, 2006). Wiretapping, surveillance, and access to private information are actions that U.S. citizens are certainly not accustomed to. It will take some "getting used to," even if it is in the name of combating terrorism and providing security for the homeland.

Ethics and Intellectual Property Rights.

We hear the term and frequently read about it, but what exactly does "intellectual property" mean? As defined at the *Convention Establishing the World Intellectual Property Organization,* Stockholm, July 14, 1967, "intellectual property includes the rights relating to: literary, artistic and scientific works, performances of performing artists, phonograms, broadcasts, inventions in all fields of human endeavor, scientific discoveries, industrial designs, trademarks, service marks, commercial names and designations, protection against unfair competition, and all other rights resulting from intellectual activity in the industrial, scientific, literary or artistic fields. Intellectual property is a creation of the intellect that has commercial value" (What Is Intellectual Property, 2005). This lengthy definition illustrates that there is a multitude of non-physical items that fall into what is called "intellectual property." If it's non-physical, then how does one steal it from another? The simple answer is that the idea is copied, such as copying the design for an automobile, or copying the formula for a prescription drug! In these examples, the owner of the automobile design and owner of the drug formula would have obtained exclusive right of ownership and use by patenting the design and formula. Ownership of "intellectual property" is generally demonstrated by registering the intellectual item as a patent, copyright, trademark, or trade secret.

I touched on this topic back in Chapter 1 only to mention that the "stealing of intellectual property" is a problem around the globe, especially in Asia. Well, it has become more than a problem. It has reached a crisis stage! Globalization and "new-age innovation" have inundated the world with digital information, software products and services, and traditional products. Car parts, Harley Davidson Motorcycles, household products, and toys—to name a few—have been copied in Mexico, China and many other regions of Asia. To this point, "it is a basic reality that the Chinese have demonstrated a huge capacity for theft of intellectual property in everything from computer programs and compact discs, to automobiles and designer jeans" (Lieberthal, 2004). I must apologize to my Chinese readers. I use this example only to illustrate that protecting intellectual property rights is a documented major problem in the global economy. Some choose to abuse the basic rights granted to the creators of this property. However, on a positive note, slow progress is being made toward solving the problem as the Chinese Legal System undergoes major changes, and a revamping of Chinese law takes place. Completion is expected in 2010. Meanwhile, the United States, Britain, and the World Trade Organization are pushing China to increase the enforcement of existing laws. Fixing, or perhaps just slowing, the widespread violation of intellectual property rights will take time.

In the United States, and much of the Western World, there are strong laws governing who owns and who can use intellectual property. In part, these laws are based on the ethical premise that it is not "right" to freely use or obtain financial gain from the ideas and creations of others—without, of course, permission or compensation to the creator for such use. Violation of this premise (violation of intellectual property rights) is generally considered "stealing," and carries a substantial penalty.

In today's digital economy, it just might be that "digital intellectual property" will be one of the most valuable assets to own in the future—if it can be protected from theft and illegal use (How Has the Electronic Age, 2005).

<u>Policing world trade: (the "wobbly wheel," "jack-in-the-box" effect).</u>

Maintaining fair trade and promoting ethical business practices among companies in a single country can be hard enough. Trying to police global trade and ethical practices around the world is nearly impossible. As globalization moves faster and faster, and more companies compete for a competitive advantage, the need for enforceable guidelines for fair trade and ethical business practices becomes extremely urgent. One-upsmanship will have its finest hour (or perhaps worst) as companies fight to grow and earn profits in the vast new markets of the developing nations. Threatening actions and "name calling" are already common procedures when individuals and companies lack a competitive advantage, or are in fear of losing their advantage.

For example, the U.S. continues to pressure China to allow their exchange rate to float so that Chinese export prices for goods going to other countries, including the U.S., won't have such an unfair advantage over other countries' prices. Do we really think that China's export levels will change significantly by simply forcing the country to further modify its monetary policy regarding its exchange rate? After all, a shirt can be made in China with 85 cents an hour labor, compared to $10.00 in the U.S. It will take a huge adjustment in the Chinese exchange rate to make up this difference. In addition, if China's currency becomes stronger against the dollar, as many predict will happen, the result will be higher prices to shoppers around the world—including the millions of us who shop at Wal-Mart each year.

Further, this monetary argument states that higher Chinese prices will give European and U.S. firms a better chance to compete with Chinese companies. Forcing China to discontinue control of its currency exchange rate doesn't seem to solve the gap between 85 cents and $10 per hour labor costs, although it makes sense from a "fair play," and "fair trade" point of view. Perhaps the 85 cents per hour needs to be considered from a human rights and subsistence level perspective. Remember back in Chapter 3 and the discussion about not wasting resources trying to compete based on "cheap labor?" Well, trying to compete directly with 85 cents per hour labor just may be a waste of resources. So, do we need a global "currency exchange police force?" No, but we do need standards and guidelines. Will the World Trade Organization take the lead?

The above "currency control" example is but one issue. There are many compliance, governance, accountability and ethical issues that need attention as global trade grows at an amazingly fast pace. Just pick one: environmental, import/export tariffs, local subsidies to companies to protect competitive positions, alliances to gain competitive advantages, shipping and transportation regulations, price fixing, tax favoritism, corporate transfer pricing schemes, banking relationships, etc. Who will lead the governance effort and whose standards will apply? How will we ever reach a common ground for global trade standards? Or, will we continue to ride on a "wobbly wheel" set of mixed standards, making slow progress as we learn how to live and do business in the new global economy? This is the next frontier for governance, compliance, accountability, and ethics!

These issues continue to exhibit "jack-in-the-box" characteristics and pop up every day, somewhere in the new global community. For example, in March 2006, the European Union advised the World Trade Organization that it would "reintroduce trade sanctions against the United

States unless Washington complied with a WTO ruling against tax breaks for U.S. companies operating overseas" (Europe Warns of Sanctions, 2006). The WTO judged that the "U.S. Foreign Sales Corporation" law breached global trade rules by giving illegal subsidies to some U.S. businesses, which included Microsoft and Boeing (Europe Warns of Sanctions, 2006). Meanwhile, on the other side of the world, the Chinese government continues to require certain banks to provide lending to local businesses at favorable interest rates. These artificially low rates reduce local business costs and protect the business from imported goods that take away their market share. I suppose this would be something like the U.S. government requiring Bank of America to provide General Motors with lending at 1% interest to help lower GM's cost structure in order to allow the company to be more competitive with Toyota. I don't think this will happen, but it puts the Chinese example into perspective.

I'd like to come back to the WTO (World Trade Organization) for a moment, since this great organization continues to play a major role in bringing about governance, compliance, and accountability with regard to "fair trade" among the nations of the world. Or, at least we can say, among the members of the WTO who have agreed to be a part of this process, and abide by WTO guidelines and rulings. An example of how the WTO is working to be the "world's arbitrator" of "fair trade practices"—which is a tall order for any single organization—can be seen in the recent dispute between the United States and the tiny twin-island Caribbean nations of Antigua and Barbuda. The dispute involved allowing U.S. gamblers to access and place bets at offshore Internet gambling sites, whereas U.S. law generally bans Internet gambling. After hearing the dispute, the WTO ruled against the U.S., and in favor of Antigua, stating that Internet gambling was within the law as it was written. The WTO gave the U.S. one year to comply or rework the law. As of the writing of this book, the U.S. has yet to comply with the WTO ruling and the deadline has passed (Alm, 2006). This doesn't sound like one of those "earth shattering" issues unless, of course, you think that Internet gambling (which the United Kingdom and several other developed countries have already approved) would be "bad" for the U.S. More importantly, and notwithstanding the whole issue of gambling, this "little case" demonstrates that all nations now have a global platform (the WTO) to resolve differences, no matter how large or small the issue, and no matter how large and powerful a country might be. This case also demonstrates that globalization and the Internet reach around the world, making "fair trade" issues more complex to deal with. Resolving disputes within the borders of a single nation or region might be possible, but resolving issues in the setting of a "world community" can be an extremely difficult task. This is exactly where we are today, now that *The World Is At Your Door!* Perhaps the WTO can be our vehicle for arbitrating the world's "fair trade" issues—even if it has a "wobbly wheel" once in a while!

Now for some better news. What is happening, and it's actually been going on for some time, is that individual companies (and in many cases countries) are taking the lead globally, when they can, to foster governance, compliance, accountability, and ethical practices. For example, Motorola, GE, GM, Wal-Mart, Sony, Coca Cola, Nike, Ikea, Siemens, Ford—to name a few—have developed and strengthened their own governance and integrity programs to include global business requirements. Firms have made these procedures applicable to worldwide operations. Companies are taking the lead today with regard to governance, accountability, and ethics—it's not perfect but positive results are happening around the world. Fair trade is happening, along with human rights improvements.

Now, I know you've been asking as you read this chapter: what does "right" mean when it comes to conducting business in the new global economy? Defining "right" is, of course, frequently an extremely difficult task. However, I believe that common practices and guidelines will emerge as the countries of the world trade goods and services and work through legal, ethical, environmental, and human rights issues. Doing what is "right" will come to mean doing it on a global basis; not just at corporate headquarters. It is an approach that echoes Dr. Martin Luther King's well-known statement: "that the time is always right to do the right thing." However, if you are in one part of the world, "right" might mean that bribing governmental officials to receive favorable treatment is acceptable. In another, bribes are against the law and carry penalties. So, we are back to the issue of whose standards will apply? More importantly, who will take the lead in establishing the world's "fair trade" and "human rights" standards?

Take, for example, the U.S.-based Proctor and Gamble Company. They, like many great companies, have a strong set of governance, compliance, and ethical standards by which all employees are held accountable. These standards are applied to all operations (and peoples) around the world, wherever located. In other words, if it is not "right" to work people extended hours without pay and rest periods in America, then it is not right in Brazil or China either. If it is not "right" to bribe officials for government contracts in Great Britain, then it's not right in India, China, or Croatia either. If it is not "right" to ignore environmental concerns to gain a competitive advantage in one country, then it is not in another.

In the end, the issue that always remains is the determination of what is "right." Conventional wisdom says that we should all know "right from wrong." This is not always the case. For individuals who venture into global businesses for the first time, the experience can be like a walk through a Vietnam minefield, or down an Iraqi war torn city street.

Take a look at the websites for any of the companies previously mentioned in this chapter and you will see that global considerations are now at the forefront of their governance, compliance, and ethical programs.

Therefore, if you are ready to join the ranks of those doing business in the new global economy, then the following is a list of items that will require your careful consideration. It is common to see companies develop global policies and detailed procedures that cover all of these items.

International Trade Controls

Complying with Competition Laws

Money Laundering Prevention

Improper Payments

Customer Relationships

Supplier Relationships

Working with Governments

Intellectual Property

Fair Employment Practices

Environmental Health and Safety

Integrity, and Raising Integrity Concerns

Conflicts of Interest

Outside Business Relationships

Code of Conduct

****

It is, indeed, great to see public and private firms taking leadership roles in doing business globally in an ethical and compliant manner. And, while this process is in its infancy, as more and more companies join the effort, standards and practices will emerge and become acceptable for the common good of all. In the meantime, expect the "wobbly wheel" and "jack-in-the-box" effects to prevail as globalization reaches out to all nations of the world.

Recommended Action Items.

1. Before venturing into doing business globally, sit down with your leadership team and establish basic global policies and procedures in the areas given in this chapter that will guide the actions of everyone in the organization. Where possible, make the global policies and procedures consistent with those used domestically.

2. Check out your government's list of countries where firms are banned by law from establishing trade relations. For example, the United States currently bans trading relationships with Iran, Libya, Syria, North Korea, and Cuba. And, the delivery of particular kinds of products and services are banned in many countries throughout the world. This information, and a tremendous amount of other useful information can be found on the U.S. Department of Commerce's website (http://www.commerce.gov/). Note particularly the "Country Lists" that indicate when special licensing/clearances are required in order to conduct business with a country. Other countries have similar requirements and control organizations, but none seems as thorough a process as that found in the U.S. and the U.S. Department of Commerce.

3. If your organization will be doing business in a foreign country through a joint venture, directly with a vendor, or directly with consumers, investigate the potential joint venture partner, vendor, and practices in the foreign country before entering into any type of agreement. Information is often available through the World Trade Organization (http://www.gatt.org/), the World Bank,

and other companies already doing business in the country you want to enter. Further, the U.S. Department of Commerce maintains offices in many countries and can often provide information on local companies/governments. In addition to commercial and financial information, these offices often know about corrupt practices, human rights abuses, and environmental issues that may surround a foreign company/country. The central office for the U.S. Department of Commerce maintains helpful information and guidance in their data bases under "Know Your Customer: Guidance and Red Flags." And, don't forget to ask your potential foreign partner a lot of questions so that you can personally assess the ethical, governance, and compliance status of the firm and country where you expect to conduct business. If you don't have the proper internal resource, seek out a consultant who is experienced in doing business in the country in which you anticipate doing business. There are also many legal firms that are experienced in foreign operations; many specialize in certain countries. Through this investigation process, identify the foreign company's practices that conflict with your domestic policies/values. For example, you will recall our discussion in this chapter where censorship, payments to officials, and certain forms of kickbacks are acceptable in several countries around the world, but not legal or condoned in most of the "Western World." You must next sort out whose standards will apply, and determine whether to say no to doing business with that foreign company or country, or continue with the business venture. To help with ethical issues, the International Business Ethics Institute (IBEI), http://www.business-ethics.org/ (a non-profit organization) provides useful information and education that assists businesses in making ethical business decisions. My recommendation is to turn away from those transactions with organizations/countries that don't adequately protect employees' human rights and the environment, or don't meet your ethical and legal standards.

4. Publicly traded U.S. firms must become familiar with the provisions of the U.S. Foreign Corrupt Practices Act (FCPA). The Department of Justice, the Securities and Exchange Commission (SEC), and the Department of Commerce provide detailed information regarding compliance with this act. In general, the FCPA prohibits corrupt payments to foreign officials for the purpose of obtaining or keeping business, and it requires the appropriate corporate accounting for all types of payments to foreign governments.

5. If possible, attend a free training course offered by the International Business Ethics Institute (IBEI) that focuses on the following questions: (Source: IBEI, http://www.business-ethics.org/pubspeaking.html)

   - How can you globalize your ethics program without sacrificing company standards?
   - How can you develop an effective global code of conduct?
   - What can you do to ensure training and reporting channels are appropriate for international employees?
   - How can you continuously assess risk and new regional issues?
   - How can you respect local cultures and not sacrifice corporate values and ethical practices?

6. Read the following book that provides a wealth of information for both large and small businesses desiring to participate in international business and the globalization process that is occurring today: *Corporate Ethics in a Time of Globalization,* by Klaus M. Leisinger & Karin M. Schmitt.

7. As we have been discussing in this book, the new global economy has been largely created and nurtured by the rapid growth of information technology—namely the Internet and "World Wide Web." The use of this technology, however, has brought about abuses and ethical issues regarding privacy, security, theft of information, destruction of information, and the theft of intellectual property (Phukan, 2001). For this reason, large and small multinational organizations that conduct business in the new global economy must analyze each of these risk areas in relation to the products and services being sold. Then, appropriate procedures must be implemented to protect the organization's products, services, and intellectual property.

"It takes 20 years to build a reputation, and five minutes to ruin it."

Warren Buffett, Chairman and CEO, Berkshire Hathaway

Chapter 7

The Standard of Living and Quality of Life Argument

"China's growing markets and voracious appetite for the world's goods and services are making companies and their workers wealthy, from Latin American cattle ranchers to French vineyards. In the U.S., the ever-increasing flood of low-priced Chinese products has enabled rising standards of living for years (even as it has made job security in some areas more tenuous)."

Michael Elliott, Author, Time Magazine's June 27, 2005 Report: "A New China Rises"

I hear it all the time. Globalization is lowering the standard of living and quality of life in "developed nations," while raising them in many of the "developing countries" around the world. Put simply, there is fear in the U.S., Western Europe, and much of the Western World that China, India, and the rest of Asia, with their extremely "cheap labor" (by Western standards at least) will pull down wages, eliminate jobs, and lower overall living standards. I don't believe it's a case of "Western World" nations wanting to deprive poor countries and peoples of developing nations of a decent standard of living. It's fear that, in so doing, Americans and others will have to take a step back in their quality of life and high standard of living. As Michael Elliot so succinctly put it in his June 27, 2005, *Time Magazine* Report, "A New China Rises," "the U.S. and China are intimately linked—for better or worse. Can we make room for each other?" (Elliott, 2005)

And, this year for the first time, *Fortune Magazine's* 2006 report on the "100 Best Companies To Work For," begins with the following: "It had to happen—Globalization's pressure is turning the screws on even the best U.S. companies, making it tougher than ever for them to treat employees well. Globalizing everything creates merciless cost pressures no one can avoid. So, yes, Delta and United are cutting pensions, and General Motors is reducing medical benefits and company pension contributions. And so are many of America's best employers. Back in 2001, 33 companies on the "100 Best List" paid 100% of employees' health-care premiums. Today, only 14 do. Pensions are a similar story" (100 Best, 2006).

Ranking the world's quality of life/standard of living.

International Living reported in January 2006, that, for the first time since serious records on the subject of "quality of life/standard of living" have been kept, rankings had shifted dramatically.

The "Quality of Life Index" is based on data from a wide range of very reputable global sources, and takes into account: cost of living, leisure and culture, economy, environment, freedom, health care, infrastructure, risk and safety, and climate. Here are the top 10 "quality of life" nations: (International Living, 2006)

1. France
2. Switzerland
3. Australia
4. Denmark
5. New Zealand
6. Austria
7. United States

8. Sweden
9. Finland
10. Italy

At the top of the *International Living* survey this year, France took the grand prize for quality of life while Iraq was ranked as having the worst quality of life. Iraq's ranking is, of course, not surprising since a state of war continues to exist in that nation. France got good marks for healthcare (#1 in the world), leisure, environment, culture, and freedoms for its citizens. In addition to being the country with the number one health care for its citizens, France is also number one as a tourist destination (China is #5 and the U.S. is #3) and number two in terms of having the most cultural heritage sites. However, we must not confuse "quality of life" with a cheap "cost of living" since France ranks high in overall living expenses in urban areas. Like many countries, though, different regions will have varying costs of living, and this is certainly the case in France where there are many opportunities to live at reasonable and often inexpensive prices (International Living, 2006).

What is surprising is that the U.S. dropped all the way to number 7, losing its 21-year reign at the top. This drop in rank is due largely to a slowing of economic conditions, on-going and increasing infringements on personal freedoms, and the declines seen in recent years in the middle class. Other areas impacting the general U.S. population can be seen in credit card debt, which is at an all-time high, averaging $9,312 per household. At the same time, the savings rate for Americans is the lowest it has been in 73 years (Wallechinsky, 2006). More specifically, hurricane disasters, rising energy prices, post 9/11 fears and constraining measures, the war in Iraq, globalization's impact on employee benefits programs, and inflationary pressures were all cited as underlying causes for the drop in the U.S.' ranking. For many years, the standard of living and quality of life for middle class and professional workers in the United States has risen substantially due to good paying jobs, exceptional housing, and good healthcare. For example, *Money* magazine's 2006 annual survey of the best jobs to have in the U.S. lists Software Engineer (average salary $80,500) as number one, followed by College Professor ($81,500), and Financial Adviser ($122,500). All of the top 50 jobs in the survey pay more than $50,000 per year, which is two to four times greater than in many other countries around the world (Best Jobs, 2006). In terms of housing, the U.S. has excelled at providing opportunities for "cheap financing" and reasonable home prices. To this point, the average number of square feet in a typical U.S. home in 1950 was 983, whereas today it is in excess of 2,300 sq. feet (LeMoult, 2006). Healthcare has generally been available to the masses in the U.S., whereas many countries still struggle to provide healthcare. In recent years, however, the middle class in the United States has begun to see declines in some areas of their standard of living and quality of life. Their "real median household income has declined 3% from 2000 to 2004 and the percentage of households earning $25,000 to $99,000 shrank 1.5% during the same period" (Wallechinsky, 2006). In 2005, real average weekly earnings decreased approximately ½ of one percent.

China ranked 93, India 87, "Russia" 78, and South Korea 57 on International Living's list of emerging nations. Interestingly, Ireland has been on many lists as a nation that has significantly improved the quality of life for its citizens. The *Economist* magazine ranked it number one this year, while *International Living* sees it as number forty on its list (International Living, 2006). The criteria for ranking countries is different, which accounts for the variation. I like the *International Living* list better since it deals with a broader range of <u>existing</u> conditions in a country and does not deal with "improving conditions." Ireland is improving but does not yet get high marks in terms of cost of living, travel facilities, infrastructure (energy, water, transportation, highways) and banking for its citizens and businesses. Ireland is benefiting from globalization and is a now a key center for software development and computer science. All of the world's major software firms have operations in Ireland.

When my wife returned from her 2006 trip to China, she shared her observations regarding how people in China, and other parts of the world she has visited or studied as an educator, feel about their standard of living and quality of life. "People are the same everywhere when it comes to certain basic needs and feelings," she remarked. "They want to have food, clothing, shelter, and to be free from sickness. They all want to be loved and they all love and take care of their children. And, they all want to be treated with respect and courtesy, no matter what their walk in life might be." The globalization process that is occurring today is bridging some of the gaps that exist in providing many of these basic needs to people in both developing and developed nations around the world.

For whom the bell tolls—let it include those in critical need.

As mentioned in an earlier chapter, the WTO (World Trade Organization) currently defines poverty as earning $1.00 per day or less in the southern climatic regions of the world, and $2.15 per day in northern countries where people must spend more on keeping warm. I've discussed in earlier chapters globalization's favorable and unfavorable impacts on those living in poverty, and on those living the "middle class" lifestyle as well. For those who live in poverty, globalization can bring jobs that, in turn, can provide income for food, clothing, healthcare, shelter, and a generally better way of life. At the same time, this labor force may be exploited, to a degree, when the goods they produce provide exceedingly high profits for large corporations around the world. In the final analysis, though, those in poverty are moving upward on the WTO's charts as a result of globalization and the free exchange of goods and services among nations never before able to participate in the global economy. As human beings, we will not be able to escape this fact. For those of us who happen to be a part of one of the developed nations in the global economy, we must not lose sight of the critical human needs still existing around the world. To this point, Mr. Jack Welch, in his recent book, *Winning*, says "the only question he received while on tour across the world to discuss and promote his book that left him absolutely speechless and without an answer, came from a lady in the audience at a Copenhagen breakfast meeting. Welch was asked by this individual, who was about to be transferred to a company's West African operations, if he had any words of guidance on how to manage a business and deal with a workforce in a country where 40% of the employees are HIV positive, and many still live below poverty levels" (Welch, 2006). Fortunately, the corporate cultures of the world's great companies take helping people and protecting the environment and world community into consideration when conducting business. Globalization can include the well-being of those in critical need and have a positive impact as well.

<u>The Globalization of Mr. or Ms. Deep Pockets.</u>

The fact that the globalization process is distributing the world's resources and riches can be seen even at the top of the affluence ladder. In early March, 2006, as I worked on this chapter, the billionaire's list came out—*Forbes Magazine's* list of the world's richest people. Clearly, changes are occurring in the list. For many years, the United States dominated the top spots. For example, in 2004, all top ten spots were occupied by individuals from the United States. In 2005, 5 of the top 10 spots were occupied by U.S. individuals. Now in 2006, only 3 of the top 10 spots are U.S.

residents. More specifically, for many years the Walton family, founders of Arkansas (U.S.A.) based Wal-Mart Stores, Inc., dominated the top 10 spots on the list. This year, 2006, none of the Waltons appear on the top 10 list, compared to 1 in 2005 and 5 in 2004. The 2005 and 2006 lists are given below: (Forbes, 2006) (Country means residence)

2006		2005	
Name	**Country**	**Name**	**Country**
1. William Gates III	U.S.	William Gates III	U.S.
2. Warren Buffett	U.S.	Warren Buffett	U.S.
3. Carlos Slim Helu	Mexico	Lakshmi Mittal	U.K.
4. Ingvar Kamprad	Swit'lnd	Carlos Slim Helu	Mexico
5. Lakshmi Mittal	U.K	Prince Alwaleed	S.Arabia
6. Paul Allen	U.S.	Ingvar Kamprad	Swit'lnd
7. Bernard Arnault	France	Paul Allen	U.S.
8. Prince Alwaleed	S. Arabia	Karl Albrecht	Germany
9. Ken Thompson	Canada	Larry Ellison	U.S.
10. Li Ka-shing	Hong Kong	S. Robson Walton	U.S.

I was disappointed that my favorite domestic goddess, Martha Stewart, who joined the list last year (2005), dropped off this year. However, 102 new names joined the list of billionaires, bringing the total to 793. Many who joined for the first time were invested in "new-age innovation" products and services, such as solar energy, electricity generating wind farms, hi-tech hardware and software products, and international trade.

Unions and globalization.

I almost overlooked the impact of globalization on unions and their membership as the globalization process continues to put significant pressure on wage rates in all nations. In 1980, 1.5 million U.S. workers were members of the UAW (United Auto Workers) Union. Today, membership stands at about 600,000. In 1950, one in every three Americans had a union job, but today in 2006, the number is only one in ten (Stahl, 2006).

All is not bad news for unionism. A new international union, the SEIU (Service Employees International Union), has emerged out of the AFL-CIO and now has over six million members, making it the second largest Union in the U.S. Andy Stern, who previously worked at AFL-CIO headquarters, is its president and intends to organize service workers—such as janitors, security workers, and day care center workers—around the world. One of the main goals of the union is to help raise low-paid service workers out of poverty and into a middle class way of life. So far, the union is being successful with its "Partnership with Corporate America" program and collaborative work with employers who are now competing in a global environment (Stahl, 2006).

Over the years, unionism has helped create a middle class standard of living and quality of life for many employed in industries in the U.S., as well as other regions of the world. Unionism seems to have helped mainly those with the equivalent of a "high school" education, and resulted in better pay rates and higher standards of living. Employees who were union members generally did not have to compete on a global scale and were "protected" by agreements between a union and the employer. Now that competition for wages and products and services is on a global basis, there is little "protection" for employees and the companies they work for. The competitive playing field is in fact, mostly level.

The impact of this competition is seen quite vividly at General Motors and Ford where wages and benefits are high compared to world standards. I have discussed the automotive industry quite extensively in other chapters in the book, but, in a nutshell, these automakers can no longer remain competitive with the union wages and benefits being paid and required in the future. From an individual's point of view, the question that weighs heavily on union employees' minds is whether their livelihood and standard of living are in jeopardy due to this global competition. From the company's perspective, the question is whether the company can continue to exist, given the impact of globalization and "cheap wages" readily available elsewhere. Answers will not come easily since it appears that many firms are not yet equipped to compete in a global economy. U.S. automakers faired well when they had high market shares, and mainly faced local competition. For example, until recently, SUV's (Sport Utility Vehicles), or "gas guzzlers" as my wife, Nicki, calls them, were selling at record highs. Now, with globalization and the price of energy soaring, a shake-up in the industry is underway. For other companies, such as Toyota and Honda, who have lower wages/benefits and cost structures to maintain, business is good and profits are soaring. In fact, my local paper reported today that "General Motors and Ford saw sales fall again last month despite some popular new models, but Toyota and Honda reported increases over sales for the same period a year ago. And, Toyota's U.S. sales set a company record for the month" (GM–Ford, 2006). Meanwhile, U.S. automakers are undergoing what seems to be the biggest challenge in their history. As Toyota becomes the largest auto manufacturer in the world, which is estimated to happen sometime in 2006 or 2007, our hope is that it will continue to build manufacturing facilities in the U.S. and other parts of the world to employ many of the displaced workers from General Motors and Ford.

We are back to the dilemma. What will happen to the 86,000 employees who are soon to be displaced by U.S. automakers cutting back and reorganizing to compete in the new global economy? Will the impacted employees experience a lowering of their standard of living that will not return soon, if ever? What will happen to these companies who have built the auto and other industries into what they are today? And, on an emotional level, is it appropriate to "level" U.S. and other developed countries' wages in the name of globalization? Hopefully, this book touches on some answers to these questions and more. However, if I may be so bold, here are my top four approaches (potential solutions) to this seeming dilemma between globalization and standards of living. As you read these, you will see that the subjects and chapters included in this book are also tied to the solutions offered.

One; while I don't see that moving toward protectionism or isolationism will benefit anyone in the global economy, some governmental actions are needed. These include programs for transitional assistance for individuals and organizations that would help each during the disruptions brought about by globalization and the movement toward a broader-based, globally competitive economy. This does not mean subsidies like those used by the Chinese government which allow certain businesses (mainly those that are state-owned) to receive interest-free loans and extended payments.

This practice has resulted in the banking crisis that exists in China today. This also does not mean protective tariffs that shelter inefficient and nonproductive businesses. For transitional assistance programs to work, they will need to be on a "repayment" basis, and not aimed at protecting businesses that cannot eventually compete on a worldwide basis. For this reason, there would need to be time limitations placed on the assistance to ensure that individuals and businesses work toward and make the transition, rather than remaining static and hiding behind the program assistance. (It is interesting to note that the United States government did, at one time, provide a loan to the struggling Chrysler Motor Corporation before it merged with Daimler Benz. Today, Chrysler has repaid the loan and moved on with Daimler Benz to be a great global company.)

Second; competing in the new global economy requires "new-age innovation," not just with regard to products and services provided by individuals and companies, but in improved processes, procedures, and business models. The chapter you have already read, "Artistic and Creative Visions for Innovative Organizations," discusses these activities and provides examples of how many of the organizations are already making progress in the transition. Individuals and organizations will need to develop proactive strategies that provide a road map to achieve a sustainable position in the new global economy.

The third area, which is covered in detail in chapter 4, "Education—The Great Equalizer (Actually the Most Important Chapter!)," requires retraining of individuals for employment in the new global economy. This includes retraining programs for complete changes in skills, or transitional training for jobs in similar, or the same industry. For example, we talked about the fact that as jobs are eliminated by U.S. automakers and airlines, new or similar jobs are being created as offshore automakers, such as Toyota and Honda, continue to locate in the U.S., and new regional airlines begin and expand service. Another example of globalization creating (not eliminating) jobs, but requiring retraining, can be seen from our earlier discussion of UPS (United Parcel Services) where 5,000 jobs are being created due to the increase in global trade.

Fourth, and last; individuals and nations will need to work with the WTO (World Trade Organization) and other global organizations to bring about needed changes to ensure "fair trade." If "fair trade" standards are not established, then a country can gain a competitive advantage that otherwise would not exist. For example, individuals will continue to lose jobs and companies in the developed nations of the world will continue to go out of business as long as a country, such as China, controls its exchange rate and protects its internal industries. I'm not saying that the U.S. or Britain can ever compete with an 85 cents hourly wage, but when the playing field is equal, then everyone has a chance to do what they do best. I call this *balancing the world's supply chains.* With fair trade and no artificial barriers, each country will be able to participate on their own merits and rise to their level of competency.

Living in a world of scarcity and abundance.

The quality of our lives and our standard of living depends on whether we live in an area of the world dominated by "abundance" or "scarcity" (Palmer, 1990). For example, many of us live in a world of scarcity when it comes to energy (oil), while such nations as Saudi Arabia and Iran live with an abundance of oil. According to the World Bank, scarcity is common when it comes to food, clothing and shelter and 1.2 billion people in the world live on less than $1.00 per day (World Bank—Who Is, 2006). Specifically, the scarcity of food results in hunger being the number one cause of death in the world today. At the same time, many nations have an abundance of food, and, in some cases, governments have resorted to paying farmers not to raise crops or produce milk. This is true, for example, in the U.S. where land banks and subsidies on certain items attempt to restrict supply. This wide gap between scarcity (people dying of hunger, for example) and abundance (farmers with the ability to produce wheat, corn, and soybeans sufficient to feed the world) will remain one of the great mysteries of our time. I will suggest that it has a lot to do with wealth, power, politics, capital investments, and social structures—or, more specifically, the unequal distribution of these forces.

Parker J. Palmer, among others, wrote some years ago that, in a world of scarcity, "only people who know the arts of competition, even of making war, will be able to survive. But in a world of abundance, acts of generosity and community become not only possible but fruitful as well" (Palmer, 1990). He went on to propose that much of the world has chosen to act under the assumption of scarcity "where competition (a way of allocating scarcity), rather than cooperation (a way of sharing abundance), is widely regarded as the only way to conduct our affairs, to make things happen" (Palmer, 1990). Indeed, scarcity seems to explain the heightened competition for the world's supply of oil, food for nourishment, precious metals, and natural resources.

Living in America, as I do, we have experienced mostly abundance and a high standard of living. Americans do share some of this "abundance" and are considered to be among the most generous people in the world when it comes to helping others. On the other hand, the U.S. has about 5% of the world's population but consumes 25%–30% of the world's resources (25% of oil supplies, for example). However, the allocation of the world's oil and other natural resource supplies is changing as China, India, Eastern Europe, and several South American countries are experiencing wealth accumulation and now demand increasing supplies of these items as they move toward improved standards of living.

So how is the globalization process helping those who live in areas of scarcity? The dependency and interconnectedness of individuals, organizations, and countries, brought about by globalization can help mitigate the threatening nature of competition and aggressive actions among the world's nations. The spread of globalization is providing jobs and raising standards of living and the quality of many people's lives in places where poverty has been widespread for decades.

****

How we ultimately use globalization to interact and prosper as citizens of the new global economy and community remains to be seen. Will we take the gentler road of collaboration, cooperation, and the sharing of abundances, or will we continue to intensify competition and fight over scarcities in oil, natural resources, real estate, food, capital investments, and wealth accumulation?

Recommended Action Items

1. Stop using the phrase "someone has to do something about this unfair global competition." Rather, you/your company will need to function in a proactive manner to maintain your standard of living and quality of life in the new global economy. In many ways, you are responsible for your own rescue if you are being adversely impacted by global competition.

2. Local, state, and national transitional assistance programs will be needed for individuals and organizations during the initial globalization process. However, such programs

must be controlled in a manner that prohibits them from becoming another "entitlement program."

3. Organizations will need to establish processes, procedures, and business models that recognize standards of living on a global basis. With the changes being brought about by globalization, workers in London, for example, may work for the same employer as the worker in Kansas City, Missouri, and as the worker in Beijing, China. Each location will have different healthcare and living conditions.

4. Retraining will be the name of the game. "Jobs will come and go rapidly. Competing for jobs in the global economy will require the constant modification of job skills and learning new jobs" (Friedman, 2005).

5. Depending on your job, career, and skill level, joining a union might be appropriate for you. The new SEIU (Service Employees International Union) and long standing AFL-CIO were discussed in this chapter. In either case, the trend today is toward employee/employer collaborative efforts to create a win-win environment for all. Heightened global competition, brought about by the globalization process, will require a partnership between workers and employers.

6. Consider living in a different part of the world where your money will provide a higher standard of living. For example, certain areas of Central America and Mexico provide excellent living conditions at cheap rates, compared to the U.S., Canada, and Western Europe.

"U.S. companies dominated international trade and commerce in the mid-1960's. Millions around the world looked for the "Made in America" label when they purchased products, convinced that U.S. goods meant top-of-the-line quality. On the domestic front, salaries and wages were rising and millions of Americans were enjoying the benefits that go with middle-class life."

Jeremy Rifkin, Fellow at the University of Pennsylvania's Wharton Business School and CEO of The Foundation on Economic Trends in Washington, D.C.

"It is simply unacceptable in this day and age that hunger and malnutrition remains the number one cause of death worldwide."

James T. Morris, Executive Director of the World Food Programme

---

Chapter 8

Energy (Crisis?)—Globalization & Innovation at Their Best (or Worst)

"In the final analysis, the market will decide whether there is enough oil in the world, and if there is not, then investors will move to develop alternatives to oil."

Turki Al-Faisal, Saudi Arabian Ambassador to the United States, February 2006, U.S. Public Television Interview

---

"New-age innovation" and globalization will have everything to do with *solving the world's energy shortage.* I'm not calling it a crisis, at least not yet. However, have you topped off that SUV (Sport Utility Vehicle) lately with gasoline selling in the $3.00 (U.S. dollars) per gallon range (May 2006)? Or, have you received a natural gas heating bill that has doubled since a year ago? Or, have you bought gasoline anywhere in Europe where the price has been in the $6.50–$7.50 (U.S. dollars) per gallon range for some time? Or, if you live in the United Kingdom, have you experienced the 2006 annual 30% hike in home heating oil, or 28% in Germany or 20% in Japan? (U.S. Energy Information, 2006) And, yes, I did say *"solving the world's energy shortage"* when I started this chapter! Let me step back a moment, though, and ask if you've been seriously doubting lately if there can be a solution, as a growing number of people, businesses, communities, and governments around the world suck up an ever-decreasing supply of fossil fuels (oil products). It is certainly easy to get this message since there is definitely no shortage of literature and media coverage of the subject.

The magnitude of numbers often tells the story better than words. Here are the top 10 daily consumers of oil in the world today, and each has an ever-growing demand: (What's Hot, 2006)

(Numbers represent "barrels per day")

1. United States – 20.0 million
2. European Union – 14.6 million
3 China – 6.4 million
4 Japan – 5.6 million
5. Russia – 2.8 million
6. Germany – 2.7 million
7. India – 2.3 million
8. Canada – 2.2 million
9. South Korea – 2.2 million
10. Brazil – 2.1 million

As Thomas Friedman put it in one of his recent *New York Times* articles: "We can't tell China (and the rest of the world) not to use so much energy, especially given what energy gluttons Americans are. We can lead only by example. The Bush team, though, can't do that because it won't ask Americans to do anything hard on energy or the environment" (Friedman, 2006). I'd like to add to his statement that we also need to ask "Corporate America" to focus on more energy-efficient vehicles for businesses and consumers, more energy-efficient production/office facilities and alternate energy sources. As we'll be discussing in detail in this chapter, there is a flurry of activity in this arena—

perhaps a little late, but, nevertheless, we are on the way with some new-age innovative solutions. I say a "little late" since American consumers have continued to buy large "gas guzzlers" such as Suburbans and other large SUV's in record numbers up until this year (2006). In early 2006, and for the first time in many years, sales declined for these large vehicles, while sales of hybrids and smaller vehicles significantly increased.

While we're looking at the numbers, and if you wonder how gasoline prices per gallon stack up around the world, here is a sampling of the International Monetary Fund's rankings as of December, 2005:

Country	Price Per Gallon (U.S. $)
Turkey	$ 6.80
Norway	6.25
Britain	6.00
Germany	6.00
Italy	5.95
France	5.75
South Korea	5.25
Poland	4.95
Japan	4.50
Finland	4.00
Australia	3.80
India	3.75
Brazil	3.10
Canada	2.90
South Africa	2.90
United States	2.65
Jamaica	2.30
Mexico	2.15
Argentina	2.05
China	1.80

Russia	1.60
Saudi Arabia	.85
Indonesia	.65
Venezuela	.55

Many countries have "toyed" with the idea of using tax pressures to curb the excessive use of gasoline; some are doing it, while others are hesitant. Interesting to note is the portion of the price per gallon that goes for taxes. This spread ranges all the way from about 10 cents per gallon in Venezuela, to $5.00 per gallon in Turkey. Yes, I did say $5.00 in taxes in Turkey. I would say that governmental action in Turkey is attempting to curb driving, or at least curb driving anything but the most fuel-efficient vehicles. In between, we have France with $3.70 of the $5.75 per gallon price going to taxes. Japan's taxes are about $2.45 per gallon, Canada's tax is about $1.00, and the U.S. about 50 cents. Saudi Arabia has no taxes and in China, the price per gallon includes 90 cents for taxes. Taking taxes out of the total price per gallon for the top 20 countries above indicates that everyone in this group pays about $2.10–$2.15 per gallon for gasoline only, and the rest is taxes. In the future, we could see higher taxes used as a mechanism to help control the demand and consumption of gasoline. I'll look at prices much differently now that I know this tax breakdown, but I still don't like the price where I live. What about you? (Emerging Market, 2006)

<u>Supply and demand.</u>

Currently, the world's supply of oil barely keeps up with demand. Forecasts call for production to peak somewhere around 2010. It follows that, if consumption keeps growing, especially as it is doing in the developing nations of the world where consumption is growing at double digit rates, then the logical conclusion says we're in for shortages—

perhaps even a crisis. Shortages—unless we get busy solving this problem!

Therefore, let me be one of the first to write, perhaps announce, that *solutions* (meaning more than one) to the energy shortage (crises if you prefer) exist and are under development today, as I write this book in 2006. Have you ever wondered why our political leadership in the U.S. has not responded to the nation's concerned citizens and pushed harder for solutions to our energy woes? Don't we need to *take action and do something*, rather than continually debating what the energy initiatives (political agendas) of the party in power should or should not be? Proactive initiatives—coupled with governmental, corporate, and individual collaborative actions—can solve this issue. History tells us that such actions can be successful.

Actually, I'm not really the very first to state solutions to energy shortages. Winston Churchill was the founder of "alternative energy source thinking" back in WWI, when he began converting battleships from coal to oil. Nevertheless, all indicators today point to the fact that there will be a continuing stream of additional solutions (many not yet thought of) as we move forward in time. The list that follows demonstrates *solutions* that currently exist, or at least where solutions are originating (not in order of importance).

- ***Collaborative efforts*** among the nations of the world to reduce energy usage. **This can be a major solution.**
- ***Canadian Oil Sands.*** The oil sands in Canada are estimated to contain 175 billion barrels of oil. Only Saudi Arabia has more proven oil reserves. Predictions are that this heavy crude oil can be purchased for $20 to $30 per barrel less than "West Texas intermediate crude" oil over the next 3–5 years (Everly, 2006). As I write in March 2006, the cost per barrel of U.S. oil has reached a high of $70+. Suncor

Energy, a major producer in the Canadian oil sands, has purchased a refinery in the USA (Colorado) and is also talking to China and India about supplying more oil to these, and other countries. A major pipeline from the oil sands in Western Canada now extends from Edmonton, Alberta, Canada to Cushing, Oklahoma, USA. More refiners are being sought in the U.S. to process the heavy crude from the pipeline into gasoline and other products. The issue here is that the U.S. only gets 5% of its oil from Canada; therefore, volume needs to increase substantially in order to bring down the overall average price per barrel, so that consumers like you and me will see a difference at the pump. Refiners are working on this issue as I write in early 2006. This is an example of how countries in North America and Asia are linked and dependent on others for their energy supply. And, according to Swapnesh Malhotra, a spokesman for India's energy department, "Life depends on energy. We will get it anywhere we can" (Petit, 2006).

- ***The Gulf of Mexico***. Expanded drilling is needed to tap into additional supplies that exist in this area. Several oil companies are erecting new platforms as quickly as possible, while rebuilding those damaged or lost by hurricanes.
- ***The territory previously called the Soviet Union.*** Many of the republics that previously made up the Soviet Union have extensive oil (and natural gas) reserves, which constitute the eighth largest reserves in the world. China is currently talking with Russian President, Vladimir Putin, to increase oil and natural gas supplies for China's use. Pipelines from Siberia are expected to be extended into China to supply oil and natural gas.

- ***Windmill Farms.*** These are springing up everywhere across the United States, Europe, and, to a lesser degree, other parts of the world. Be sure and read the section later in this chapter labeled, *The Answer is Blowin' in the Wind!* You can even hum along as you read the section—if you'd like (but keep your day job!). You'll understand what I mean when you read it.
- ***Hydrogen Power.*** London's bus transit system is already using a fleet of hydrogen-powered busses; Hamburg, Germany has a fleet running on hydrogen based fuel cells; General Motors and Shell Hydrogen are collaborating on the commercialization of this new technology. GM is developing vehicles that run on hydrogen fuel cells, and the Shell Hydrogen Company is providing the hydrogen refueling station and dispenser. BP, British Petroleum, is developing the world's largest hydrogen-fueled power plant in Southern California.
- ***Small independent drillers*** in "oil patches" around the world are once again needed as suppliers of petroleum.
- ***Ethanol fuel.*** (From corn and sugar cane.) The supply of E85, a blend of fuel with 85% ethanol and 15% gasoline, and automobiles capable of burning this fuel, are increasing daily. New to the ethanol scene is cellulosic ethanol, which is made from straw, corn stalks, and other agricultural by-products. Ethanol production has increased 18% per year over the past five years, 2002–2006, and there are currently 31 new production facilities under construction in the U.S., compared to 16 in 2005 and 15 in 2004 (Alternative Investing, 2006).
- ***Biodiesel fuels.*** "Bio fuels" are called "biomass" energy, which means "fuels made from plants." Biodiesel comes from oilseed, such as pumpkin,

hemp, grape, and corn seeds. The number of vehicles that run on diesel and biodiesel fuels is growing each year. They are more fuel-efficient than regular gasoline-powered vehicles. Did you know that you can buy the equipment to press oilseeds and produce your own biodiesel fuel? Check out the Internet.

- ***Natural gas.*** Expanded exploration, development, and use of this clean burning energy source is needed.
- ***Solar (sun) power.*** Progress continues to be made in bringing this source of energy to the point of commercial viability. Many homes and businesses today have solar panels for energy production, but the cost remains high.
- ***Modified vehicles.*** "Micro Cars," "Smart Cars," electric "City Cars," electric "Scooters," and electric "Bicycles" represent a growing number of vehicles that have been modified to enhance energy efficiency. Are you ready to purchase a "Zappy 3 Scooter" for short trips around town?
- ***Coal.*** This cost-effective energy source is currently plentiful and readily available. The United States gets 56% and China gets 44% of its electricity from coal-fired generating plants. In terms of total energy consumption, China relies on coal for 65% of its needs. I am reminded of the importance of coal as an energy source each time I am forced to stop and wait at a railroad crossing for a coal train to pass. For example, it takes three of these 100-car trainloads of coal per day to fuel the massive Gibson electric power generating plant in Indiana (USA). The U.S. has the largest quantity of the world's coal supply with 27%, followed by Russia (17%), China (13%), and India (10%). In terms of who uses it the most, China is way ahead of all other countries and is expected to widen its first place lead by doubling

usage by 2025. A major limitation on burning coal is the fact that it emits carbon dioxide pollution. During my wife's trip to China in 2006, some members of her tour group wore masks in cities where coal was burned for energy, heating, and cooking without pollution control equipment. Pollution is a major problem in China, and many countries around the world (Appenzeller, 2006).

- ***Nuclear power.*** Once again, interest in nuclear generation of electricity is growing around the world. See later section in this chapter titled "Nuclear Power: Saving the World! Not Risking the World!"
- ***Geothermal energy.*** Do you think they would mind if we harnessed "Old Faithful?" "Geothermal energy literally means "heat from the earth"—geo (meaning earth) and thermal (meaning heat). This underused energy source is accessed by drilling water or steam wells in a process similar to drilling for oil. This energy is clean, emits little or no greenhouse gases, and reliable" (Geothermal Energy, 2006).
- ***Fusion energy***. "Fusion" is an energy source different from nuclear "fission." "Fusion" relies on the nuclear reaction of two hydrogen atoms. Hydrogen atoms are, of course, plentiful as they are found in water. Although fusion is a nuclear process, the products of the reaction are not radioactive; an important distinction between fusion and fission (the process used to generate electricity in nuclear power plants). Scientists have been working over 40 years to overcome significant scientific and engineering challenges associated with fusion. If successful, "fusion" as a source of energy is considered to be inexhaustible. A <u>gallon</u> of water, the source for the hydrogen atoms needed for fusion, contains the energy content of <u>300 gallons</u> of gasoline! (What Is Fusion, 2006) In 2005, a six-member consortium

(China, the European Union, Japan, Russia, South Korea, and the United States) agreed to build an experimental fusion reactor at Cadarache in France (Nuclear Energy, 2006). This is a good example of the global collaboration needed to solve energy issues.

- ***Hydropower.*** Tides coming in and going out, ocean currents, and waves are predictable forces to harness for power generation. Tidal turbines are set to be built in New York City's East River. Portugal, Scotland, and Britain already have prototypes (Aston, 2006).
- ***Extended life battery power.*** Innovative technology is progressing in the development of extended life batteries for use in hybrid vehicles and as power sources for a wide range of consumer and industrial products. The Zap Company, a major manufacturer of electric cars, just announced a new lithium battery that has at least twice the life of existing batteries. One of its alternative uses will be to power various hand-held devices, such as music players.
- ***Cooperative efforts*** between governments and private industries/organizations to develop alternate energy sources. For example, the Midwest Research Institute in Kansas City, Missouri, currently manages the U.S. Government's Solar Research facilities in Colorado.
- ***Leadership*** from the world's "powerful and wealthy" individuals and nations to take action immediately. For example, Microsoft's Bill Gates and Virgin Atlantic Airline's Sir Richard Branson, have each begun investing in various types of alternate energy sources.
- ***Alaska***. "Run reindeer run" because more drilling for oil and natural gas is likely in the future.

- ***Hybrid*** and more fuel-efficient automobiles/ transportation vehicles. Have you been to Yosemite National Park in the United States and ridden on the General Motors Advanced Hybrid Electric Technology shuttle buses that carry visitors and personnel around the park?
- ***Technological breakthroughs*** that enable development of undiscovered (as of now) alternative fuels. This is an example of "new-age innovation" at work.
- ***Steamflooding*** to extract heavy oil that was previously unrecoverable in an oil field.
- ***Favorable tax and import/export regulations and tariffs***.
- ***Continuation of special tax credits for hybrid vehicles***, such as the Honda Civic, Toyota Prius, and Ford Escape. According to *Edmunds.com*, the world's authority on auto rankings, these autos are expected to be assigned credits of $4,000, $3,150, and $2,600, respectively.
- ***Capital spending incentives*** for energy conservation and the development of alternative energy sources.
- ***Allowing drilling on federally-owned lands*** with oil and gas reserves. This controversial issue will require compromises between government agencies and concerned citizens. Consideration for environmental concerns and energy needs is critical for satisfactory resolutions.
- ***The Mid East***. Explore and extract large untapped reserves believed to exist in such areas as Iraq.
- ***New hydroelectric facilities.*** China is currently working on the world's largest facility, in terms of power generating capacity, at the Three Gorges Dam Site on the Yangtze River at Sandouping Village,

China (to be completed in 2009). This dam, with its 26 generators, will produce electricity equivalent to 18 nuclear power plants and is anticipated to supply about 10% of China's electricity needs. Sun Yat-sen first proposed building a dam on the Yangtze as far back as 1919. Due to unfavorable economic and political conditions—and due to the fact that the dam sits on a seismic fault—dam construction did not begin until 1993. The world's current largest dam, Itaipu, is shared by Brazil and Paraguay. According to the World Commission on Dams, Brazil, India, Turkey, and China continue to build dams on a large scale. "Hydropower currently provides about 19% of the world's total electricity supply and is used in over 150 countries, with 24 of these countries depending on it for 90% of their supply" (Quick Guide to Dams, 2006). Hydropower, which is a clean and renewable energy source, will no doubt continue to play a major role in meeting the world's growing electricity needs.

- ***Wear a sweater in the winter.***
- ***Sit in the summer breeze.***
- ***Work from home*** (via the internet), which saves gasoline for daily travel to and from work. Minimizing business travel by using a number of communications tools will also save energy. Where practical, employers need to modify procedures that allow jobs to be performed offsite, such as a person's residence.
- ***Improving the gas mileage*** for new autos—GM, Ford, and others are making significant strides. It's about time!
- ***Take the alternative energy-powered buses*** that are beginning to show up in major cities around the world. Or, simply take advantage of existing public transportation in your area. What is the status of public transportation systems in your community?

- ***Practice what you preach—lead by example***. U.S. Congressman from Missouri and former mayor of Kansas City, Emanuel Cleaver, is proposing a rules change that would require members of the U.S. House of Representatives to lease energy-efficient vehicles. "Surely Congress cannot sell the American public on the need to abandon its gas guzzlers when they observe members of Congress proudly driving them" (Kraske, 2006). It remains to be seen if this proposal will pass. Each individual has a stake in the energy conservation effort, whether it is driving a fuel efficient vehicle, riding public transportation, turning off the lights when you leave the room, conserving water—to name just a few examples. While we may not immediately see the results of our small individual efforts, the cumulative effect of everyone doing their part can make a significant difference in the conservation of energy.

- ***Ride a pedal or motor bike!*** 5 million people in India ride motor bikes. 600,000 people in Amsterdam (Netherlands), a city of only 740,000 people, ride conventional pedal bikes. (I know this personally, as I tried to walk the streets of Amsterdam on vacation. You can get run over very easily if you don't obey the "bike path" signs.) The United States has its national *Bike to Work Week* each year. Specifically, Chicago's Mayor Daley promotes the *Bike Chicago Campaign*, which encourages the use of bikes as an alternative to automobiles. Will Americans be able to modify their love affair with the automobile in the name of conserving energy?

- ***Thermoelectric devices*** attached to chimney stacks and vehicle exhaust pipes to convert heat into electricity. Mr. Mercouri Kanatzidis at Michigan State University is already working on these devices. Savings on fuel costs for an automobile could be 10%. Electricity converted from heat passing through a power plant's pollution control system and smoke stack could be significant (Thermoelectrics, 2006).

- ***U.S. government sponsored prize money*** for scientists, inventors and entrepreneurs to compete in the development of alternative energy sources, such as the $10 million prize offered for research into hydrogen as an alternate energy source.
- ***Public Awareness for energy conservation and the development of alternative energy sources.***

You might be wondering about the "*Wear a sweater*" entry in the above list. It is my way of symbolically saying that there is a need to be forever aware and proactive when it comes to the conservation of our limited sources of energy, or any of the earth's natural resources. As Mr. Clyde Prestowitz, in his latest book, *Three Billion New Capitalists: The Great Shift of Wealth and Power to the East* puts it: "three billion people from China, India, and the new countries from the old Soviet Union Bloc, will demand an ever-increasing amount of energy and all kinds of resources as they begin traveling the once-hated road of capitalism" (Prestowitz, 2005). This increase in headcount (people) joining the ranks of consumerism, coupled with overall fast growth in these developing countries, will require concentrated worldwide conservation efforts. And, it is very likely that supplies of energy, and perhaps certain goods and services, will be severely strained for a while.

Simply put, the energy shortage—the excess of usage (demand) over supply—cannot be solved by a single action. Multiple innovative solutions, many of which I've listed above, will be required. There are fortunes to be made from the energy solutions given above. Is there any doubt now that this global problem won't be solved? There will be some challenges, especially in the short term, as the world plays "catch-up innovation," and as supply and demand battle it out for an equilibrium. I say "world" because energy management is a global issue. Globalization and "new-age innovation" will be positive driving forces in finding solutions and bringing stakeholders (which means all of us) together for the development and management of this global issue.

With regard to several of the major alternative energy sources I included in the list above, "history is on the side of renewable energy." According to the U.S. Department of Energy's Office of Renewable Energy and Energy Efficiency, "many early civilizations used the sun, water, wind, and geothermal energy to meet basic needs. North American Indians used hot springs for cooking as far back as 10,000 years ago, the ancient Greeks used hydro power to grind flour, and the Persians used windmills to pump water" (Renewable Energy, 2006). As my wife and I toured the Netherlands recently on a vacation trip, we witnessed this historical perspective first-hand as we saw old restored windmills from the early centuries grinding grain, alongside modern day wind-powered turbines generating electricity for the modern cities of Amsterdam and Rotterdam. As I have engaged in research for this book, I am forever amazed at how history seems to find itself in the future again and again. And, so it is with the return of the basic sources of energy described above by the Department of Energy.

The short term, high altitude view tells us that shortages in global energy supplies are likely to occur as development of alternate sources attempts to catch up with demand. Many of the solutions presented earlier are still in the process of being developed, or progressed to the point of being commercially feasible. The good news is that several solutions, such as bio-fuels, solar power, windmill power-generating farms, and hybrid power technologies are already in use today, supplying energy for automobiles, communities, and businesses. The question that remains unanswered, and is likely to remain so for a long time, is whether supplies of energy of all kinds can keep pace with demand, as developing nations around the globe require more energy to power their new found wealth and growth. And, at what price? One thing is perfectly clear—fueling the world's growing economic prosperity will take a lot more energy from every possible source. As Adrian Heymer of the Nuclear Energy Institute puts it: "Meeting future energy needs will require many types of fuels" (Petit, 2006).

<u>More Buicks taking to the highway.</u>

In China, Buick automobiles (one-time dream car of America and the "Baby Boomer" generation), along with many other brands, are taking to China's roads and highways at an alarming rate. In Beijing alone, 30,000 new cars per month are purchased by the newly affluent class in that country. Come on now, you remember your father's Buick, don't you? It's the one that famous U.S. golf pro, Tiger Woods, advertises for General Motors. (I doubt he really drives one!) It is one of the main "cars of choice" in China today; a symbol of new found prosperity for millions of people who can now purchase an automobile for the first time in their family's history (Business Week, 2006). To handle this amazing growth in vehicles, China is spending heavily on new highways and infrastructure requirements for a mobile society. The same is happening in India, Eastern Europe, South America, and the other nations of Asia, but at a slower pace. By 2020, China is expected to have 150 million cars on the road, and India will have even more. Surprisingly, India is currently the fastest-growing car market in the world (Carpenter, 2005). This all translates into a never before seen growth in demand for energy! And, as I am writing this book, China is already in critical need of additional oil supplies and is shopping the world's suppliers to meet their demand. In fact, NBC news reported that Canada, Brazil, South America, and Saudi Arabia (the world's richest oil nation, and holder of 22% of the world's oil reserves), are working on long-term agreements with

Chinese officials to supply additional oil to that country. King Abdullah of Saudi Arabia began his early 2006 Asian tour by personally visiting China and its president, Hu Jintao. This was the king's first official trip outside the Middle East, and the media reported that the trip was to "talk oil deals." The United States is currently the largest customer for Saudi Arabian oil. Saudi Arabia is also building refining plants in other parts of the world to be closer to their buyers of oil, and to remedy the need for additional refining capacity. Prior to doing some research for this chapter, I was not aware that one of the current constraints on the flow of oil is the need for additional "refinery capacity." Refineries are planned for China, India, and Korea, according to Turki Al-Faisal, Saudi Arabian ambassador to the United States, in a U.S. Public Broadcasting System television interview.

Energy is indeed a global issue, and it exemplifies explicitly how we're all tied together in the new global economy—whether we like it or not! Take, for example, the joint venture between the two huge global energy companies, Royal Dutch Shell (Netherlands) and Iogen (Canada). They plan to have a commercial operation going by 2009 to produce cellulosic ethanol, which is a form of ethanol that comes from agricultural by-products such as straw, corn stalks, and other waste (Ethanol, 2006). The process to make ethanol from these by-products is much faster than corn or sugar ethanol. DuPont and Genencor, a biotechnology firm, have also joined forces to develop improved mixtures of ethanol. Currently, regular Ethanol production stands at 4.3 billion gallons for 2006, up from 3.6 billion in 2005 and 3.1 billion in 2004, representing an average growth rate of 18% per year (Alternative Investing, 2006). Ethanol/gasoline blends are becoming a significant source of fuel for motorists. On the global personality front, Richard Branson, founder and CEO of Virgin Airlines, has formed Virgin Fuels to develop ethanol fuels. Bill Gates and Paul Allen, co-founders of Microsoft, have also made significant investments in ethanol fuels (Ethanol, 2006). And, last but not least, although I never really liked but a few of his songs, the singer/songwriter Willie Nelson has championed ethanol and biodiesel fuels in TV commercials. These commercials show his tour buses running on biodiesel fuel and his Texas service station providing the fuel to motorists (mostly Texas cowboys and cowgirls, I assume). Over the years, his concern and help for farmers all over the world has been admirable. These new fuels offer outlets for farm products which, until recently, have been in oversupply. I could go on to mention the huge agricultural product firms of Cargil, Archer Daniels Midland, and many of the world's major oil companies who are also participating in developing these fuels. But I'll stop here with the point that these are examples of globalization, and global collaborative efforts to solve the world's ever-increasing need for energy.

Take a look again at the "energy solutions" list presented at the beginning of this chapter. I believe this list represents the future of energy supplies—with some yet to be discovered sources, of course.

More about airplanes and automobiles.

Over on the airline side of the transportation equation, China alone plans to build about 30 new airports over the next 5–10 years, and order 500 new regional aircraft over the next 5 years. India is doing the same, but at a slower pace. Where will the fuel come from to power these aircraft?

25% of the world's oil supply is used by just 5% of the world's population (the U.S.) (Baldacci, 2005). However, progress is being made toward using less oil and finding alternative fuels— probably much too slowly. Ethanol-based fuels and wind energy farms are growing as alternatives to traditional oil. Hybrid vehicles are starting to take hold. For example, Ford plans on selling 40,000 hybrid vehicles this year, with a growth rate of 20% in coming years. In fact, the first mass-produced hybrid vehicle built in the U.S. began rolling off Ford's Kansas City assembly line in 2004. The first Fords ever built, around the turn of the 20th century, could also run on vegetable oil. Have we come full circle as "bio fuels" (fuels made from plants) are once again being used? Have you burned any gasoline lately blended with Ethanol (made from corn)? Check it out next time you fill up. It's widespread. Fifty percent of automobile fuel in Brazil comes from Ethanol made from—you guessed it—sugarcane! (Parfit, 2005)

Toyota and Honda hybrids are also starting to be seen in significant numbers on the highways. It was interesting to note that when the *Edmund's* list of the most fuel-efficient cars sold in the U.S. came out in early 2006, the top 10 were all from non-U.S. automakers, although many of these autos are manufactured at plants physically located in the U.S. The "Top 10" for 2006 are as follows: (Edmunds, 2006) *(mpg = miles per gallon)*

#1 Honda Insight, 60 mpg city driving/66 highway
#2 Toyota Prius, 60 mpg city/51 highway
#3 Honda Civic Hybrid, 49 mpg city/51 highway
#4 Volkswagen Golf TDI, 37 mpg city/44 highway
#5 Volkswagen New Beetle TDI, 37 mpg city/44 highway
#6 Volkswagen Jetta TDI, 36 mpg city/41 highway
#7 Toyota Corolla, 32 mpg city/41 highway
#8 Toyota Scion XA, 32 mpg city/37 highway
#9 Hyundai Accent, 32 city/35 highway
#10 Kia Rio, 32 mpg city/35 highway

The 2005 list looked the same, except the Dodge Neon came in at number 10, and was the only U.S. automaker's car represented on the list. These autos sell in the $10,000 (U.S. dollars) to $13,000 range. It was interesting to note that the cheapest U.S. auto, the Chevrolet Aveo—selling for a base price of $9,995—was not on the "fuel-efficient" list (Edmunds, 2006).

Consumer Reports, which rates cars for consumers based on overall value, efficiency, safety, and quality, especially liked Japanese built automobiles. All of its automobile picks for 2006 were from Japanese companies (Naughton, 2006).

These lists certainly support the conclusion by many that the U.S. needs to significantly expand its energy conservation efforts and programs, especially when it comes to automobiles. This needs to be done immediately! We can't wait any longer!

We can't blame the oil shortage on just planes, trains, and automobiles. Other significant forces driving the soaring demand for oil and other forms of energy are products that utilize oil in their production (such as plastics) and a boom in construction in certain areas of the world (China, India). In addition, a general increase in the number of people and nations that can now afford and need oil-based products and services is growing, as Clyde Prestowitz points out in his book titled *Three Billion New Capitalists.* (Prestowitz, 2005)

Put simply, the supply side of the equation is struggling to keep pace with existing and new demands for oil and other energy sources. Prices are increasing as a result. Latest estimates place worldwide demand for oil at 84.4 million barrels per day and supply at 84.1 million; a very delicate balance (Energy Information Administration, 2005). The United States leads in demand (usage of oil). Europe is second, followed by China in third place. China, the world's fastest-growing economy and largest population, is moving up fast, as are India and other Asian nations. Even more worrisome is the fact that, ten years ago, both China and India had enough oil to export excess to other nations (Carpenter, 2005). Today, they must import to meet needs. Specifically, China's current importation rate is 3 million barrels per day (and growing). Yes, it is capitalism at work—supply and demand are setting selling prices, just as they should! Do you recall the early 1990's when oil was $15 (U.S. dollars) a barrel, compared to today's price which has reached as high as $70+?

The answer is blowin' in the wind.

It was the ever-popular sixties and seventies folk singing group *Peter, Paul and Mary* who wrote and performed *"Blowing In the Wind"* for audiences and Vietnam War protest gatherings around the world. They (PP & M) are still with us today. Do you remember them? One of my favorite lines in the song is "*the answer my friend is blowing in the wind, the answer is blowing in the wind*." How appropriate it is today. One solution to our global energy shortage is not just "blowing in the wind," it is the wind. Wind-powered electrical generators can be seen perched atop 200 to 400 foot towers across the landscapes of many countries, and along their coastlines. The largest of these "new-age innovation" windmills, with blades the length of a football field, can supply enough electricity to run five thousand homes (Parfit, 2005). Currently, Europe leads the world in wind-powered electric generation, producing electricity from wind generators equivalent to 35 large coal-fired power plants (National Geographic, 2005). North America is a distant second, but has huge potential. Specifically, Denmark and Germany (as of 2006) lead all European countries and obtain 20%–25% of their electric power needs from wind powered generators. France, Norway, Sweden, The Netherlands, Great Britain, and Ireland are also significant players in wind energy generation. "With the exception of hydroelectric power, which has little room to grow in developed countries, wind is currently the biggest success story in renewable energy. Globally, wind supplies less than 1% of electric power needs, but it's the fastest growing source of electricity today" (Parfit, 2005). Wind power is currently a $11.8 billion global revenue industry (Renewable Energy, 2006). According to the German Wind Energy Institute, "Over the next 8 years, international installed wind energy capacity is expected to triple and increase to approximately 210,000 megawatts from today's 59,000 megawatts" (Yahoo News, 2006). One megawatt of wind power will provide enough electricity to sustain several hundred households (Parfit, 2005). As costs continue to come down, we can expect to see more modern-day windmills.

Many companies, such as the General Electric Company, Siemens, Spain's Gamesa, Florida Power & Light, Mitsubishi, Goldman Sachs, and tiny Southwest WindPower in Flagstaff, Arizona USA, see significant profits to be made by supplying wind-power generated electricity, as well as parts and equipment for "windmills" (Renewable Energy, 2006). In fact, Southwest WindPower now markets a small portable "windmill" version that can light a small home, or be used where electricity is not available (remote regions, ships, sailboats, etc) (Parfit, 2005). You need a good breeze, of course! The company is testing a backyard version that can power a home—except in high peak periods. Any electricity generated by the wind turbine not used can be sold to the utility company serving the area for others to use. This sounds like "new-age innovation" to me!

On the large company side, BP (British Petroleum) Alternative Energy, North America's largest producer of solar panels, has now made wind energy one of the four pillars of its $8 billion ten year investment to build an alternative energy business. The other three pillars are solar energy, hydrogen power, and natural gas-fired power generation (Renewable Energy, 2006).

Before bringing this section on wind power to a close, I would like to share with you one last encouraging example. This example is a business using an alternative energy source, which not only helps promote a cleaner environment, but supports the on-going operation and development of wind energy farms. Right here at home in Overland Park, Kansas (a suburb of Kansas City), Sprint Nextel Corp. maintains its headquarters for worldwide operations. More than 75% of the power needed to run this massive complex that houses 15,000 workers, is supplied by a Kansas wind farm located near the historically notorious "cowboy western" town of Dodge City, Kansas. This wind farm, owned by Kansas City Power & Light, has 67 GE turbines spread over 5,000 acres and generates power equivalent to supply 33,000 homes. According to a KCP&L news release, use of this facility will reduce 175 million pounds of carbon dioxide annually from entering the atmosphere (Sprint…Wind Farm, 2006).

As stated earlier in this chapter, there are fortunes to be made in both large and small alternative energy businesses. At the same time, alternative sources of energy, such as wind, will move all of us away from dependency on fossil fuels (coal, petroleum, and natural gas), which are being depleted by increasing needs around the world.

We've been driving all day, fill'er up with hydrogen, please

Hydrogen fuel cell powered vehicles! They are already a reality, they're just not quite commercially feasible yet! "Commercially feasible" is a phrase that means "not affordable by the masses," or "affordable by only a few."

There are many great examples of collaborative efforts to solve seemingly insurmountable problems. The development of hydrogen fuel cells as an alternate to the internal combustion engine the world has long depended on to power its vehicles, is a fine example of the globalization process and "new-age innovation" at work. General Motors, Royal Dutch Shell (Shell Hydrogen), and a group of worldwide subcontractors have developed hydrogen fuel cell powered vehicles, as well as the hydrogen dispensing systems that would be needed as "re-fueling stations" of the future. General Motors has spent more than $1.0 billion (U.S. dollars) to date on this project, despite the financial condition the company is experiencing in its fight to maintain leadership in the auto industry. Test vehicles (cars and busses) are operating in Germany, Britain, and the United States.

Obstacles that remain before this technology is viable for commercial use and affordable by the masses include:

1) Financing refineries for the hydrogen fuel;
2) Storing hydrogen in liquid form or under pressure; (Dawson, 2004)
3) Financing and building a network of hydrogen re-fueling stations. Some progress has been made in this area, as a private-public consortium has already built hydrogen filling stations in Munich and Berlin, Germany; (Dawson, 2004)
4) Continuing to find investors who can afford the risks inherent in this type of development, which may take a decade or more to finalize;
5) Finding the right cost-volume-profit relationships that will sustain on-going profitability for stakeholders.

In the meantime, researchers continue to work on other potential power sources, such as "fuel cells, engines that burn both hydrogen and gasoline, and hybrid gas-electric cars" (Dawson, 2004)"

Nuclear Power: Saving the world! Not Risking the world!

The 1979 ill-conceived clouds that hovered above the near-disastrous meltdown at Three Mile Island, Pennsylvania, nuclear station, still haunt Americans today. The 1986 meltdown of one of four nuclear reactors at the Chernobyl power generating station in Russia's Ukraine countryside still haunts the residents of that region, and the nearby country of Belarus, as well (Petit, 2006). At the same time, the thought of a world without a sufficient supply of life-sustaining energy haunts us all—even more. Welcome to the on-going global debate on nuclear power.

Although there are over 400 nuclear power plants around the world, the use of "fission reactions" to produce electricity safely is a subject of significant disagreement among individuals and nations around the world. Yet, nuclear power has the capability to play a major role in closing the electricity energy supply gap today and for years to come. Nuclear-generated electricity is cheaper than gas and coal fired generation, no greenhouse gases are emitted during normal operations, and there are large fuel (uranium) reserves. On the other hand, the transportation of nuclear fuel, the disposal of radioactive spent fuel, and the potential for human error resulting in a release of radioactive emissions lead the list of concerns expressed by critics of nuclear power plants. I believe it is accurate to say that we are all concerned that humans have now harnessed an energy source so powerful that we don't trust our own ability to control it. Nuclear power is so controversial that no new nuclear power plants have been built in the U.S. since 1979. In Europe, only Finland and Ukraine are constructing new plants (Nuclear Power, 2006). The talk of building nuclear power plants around the world is frightening to many. It is a global issue with no comparison.

Today, France gets 78% of its electrical power from nuclear plants. The United States gets 20% of its electricity from 103 nuclear plants located about the country. One-half of the uranium used in these plants comes from decommissioned soviet weapons (Petit, 2006). This is an excellent example of global collaboration to turn "war machinery" into a positive use for energy needs. India has 15 plants currently on-line, with 8 more reactors under construction—more than any nation in the world—and expects to need more to meet the needs of its 1.1 billion people. Canada assisted India in getting started with its nuclear generation program, but India now has full nuclear capabilities. This capability includes the production and supply of uranium and plutonium; the required raw materials for nuclear reaction.

China now has 9 nuclear power generating stations operating, with another 30 to 35 on the drawing board. China, like India, is struggling to maintain energy supplies to support its 1.3 billion people, who are demanding more energy as consumerism and industrial production grow in that country.

Meanwhile, the U.S. is experimenting with a nuclear reactor that uses a high-temperature, helium-gas-cooled process to produce electricity and hydrogen gas." (Petit, 2006) This process has tremendous potential since hydrogen is thought by many to become a major source of energy for our future.

There is no clear global view of the use of nuclear power. But, as gas and coal reserves decline, energy costs increase, and the challenges associated with "fission reactors" are overcome, decisions regarding energy production may be easier to make. Closer relationships and collaborative practices among many of the nations of the world, brought about by globalization, can only promote better solutions to the energy dilemmas facing the world.

It all comes down to cost and profit—maybe?

From an economic perspective, conventional supply and demand economic theories would support the supposition that alternative energy sources will be rapidly developed, just as soon as it is financially attractive for investors to place their money in these projects. And, with regard to the development of alternate energy sources, Paul Volcker, ex-Chairman of the U.S. Federal Reserve Bank, said early in 2001 that "capital would flow to the areas of the highest potential return" (Volcker, 2001). Turki Al-Faisal, Saudi Arabian Ambassador to the United States, in an interview early in 2006, stated that "in the final analysis, the market will decide whether there is enough oil in the world, and if there is not, then investors will move to develop alternatives to oil."

However, new thinking on the subject says that the negative affects on our earth and its inhabitants as a result of emissions from fossil fuels will demand solutions at nearly any cost. Until recently (and perhaps still today), using alternate energy sources on a widespread basis has been largely dependent on the cost of each energy source. For example, the projected cost per kilowatt hour of the following sources of electricity appears to explain why we use one source over the other (Parfit, 2005).

Cost Per Kilowatt Hour of Electricity *(U.S.$)*

Coal	5	cents
Natural Gas	5.5	cents
Wind	6	cents
Nuclear	7	cents
Solar	22	cents

There seems to be a growing consensus among many economic, political, and industry leaders that immediate increased governmental actions will be required to mitigate a global energy crisis. New York University professor Martin Hoffert says that "jet planes, integrated circuits, computers, the internet, and satellite communications all required a big push by governments" (Parfit, 2005). And, so it is with energy. Many governments are already at the task. It would appear that, in reality, it will take a collaborative effort among governments and free-market enterprises (businesses). I believe this is exactly what is happening today. Samuel W. Bodman, the current (2006) U.S. Secretary of Energy, says that "gradual work with our private-sector partners has already begun to enter the marketplace: we are working to make hydrogen-powered cars a commercially viable option; recent breakthroughs in ethanol and bio-based products represent a promising alternative to fossil fuels; and solar cells are more efficient than ever. Such developments will not only increase energy security, but will generate more jobs and strengthen our economy" (Renewable Energy, 2006). At this same time, funding for the U.S. Advanced Energy Initiatives Programs has been increased by 22%. These are great efforts, even if they are somewhat late in the energy game.

Profit and Oil.

Globalization and competition for the world's oil supplies in 2005, and continuing in 2006, were extremely good to the mega-energy corporations. In 2005, Exxon Mobil, the world's most valuable company, earned profits of $36.1 billion—the highest profit ever for a U.S. company. The company also took over first place in terms of revenues, coming in at $340 billion compared to number two Wal-Mart at $316 billion (Elphinstone, 2006). At the same time, the firm lowered its investment in energy research and development from $2.00 to $.70 for every $1.00 distributed to shareholders (Norris, 2006). Royal Dutch Shell reported earnings of $25.3 billion (U.S. dollars), which was the largest earnings ever for a British or Dutch Company (Earning Digest, 2006). I suppose these record profits attracted the attention of so many people that the U.S. Congress was driven to hold hearings with the CEO's of all the major oil companies in November 2005. Congressmen were attempting to determine if these companies were participating in price-setting abuses. To date, no reports have been issued on the outcome of the meetings; just some talk about a potential "windfall profits" tax. I doubt this will happen, since such action would be targeting an industry that desperately needs to find more oil and energy sources for all consumers.

Fortune Magazine's 2005 top six U.S. companies, ranked by sales, included three large energy (oil) companies. These were Exxon Mobil (#1), Chevron/Texaco (#4), and Conoco/Phillips (#6). Exxon had a sales growth from 2004 to 2005 of 26%, Chevron 28%, and Conoco 37% (Elphinstone, 2006). I'll try to think positively about these high growth rates and profits when I fill up my car with gasoline this evening.

The keepers of the oil!

Many new and innovative sources of energy for use by all the world's people are under development throughout the global economy and community. In many cases, these new sources of energy—such as wind, solar, ethanol, biodiesel fuels—are already online and contributing to the needed supply. At the same time, it is also clear that "traditional oil" will continue to play a major role in supplying energy for the world. Where will future oil come from? What countries hold the keys to the oil reserves around the world? According to the Energy Information Administration's Oil and Gas Journal, oil reserves by country are as follows: (Oil and Gas Journal, 2006)

Estimated Reserves

Country	***(Billions of Barrels)***
Saudi Arabia	252
Canada	176
Iran	125
Iraq	112
Kuwait	100

Abu Dhabi	90
Venezuela	77
Russia	60
Libya	40
Nigeria	35
United States	22

Many of the countries on the list have also been areas of instability in the past. We can hope that all will embrace globalization and recognize the survival interdependency that exists among all nations—stable and unstable. Perhaps Ms. Jane Bryant Quinn, *BusinessWeek* columnist, sums up this view regarding our interdependency for oil supplies when she says, "For years to come, we'll (U.S.) be in the hands of some of the most dysfunctional governments in the world. Oil prices will rise and economic growth will slow—not this year, but almost certainly a few years out. We'll be paying in both treasure and blood, as we fight and parlay to keep ever-tighter supplies of world oil flowing our way" (Quinn, 2006). This statement reminds me of the many times we see and hear about the conflicts in the Middle East as being founded in rights to oil supplies. She ends her column by saying that "unfortunately, we're (US) investing in war (Iraq), not in crash projects to develop new energy sources" (Quinn, 2006). What do you think? Is the Iraqi War about terror or oil—or both? Will the U.S. and other nations in the world be able to move away from oil as their main source of energy, and away from dependency on others that have access to scarce energy sources?

****

To end where we started, energy is a global issue and requires global efforts to find solutions to shortages. Protectionism or isolationism, by individuals, companies or countries, will have <u>no</u> roles to play in the search for energy to sustain and grow the global economy.

Recommended Action Items:

1. Invest in local and global alternate energy source companies to boost capital investment required to develop alternative sources of energy. The current near-term "big five" potential alternative energy sources are: (1) wind power, (2) solar power, (3) biofuels (various mixtures), (4) hydrogen power, and (5) hybrid technologies (fuel cells, gas/electric power).

2. Lobby your representatives at all levels of government to develop and support alternative energy initiatives. Time has run out for political jockeying.

3. Make use of alternative energy sources, including biofuels, whenever and wherever they are available to you.

4. Be forever conservative with all sources of energy and natural resources.

5. Reread my list of solutions to the energy shortage—crises if you prefer—and determine which ones you can use to conserve energy and favorably impact your profitability.

"America represents less than five percent of the earth's population, yet consumes one-quarter of its energy."

David Baldacci, New York Times #1 Bestselling Author, Factual Statement by fictional Arab character in "The Camel Club" (2005)

Chapter 9

In Transition—It's Not a Pretty Sight, But . . .

"A focus on globalization as an opportunity, rather than a threat, is absolutely required for a firm to effectively compete and win in the new global economy!"

Phil Watlington, Author "The World Is At Your Door!"
Lead Faculty and Area Chair, Financial Planning and Control,
University of Phoenix

I need to tell you that I'm going to discuss some of the short-term bad news about the globalization process in this chapter. The "transition" the world is going through as a result of economic ***globalization***, which might be lengthy, is characterized by both positive and negative disruptions to individuals, businesses, entire industries, societies, and nations. Thus far, this book has focused mainly on the positive aspects of globalization and how organizations can formulate and implement winning strategies around innovative processes, products, and services. However, I would be remiss if I did not cover in some detail the short-term transitional bad news, and, to an extent, some of the limiting aspects associated with the "***globalization era.***" So, here it is! I must emphasize that as you read the chapter, nothing about the "bad news" negates what I have pro-actively discussed and argued previously. Stay the course!

In many ways, the ***globalization transition*** we are all experiencing is not a "pretty sight," but it offers unprecedented and tremendous opportunities for those who embrace the process, and leverage (efficiently and effectively utilize) it to their competitive advantage. Now, it might be hard to buy into these benefits if you happen to be one of the many employees, and I don't just mean U.S. employees, who have lost their jobs lately in the globalization process as their employers went in search of competitively cheap labor. For example, many jobs have been transferred to offshore organizations in Bangalore and Hyderabad, India—the currently recognized "hubs" for outsourcing all types of services from engineering to call-center operations and tax return preparation. In addition to companies seeking out cheap labor in Asia and Eastern Europe, they also see these areas of the world as markets where their products and services can be sold. In fact, I can't begin to count the number of firms I have heard or read about that are looking to the East (primarily China and India) for their future growth. It is to a point that I wonder if we all aren't just counting on China and India a little too much. What if these countries stumble, as some say could happen, in such a frenzy of growth? In the case of China, unstable banking conditions, communist controls, and growing industrial overcapacity could lead to deflation and declining economic growth (Jubak, 2006). It happened in Japan, but that country has now returned to a slow growth status. As an example of what seems to be dependence on China, Rick Wagoner, General Motor's CEO, in almost all of his interviews and speeches, talks about GM continuing to grow in China as a cornerstone of GM's turnaround strategy. I wonder if he knows that China currently has the capacity to produce 2.0 million more cars than demand calls for? (Jubak, 2006) Jeffrey Immelt, Chairman and CEO of the General Electric Company, talked about the "changing face of global competition" in his Cornell University 2004 Hatfield Fellow speech. He stated that, today, both opportunity and challenge "come primarily from places like China, India, and Eastern

Europe" (Immelt, 2004). In earlier days, many of us might remember, it was Japan that was the focal point of opportunity and challenge. Do you recall when everyone thought Japan and its growing economy and attention to quality was going to take over the world's electronic and auto industries? Today, some thirty years later, they have certainly made some progress toward this end, but no one seems to worry about it anymore, especially after their decade of economic instability. So, let's turn our discussion to the global economic transition we're seeing today and the challenges and opportunities that surround it.

When you are through with change, you are through!

Martha Stewart, the current reigning "domestic goddess" of the world and very astute entrepreneur, in her recent book *THE Martha Rules*, says it similarly several times throughout the book: "*when you are through changing, you are through*!" (Stewart, 2005) We are certainly not "through" when it comes to the transition of the world to a new global economy!

This transition (change), which is characterized by a shift in focus from local, national, and regional economies to a global economy, is taking on many faces. One of these new faces can be seen vividly by looking at the auto industry, where automakers around the world are already intensely competing globally to sell cars (and trucks) in their own home countries as well as many other countries. Several automakers, namely those in the United States, seem to be on the road to bankruptcy, while the industry as a whole is growing, and several non-U.S. automakers are earning record profits. I might add here that a similar scenario seems to be at work in the airline industry as well. My wife, Nicki, when she proof-read these statements immediately responded, "ok, that's obvious. What is new about worldwide competition to sell cars and trucks? Do you think that spark of brilliance will sell books?" Well, stay with me here.

I invite you to step aboard my new FORD Escape, or maybe we'll take the HONDA—symbolically of course—and take a short drive across the globalized landscape of the auto industry. This drive will take us across Europe, Asia, North America, and South America. When we arrive back home, you will better understand how economic globalization is transforming the world in which we live and work.

I'm going to venture out a little here as we begin our drive, and say that the auto industry is experiencing an unprecedented demand for its cars and trucks. As we drive across the landscape and see those new Toyota plants in Texas (USA), Ontario (Canada), California (USA), and Beijing (China), I might even say the industry is booming, depending on whatever definition one uses for a "booming market." What about that new 4,200 employee Nissan Motor Co. facility in Mississippi? And, the Mercedes Benz and new Hyundai plants in Alabama? Toyota is currently working with several Southern U.S. states to find a location to build yet another auto manufacturing facility. And, it is speculated that Honda will begin looking for another location in the United States by the end of the year (2006). Since 2000, the United States auto industry has had an influx of 33,000 non-union jobs from offshore car makers, but this has not been enough to offset the cutbacks by domestic automakers (Foust & Welch, 2006). As we weave our way across to India and China, what about all those new auto factories displaying the names of the major car makers of the world? Remember that urban Chinese consumers like Buicks and Volkswagens. With globalization at work, they can now afford them.

Certainly, the extraordinary demand found in the developing nations of China, India, virtually all of Asia, and Eastern Europe, is driving unprecedented growth in auto sales. This growth will continue and, in fact, intensify. A couple of simple number comparisons tell the story. In China, there are 6.7 cars per 1,000 people, and in India, there are 6.0. In the United States, there are 481 cars per 1,000 people, while in France and Germany there are 491 and 516, respectively. (Lebanon and New Zealand have the highest concentrations.) (Pocket World in Figures, 2006) I am not suggesting that China or India will approach the density of the U.S., Germany, or France in the near future, but with their large populations (1.3 billion in China, and about 1.1 billion in India), even small increases in their ability to buy cars spells big sales and profit numbers for automakers. In addition, there is still growth in many of the "developed nations." For example, in 2005 sales of automobiles in the United States grew to 17 million vehicles; the third highest level ever (Foust & Welch, 2006). At the same time, and as you will see later in this chapter, record numbers of layoffs and plant closings were announced in 2005-6 by U.S. automakers. After much reading and research, this brings us to a key point and conclusion: *The brutally competitive globalization process that is taking place in the auto industry today is one of transitioning auto production and sales from several of the older giants of the industry—specifically, Ford, GM, and Daimler Chrysler—to newer giants such as Toyota, Honda, Nissan, and Hyundai. For these newer companies, quality, innovation, cost management, productivity, and customer appeal have outpaced that found in the older companies. Further, these "newer" automakers are not burdened by the high costs associated with retirement benefits that plague the older companies. Although these "newer" automakers are non-union, their pay schedules for factory workers are considered good pay and range from $14 per hour entry level, to about $24 after 5 years of service. In terms of "productivity," the "newer" automakers produce a car in about 18 hours, compared to 20 hours for U.S. domestic producers* (Foust & Welch, 2006).

Again, I repeat, the worldwide industry is booming! Why is it that some firms are growing while others are shrinking?

Forecasted worldwide auto sales for the future tells us that unprecedented growth in the demand for new automobiles will continue as the newly affluent people of the developing nations take to the highways in record numbers. The difficult part of this globalization process is that some businesses will gain and employ more people at a wage for a good standard of living, while others will be forced to close plants, cut retiree and employee benefits, and lay off large numbers of people. In the U.S., the February 13 issue of *Business Week* reported that auto industry consultants view the domestic U.S. auto industry "as healthy as ever," but "the names on the signs in front of manufacturing plants across the country have changed" (Foust & Welch, 2006). Put simply, Toyota, Honda, Nissan, and Hyundai (including its affiliate, Kia) are building new plants in the United States and achieving record sales and earnings, while U.S. based firms, General Motors (the largest auto maker in the world) and Ford, are laying off approximately 30,000 people each and closing a dozen plants each. Hopefully, many of these displaced employees will find jobs with the other global companies who are expanding and prospering. This is the way capitalism works. This is how globalization works. We are in a transition; a transformation if you prefer, and as my title for this chapter implies, *It won't be a "pretty sight*" for some time. If you need some uplifting, this might be a good time to go back and review my chapters—"Energy Crisis: Globalization at Its Best (or Worst)" and "Artistic and Creative Visions for Innovative Organizations." You will see that all of the automotive companies, including the U.S. firms that are struggling for survival, are continuing to work on new and innovative vehicles that will appeal to buyers, conserve energy, and provide employment for the individuals who design and build automobiles and trucks around the world. I would not dismiss U.S. firms as they are the original innovators of mass transportation vehicles and automobiles, and several have nearly a hundred years of experience to draw upon and to project into the future. Further on in this chapter, we will discuss their current status as they fight for survival and struggle to keep their places as leaders in the auto industry. At this time, it appears that Toyota will overtake General Motors as the world's largest automaker in late 2006 or 2007.

Well, the drive so far has certainly been filled with some ups and downs with regard to the companies that make up the auto industry. By the way, did you check out those gasoline (petrol) prices as we traveled across Europe and Asia—two to three times that of prices in the U.S. Perhaps it's good to be nearing home. You know, of course, that we could have just as easily taken this journey on the Internet (or "www")!

Before we finish our drive, and if you haven't already picked up on it, Japanese auto makers (in particular, Toyota and Honda), seem to be riding the "yellow brick road" of gold and riches, while U.S. firms struggle for survival and for ways to stop the decline in their market shares. GM's share of the auto market has dropped from 45% in 1980 to about 26% today. Its market share in 1955 was 49.5%. Ford's share dropped only slightly from 20% to 18% in the same period (1980–2006), and for a while in the '90s its market share increased. In this same period, Toyota, Honda, and Nissan had increasing market shares (Loomis, 2006). Why is this happening? What is driving the transition of customers from one company to the other? Can globalization and "new-age innovation" be used to leverage a firm's competitive advantage in the new world economy? The answer is YES! Do you remember that *Wizard of Oz* story I talked about back in the introduction to this book, and the experiences of the fictional character, *Dorothy*, as she traveled the "*Yellow Brick Road*" leading to the *Emerald City* of success, abundance, and pleasure? Well, today's travelers on the "*Yellow Brick Road*" of global success demand to drive vehicles that are top quality, energy-efficient, price competitive, and appealing in design, style, comfort, and innovative features. This is a tall order, but delivering on these demands is what turns a “good company” into a “great company,” and a profitable one! (Collins, 2001)

Globalization Fear Factors.

In the brief timeline that follows, we will be looking at some of the significant events that have occurred (and there will be more to follow) as a result of the transition to a more global economy. These events have brought fear to many. You will need to remember that this is a short-term transitional process that “is not a pretty sight” as the title of this chapter suggests.

November 2005, *General Motors*: The world’s largest automaker—but not for long! The news media around the world reported that *GM (General Motors),* the world’s current largest auto manufacturer (Toyota is number two), is struggling with union benefits, pension contributions, and competitive pressures from Asia and Japan. They announced that 30,000 jobs would be cut and twelve North American facilities closed. As 2005 ended, GM announced that the company had lost $10.8 billion for the year. At the same time, Toyota reported that they had a record year in 2005, and profits were up 34% (Popely & Mateja, 2006). This wasn’t the end of the bad news for GM. February 2006 brought news that GM would cut its dividend in half to $1.00 per share, retirees and salaried employees would be paying more of their benefits in the future, and senior management would be receiving pay cuts and no bonuses. February also brought the bad news that Deutsche Bank, a globally respected investment and banking institution, issued an investor advisory recommending its clients sell their GM securities. GM’s well-respected bonds sank to an all time low in the $550–$600 range, from a high of $1200 in 2004. Likewise, its stock hit an all time low since 1982—$19 per share. Its stock had its all-time high of $93.75 per share back in the second quarter of 1999. All this is on top of the fact that GM has cut its white-collar payroll 10% each year since 2000, and reduced its number of engineers by 35% for the same period (Foust & Welch, 2006). Its biggest supplier of parts, Delphi, in which GM has a large ownership interest, filed for bankruptcy. By the time you are reading this book, we will all know more about the fate of General Motors. And, in all probability, we will have witnessed Toyota pushing GM out of first place in the auto industry.

January 2006, NBC Nightly News: The "late breaking news" across the world reported that *Ford Motor Company* (the 2nd largest automaker in the U.S.) would cut 30,000 jobs and close 14 facilities by 2012. Reasons stated: Inability to compete globally; loss in market share to other global automakers (Honda, Toyota); pay and benefits levels for employees cannot be supported by current selling prices; and, production capacity exceeds current demand for Ford products. However, Ford believes demand for its vehicles, especially its new hybrid cars, will improve if it can restructure the company to compete more effectively on a global basis, especially in those countries experiencing significant new car sales growth rates—China (13% growth in 2005) and India (24% growth in 2005). Ford's stock sank from $12 per share to $8 and is expected to move downward even further in 2006. It still pays $.40 per share dividend to its stockholders, but speculation says that this could end quickly if the company gets into liquidity (cash flow) problems. Ford's stock sold for as high as $29 per share back in 2001.

January 2006, "late breaking news" story from Germany: *DaimlerChrysler*, world renowned auto maker, known for its Mercedes Benz line of vehicles, stated that cost pressures brought about by globalization would require the company to lay off 6,000 employees over the next three years. 60% of the job cuts will be at its European Corporate Headquarters in Germany, mainly Stuttgart. There will also be some cuts at the company's North American Headquarters in Auburn Hills, Michigan (USA).

February 2006, The Associated Press Newswire reported: "VW Slashes Jobs." *Volkswagen AG,* Europe's number one automaker, announced that it would cut as many as 20,000 jobs (out of 340,000 world-wide) over the next three years, in conjunction with a program to restructure the entire company. It also announced that shutdown of an undisclosed number of manufacturing facilities was also under consideration. This announcement was unusual since the company had earlier reported record sales in 2005 of $126.7 billion (U.S. dollars), and profit of $1.3 billion. Profits were 61% ahead of 2004. The February 2006 announcement further stated that VW would build a manufacturing facility in Russia, continue to grow its sales in China, and introduce new brands in India—all part of its continuing global marketing strategy. For many years, Volkswagen was the leading seller of automobiles in China and much of Asia. (But, GM has now moved ahead of VW in China.) VW cited the reasons for the restructuring action as: "global competitive pressures" and "the need to bring the company's productivity up to international standards" (Associated Press, 2006). I believe one could infer from this action that the company is positioning itself to continue to be a world-class automaker. In fact, VW now owns Rolls-Royce, has signed agreements with Google to provide navigation systems for its vehicles, and is Brazil's leading automaker (Hoovers, 2006). There was speculation that the company took advantage of the fact that several other automakers, as discussed above, made announcements; so, if restructuring and productivity issues needed to be addressed, the time was right to join the pack.

Well, now, let's see if I can summarize and add up all the layoffs by the world's largest automakers. It looks like quite a transition and shake-up is going on.

General Motors	30,000 jobs (12 plants)
Ford Motor Co.	30,000 jobs (14 plants)
Daimler Chrysler	6,000 jobs
Volkswagen	20,000 jobs
Total	86,000 jobs

One has to ask: "how can this be happening if the auto industry is, in fact, growing, and the world's developing economies are demanding an ever-growing number of automobiles and trucks?" The key answers (as I currently see them) are:

1. Overcapacity exists in the industry.
2. Market share from the above automakers will move to others, who will need to add jobs to meet their new demand. Don't expect to see a one-for-one offset, since each company is looking at improving productivity. Note that one generally accepted definition of productivity is: "achieving additional output with the same or less input." This is exactly what automakers are looking for. Honda and Toyota already have a productivity advantage over many other manufacturers since they can produce an "average" car in about 18 hours, whereas it takes approximately 20-21 hours in the U.S. and Europe.
3. New and existing manufacturers in China, India, and Korea are expected to begin supplying more of the world's demand for cars and trucks. In fact, in 2005 and for the first time in history, China built, sold, and exported more cars and trucks to the rest of the world, than the world's automakers sent to China. "It won't be long before Chinese brands make their way to U.S. shores, including *Geely* and *Chery* automobiles" (George, 2006). There's some speculation that these cars could be sold by retailers such as COSTCO and Wal-Mart.
4. Older firms in the auto industry have not always kept pace with styles, features, options, and consumer preferences. In addition, as automakers aged, their costs have risen significantly, including operating expenses for

their huge facilities, and employee wage and benefit programs. Specifically, these "older automakers" have an ever-growing number of retirees and laid-off workers to support. Newer firms to the industry seem to have a cost advantage in all of these cost categories, as well as a productivity advantage—at least for now.

5. Micro Cars, sometimes called "Smart Cars," have been in use in the rest of the world for years. Small, fuel-efficient cars are a way of life in Europe, Asia, and the Middle East. These cars are just beginning to gain popularity in the U.S. More and more buyers are looking at the smaller, more fuel-efficient cars that are becoming available. GM and Ford are not yet common names when it comes to these "micro cars," but they are working on small fuel cell cars and vehicles powered by alternate energy sources. ZAP, Inc., which stands for "Zero Air Pollution," in Santa Rosa, California, appears to be the up-and-coming global leader and pioneer in alternate fuel "Micro" vehicles. The globalization of "Micro Car" technology will spread the availability of these vehicles. Embracing this niche market for alternate energy cars might help GM and Ford become more competitive with their product line offerings, as buyers become more "energy and environmentally" conscious. Are you interested in an "electric kit" for your bicycle, or perhaps an all electric "City Car?" The ZAP Company manufactures the electric car in China and sells it in the U.S. for $8,995. Running this little "baby" on electric energy costs about ⅓ the price of gasoline. No freeway driving is allowed since its maximum speed is 40 mph. Perhaps you would rather be sportier and get an 85 mph gasoline-powered "Smart Car," which ZAP imports from Mercedes Benz (DaimlerChrysler) in Germany. The first cars are being sold in the United States this year (2006). ZAP has to modify each one to comply with U.S. auto and environmental standards. These cars were available in Europe and other parts of the world 8 years ago. They are priced at $20,000 to $25,000 (U.S. dollars), and they get about 40–50 miles per gallon of gasoline (ZAP, 2006). The one I like has a built-in iPod playback and charging system. Do you think U.S. drivers will transition

from those gas guzzling $36,000 Ford Explorers and GM Suburbans to a "Micro" vehicle?

More late breaking news…

Just as we are finishing up with this section, news is being reported with regard to globalization's impact on one of the world's largest electronics retailers. Radio Shack announced today (February 16, 2006) that it would close 400 to 700 stores and two distribution centers in an effort to improve its declining profitability, citing competitive global price pressures as a main cause. Their 4th quarter earnings plunged 62%, from $130.9 million (U.S. dollars) last year to $49.5 million this year. It is easy to see how this is happening. Individuals and companies can easily purchase many of the items offered by Radio Shack and other retailers right off the internet from a large number of suppliers around the world, at substantially discounted prices. Personally, I just purchased a video storage device for a camera on the internet from an unknown vendor in Hong Kong for 50% less than Sony's price here in the U.S. It arrived in less than 5 days and was packaged in "official" (looking) Sony packaging. I question if it really was made by Sony. I wonder how the vendor got a supply of these Sony products to sell. It works just fine. Maybe I just benefited from the globalization process! Perhaps we are all benefiting from globalization each time we visit that ever-popular, and sometimes not-so-popular, Wal-Mart! What do you think?

CIA Report (2000), "Global Trends 2015."

"The rising tide of the global economy will create many economic winners, but it will not lift all boats. It will spawn conflicts at home and abroad, ensuring an even wider gap between regional winners and losers than exists today. Globalization's evolution will be rocky; marked by chronic financial volatility and a widening economic divide…

Regions, countries, and groups feeling left behind will face deepening economic stagnation, political instability, and cultural alienation. This will foster political, ethnic, ideological, and religious extremism, along with the violence that often accompanies it" (CIA Global Trends, 2000).

The above quote, from the "CIA Global Trends Report," clearly states a point of view that many have regarding globalization. It is a view that globalization can be a divisive force between those "winning" and those "losing." Alan Greenspan, former Chairman of the U.S. Federal Reserve System, spoke about divisiveness in terms of a growing inequality between those who do the work, and those who provide capital and oversee the work. In his 2005 mid-year speech before the U.S. Congress, he remarked that there was "growing evidence of anti-globalization sentiment and protectionist initiatives" (Frank, 2006). Barney Frank, the ranking Democrat on the House Financial Services Committee, in his report on the meeting with Greenspan, agreed that, thus far, an "economy marked by globalization has seen real wages for average workers erode and health and pension benefits decline. Meanwhile, corporate profits and pay for the top 2% of the population (U.S.) have soared" (Frank, 2006). This view points out that globalization is having some short-term negative impacts on "average workers," especially those in the Western World. Many in developing nations are seeing real gains. It is hard to put this into perspective, but a real gain in a poor developing nation might be one nutritious meal a day. In most of the Western World economies, real increases might be measured in terms of improvements in an already high level standard of living.

Speech by Jerry Mander of the International Forum on Globalization, at the World Affairs Council, San Francisco, April 2003.

" .... the survival of a globalized economy can only be achieved via an impossible formula: a never-ending, always expanding supply of inexpensive resources, new markets, and cheap labor. But it's a process that cannot go on forever on a finite planet. Many global resources are already seriously depleted: oil is becoming among them. Markets in many countries are also nearly saturated. People can buy only so many cars, and so much stuff. And, cheap labor is less and less willing to be cheap… What they (cheap labor) clearly see are corporate CEO's making millions while their own wages decline or stagnate, if they have a job at all. Meanwhile, the world's environmental systems—from climate to water to oceans—are near collapse from the expansive, intrusive pressures of the system. Economic globalization was to be a panacea for all the world's problems—poverty, war, even environmental degradation. It was going to bring freedom, free markets and free trade .... it was to be the rising tide that will lift all boats" (Mander, 2003).

Question & Answer Session with Jack Welch, former Chairman and CEO, General Electric Company.

"I don't want to sound like a *Pollyanna* about China. Its presence is a real game-changer in business today, even if trade restrictions get enacted, its currency is allowed to fluctuate, and intellectual property laws are passed. No political solution in the world is going to make it go away. You can look at the situation and feel victimized. Or you can look at it and be excited about conquering the challenges and opportunities it presents. Pick the latter. You can't win wringing your hands. Think of China as a market, an outsourcing option, and a potential partner. China can be more than just a global competitor" (Welch, 2004).

Merger Mania.

It's on the news, in our papers, and in our faces every day. The mega companies of the world, as well as some smaller organizations, continue to combine, split, sell, diversify, and reorganize in response to the new global economy, and the "competitive survival instinct." I am not suggesting that globalization and the rise of the new world economy are the only reasons driving merger and acquisition activity, but I will argue that they are key drivers—perhaps one could even say, "the key drivers." Following is a list of the major participants in the "Merger Mania" we have seen in recent years: (1998 to April, 2006)

- Walt Disney Co. (CEO Roger Iger) and Pixar Animation Studios (CEO Steve Jobs), January 2006 – ***merger*** valued at $7.4 billion.
- Boston Scientific Corporation ***purchase*** of Guidant Corporation in January 2006 for $27.2 billion. Both companies design, manufacture, and market medical devices.
- New York Stock Exchange ***merger*** with Archipelago – $9.0 billion.
- Hewlett-Packard ***purchase*** of Compaq – $25 billion.
- Swiss Re Insurance ***purchase*** of GE Insurance Solutions – $6.8 billion.
- Paramount Pictures ***purchase*** of Dreamworks – $3.1 billion.
- U.S. Air ***merger*** with America West Airlines – $1.5 billion.
- Sprint ***merger*** with Nextel – Telecom – $35 billion.
- Verizon ***merger*** with MCI – Telecom – $8.4 billion

- SBC ***merger*** with AT&T – $16 billion
- J.P. Morgan Chase ***purchase*** of Bank One – $59 billion.
- Bank of America ***merger*** with FleetBoston Financial – $47 billion.
- Sears ***merger*** with Kmart – $11 billion.
- Proctor & Gamble ***purchase*** of Gillette – $54 billion.
- Chevron ***merger*** with Texaco – $35 billion.
- MCI Communications ***merger*** with WorldCom – $44 billion.
- Citigroup ***merger*** with Travelers Group – $73 billion.
- Exxon ***merger*** with Mobil Oil – $77 billion.
- Gas Natural ***purchase*** of Endesa (Spain) – $51.2 billion.
- Vodafone ***purchase*** of Mannesmann (U.K.) – $130 billion.
- AOL Time Warner ***merger*** with America Online – $166 billion.
- British Petroleum ***merger*** with Amoco – $110 billion.
- Daimler Benz ***merger*** with Chrysler – $35 billion.
- Phillips Petroleum ***merger*** with Conoco – $15 billion.
- Whirlpool Corp. ***purchase*** of Maytag Corp. – $2.6 billion.
- Attempted ***acquisition*** – NASDAQ offered to purchase the London Stock Exchange for $4.2 billion. (Rejected March 2006.)
- Currently in progress (April 2006) – AT&T (formerly SBC) ***purchase*** of BellSouth – $67 billion. This combination of companies will create the largest amount of capital invested in any company anywhere in the world – about $280 billion! (Colvin, 2006) Do you recall some years ago (1984) when the U.S. Justice Department had a hand in breaking up the "Ma Bell monopoly" in the name of "fair trade?" Seems like a few of these companies might be getting back together again, if the acquisition is

approved and completed. By the time you are reading this book, we'll all know the outcome.

2006 promises to be another record year for M&A (Merger and Acquisition) activity, as companies seek to become larger, more powerful, and more resilient in the age of globalization. In this regard, "Merger and Acquisition" activity in Western Europe during the first half of 2006, was reported in *USA Today* as the number one driver of heightened economic growth in that region of the world. Interestingly, "Outsourcing" and "Globalization" were cited as numbers two and three. With regard to outsourcing, European nations continue to shift jobs to Eastern Europe and Asia to lower labor costs, just as the U.S. and other industrialized nations have been doing for some time. And, with globalization at work in the region, Eastern and Western Europe are attempting to become more integrated to allow for easier and more open cross-border trade and investment (Block, 2006).

In the end, the broader and magnified pressures of "world competition," brought on by globalization, seem to be driving merger and acquisition activity around the world. Being bigger generally means that a company has more resources and economic wherewithal to tackle "large scale projects," such as the massive infrastructure and energy needs in many of the developing countries. I believe there's some truth to this, but there are numerous opportunities for small and medium size companies as well.

The Global Economic Olympics.

When the official numbers are reported for 2005, the prediction is that China will trump France and Britain and move up from number 7 in 2004 to number 4 on the list of the world's largest economies (as measured in terms of GDP—Gross Domestic Product) (CIA Global Trends, 2004).

The transition and reshuffling of the world's economies, primarily as a result of globalization, have been and continue to be dramatic. Here's how the top 10 economies stack up: (Source: World Fact Book, 2006)

Rank	2000	2003	2004	2005(Est)
1	USA	USA	USA	USA
2	Japan	Japan	Japan	Japan
3	Germany	Germany	Germany	Germany
4	France	Britain	Britain	**China**
5	Britain	France	France	France
6	Italy	Canada	Italy	Britain
7	**China**	Italy	**China**	Italy
8	Brazil	Spain	Spain	Spain
9	Canada	**China**	Canada	Canada
10	Spain	Brazil	India	India

The above rankings represent history. More importantly, what does the future hold for the world's economies as globalization takes a firm hold on the way the world functions economically, politically, and socially? There are many views on the subject, but all conclude that China will become the world's number one economy in the near future. In twenty years, the projected view looks like the following: (compared to 2005) (Source: Cylist, 2005)

Rank	2005(Est)	2025(Est)
1	**USA**	**China**
2	Japan	USA
3	Germany	**India**
4	**China**	Japan
5	France	Brazil

6	Britain	Russia
7	Italy	Britain
8	Spain	Germany
9	Canada	France
10	**India**	Canada

It is interesting to note that China is projected to move into first place by 2025, beating out the USA and Japan, who have held first and second places for many years. In answering the question as to what drives economic growth, four measures are generally used: (Bergheim, 2006)

Population growth

Investment

Human capital

Trade openness (globalization)

By applying these four measures, economic growth rates for the top 10 countries over the next 20 years are forecasted as follows: (Bergheim, 2006)

Rank	**Country**	**% Growth 2006–2025**
1	India	5.5%
2	Malaysia	5.4%
3	China	5.2%
4	Thailand	4.5%
5	Turkey	4.1%
6	Ireland	3.8%
7	Indonesia	3.5%
8	Korea, So	3.3%
9	Mexico	3.3%
10	Chile	3.1%

Others:

11	USA	3.1%
14	Brazil	2.8%
15	Canada	2.4%
21	Britain	1.9%
22	Sweden	1.8%
24	Denmark	1.7%
27	Germany	1.5%

The above rankings are certainly very revealing in that they support what we are reading today in 2006. Rapid economic growth will continue in the developing countries of the world who have recently embraced capitalism, consumerism, and globalization. China, India, and Malaysia are at the top, while many of the "more mature" countries of the world are at the bottom. Asia, Malaysia, and Indonesia dominate the top 10. It is very interesting that Ireland slips into the middle of the pack at #6. Notice that countries once considered dominant economies have moved down in the rankings. Japan and France are even further down on the list.

There is one more important ranking I'd like to share with you. Depending on one's point of view, it might be the most important—important in the sense that businesses, individuals, and entire nations are seeking competitive advantages as they transition to effectively participate in the new global economy. Thanks to the United States and its Central Intelligence Agency ("The CIA"), *competitiveness among nations* is measured and ranked as follows: (using return on investment and productivity data) (Easton, 2005)

Rank	**Country**
1	Finland
2	United States
3	Sweden

4	Denmark
5	Taiwan
6	Singapore
7	Iceland
8	Switzerland
9	Norway
10	Australia
11	Netherlands
12	Japan
13	U.K.
14	Canada
15	Germany

Not shown are France ranked #30, China #49, and India #50. With regard to China and India, their rankings and the others shown above demonstrate that we are perhaps confusing size and growth with economic and competitive strengths. China and India certainly have the highest GDP (Gross Domestic Product) growth rates and are destined to become the world's largest economies, but this does not mean that they will be strong in every dimension of economic and commercial activity. Banking, legal, and capital market structures are weak and lacking in performance standards in both of these countries. In China, the Communist government often steps in and directs banks to make loans to homeland firms that are not creditworthy by any standards. The Chinese government often subsidizes its State Owned Businesses, to make sure they can be competitive. Until recently, few IPO's (Initial Public Offerings) took place in China and India. Intellectual property laws, while relatively strong in China, are poorly enforced. Stable stock markets from which to raise capital and trade securities have been weak in both China and India. Healthcare for the citizens in these countries is severely lacking, and the overall quality of life remains poor, but improving every day. My point here is that China, India and the other developing nations of the world are not to be feared just because their day is now, and they are experiencing unprecedented growth rates, and have massive amounts of cheap labor. It takes more than growth and cheap labor to build strong economies, especially a global economy.

The capitalistic forces of supply, demand, and competition will certainly balance the strengths and weaknesses among all nations in the new global economy. This is exactly the transitional process that we are in the midst of today. There will be room in the new economy for all who leverage globalization, rather than fear it.

What are we to make of all this change? We are in a transition that continues to level the world in terms of opportunities for global trade. It is a transition like no other we've seen in recent history. It is a transition to a world economy that knows few borders and barriers. The Internet and "new-age innovation" are driving communications and bringing people together for commercial, political, and social reasons.

As we have touted the benefits of the new global economy, perhaps we overlooked the difficult transition requirements placed on people, businesses, and communities. As Senator Hillary Rodham Clinton (wife of ex-U.S. President Bill Clinton) remarked in her July 2005 speech before The Aspen Institute's Idea Feast, "It continues to amaze me that the Administration, which has seen soaring rates of offshore outsourcing and a net loss of US jobs on its watch, has made no provision that really will assist US workers harmed by our trade agreements" (Clinton, 2005). While there may be some political jockeying going on in this statement, there is a need for assistance, not just in the United States, but in all nations that are a part of this difficult transition to a new global economy and world community. Those of us who live in reality know that we're all interdependent participants in a major business, economic, political, and in many ways, social transformation. Globalization: ***"It's not a pretty sight, but. . .!"***

"Companies begin to age or decline when they resist change or new ideas, and focus on controlling how things get done, and who is involved."

Jack Veale, Principal PTCFO, Inc. Consultant in Change Management

---

"The biggest danger to U.S. workers isn't overseas competition. It's that we worry too much about other countries climbing up the ladder and not enough about finding the next higher rung for ourselves."

Michael J. Mandel, Economist and Writer, New York. As found in "Businessweek Online," August 25, 2003, "Commentary: Outsourcing Jobs: Is It Bad?"

Well, what I'm trying to say is that we have to wake up to the fact that we're in a global economy and people have to change."

Andy Stern, Leader SEIU
(Service Employee's International Union)

CONCLUSION

How we interact as citizens of the new global economy and community remains to be seen. Will we take the gentler road of collaboration and cooperation, or will we continue to fight over religious beliefs, skin color, scarce natural resources, real estate, oil, ideology, political agendas, and wealth accumulation?

Phil Watlington, Author "The World Is At Your Door!"
Lead Faculty and Area Chair, Financial Planning and Control,
University of Phoenix

Thank you for taking this journey with me. Our virtual journey of words and visualization started **"On the Road To the Airport, Or On the Internet"** (Chapter 1), where we became grounded with an understanding of globalization. We looked at such globalization activities as offshoring, outsourcing, insourcing, and backshoring, not just in terms of how to lower costs on products and services, but also as vehicles for businesses to tap into other countries' markets where goods and services can be sold. We found this transitional period in history, called "globalization," to be about more than commercial transactions and global economics. It is really about opening doors and getting to know people around the world. It is about learning to work together and coming to the colossal realization that we are all dependent on each other. To a degree, we are each others' keeper, whether we like it or not. And, through events in past and present history and the communications mediums of the Internet and World Wide Web, we are now neighbors in a global community. How we interact as citizens of this new global community remains to be seen. Will we take the gentler road of collaboration and cooperation, or will we continue to fight over religious beliefs, skin color, scarce natural resources, real estate, oil, ideology, political agendas, and wealth accumulation?

Next, we explored the role of "new-age innovation" and the use of **"Artistic and Creative Visions for Innovative Organizations"** (Chapter 2) as tools for surviving and thriving in the new global economy. Our focus was on a renaissance in inventiveness that extends well beyond laboratory-based research and development models of the past. Inventiveness now encompasses web-based virtual and collaborative business processes, specialized organizational structures, and new (and often simply improved) customer centric products and services. These new-age innovative products and services embrace not only needs, but pleasure, entertainment, and anticipated customer satisfaction. Delighting the customer by delivering more than anticipated—the Sony postage stamp-size memory stick that holds 1,800 photos, Apple's new "4GB pencil thin 1.5oz. nano iPod digital player" with access to 1,000+ recordings/audio books, and Proctor and Gambles' new "Swiffer electrostatic dust mop" are examples of "new-age innovation" and design theory "ideation" at work. Certainly, Steve Jobs of Apple Computers, and Bill Gates of Microsoft, will be joined by many others who will continue to apply creative and imaginative knowledge-based technologies to gain a competitive advantage in this new global economy. China and India, once world leaders of inventiveness, will return as 21st century economic and inventiveness powers. At least in the foreseeable future, every day will be tomorrow in the new global economy and new age of inventiveness! Innovation has worked in the past. "New-age innovation" will work today and in the future!

There was simply no detour around understanding and attempting to sort out how to deal with the fact that in many "developed countries" around the world; **"The Cost of Labor is Four Times Greater Than in China and India—Now What?"** (Chapter 3) China has become much of the world's preferred location of choice for manufacturing. In this regard, leveraging manufacturing supply chains to establish a cost advantage for your organization will generally be the best strategic direction. For highly labor-intensive manufacturing organizations, the offshoring or outsourcing of this activity will be a must. But, as we saw with the automobile industry in the U.S., companies from Asia, Europe, and Japan are successfully locating in the U.S. with lower wages and benefits. So, this means that, before leaping into offshoring and outsourcing activities, a close look at cost structures and core competencies is required when making effective competitive decisions. These competitive type decisions are being played out at GM and Ford today, and the results so far have been that these organizations' cost structures, primarily wage and benefit programs, will not allow them to be competitive and maintain or grow their market share in the new global economy. These great companies, rich in history and inventiveness, face a transition like none other in their histories. Many people in the global community depend on them for their livelihood. I hope they can be with us for another 100 years!

Just as China has "cornered" the market for manufacturing, India has a grip on services. Everybody knows it. At this time, the savings are extremely significant and to ignore leveraging labor costs in India is to ignore being successful in today's new competitive environment. Bangalore and Hyderabad, India, have become household names for locations for call center operations, engineering, research, and information technology activities. Beware, however, that "red flags" are beginning to surface as pay scales are literally doubling every year in India for many jobs, mainly information technology (IT). Even at this rate, it will be some time before there will not be an advantage to leveraging low-wages in India.

And, don't overlook Wuhan, China, which is becoming the "Bangalore" of China for information technology (IT) work, or many of the eastern European nations where computer technology and software workers are plentiful (at least at this time).

"Education—The Great Equalizer (Actually the Most Important Chapter!)" (Chapter 4) dealt simply with the fact that knowledge is the basis in the new global economy upon which solutions to complex (and not so complex) problems will be found. It is the key to achieving a competitive advantage as an individual, company, or entire nation. As one reads the literature, there is great concern—especially in the U.S. and countries of Western Europe—that education in the technical disciplines, mathematics, and sciences are declining, or not keeping pace with the rest of the world. These are the disciplines that typically drive innovation and higher standards of living. As Thomas Friedman, well-know author of *The World is Flat, A Brief History of the Twentieth-First Century*, writes with regard to a futuristic view of education: "One of the most important needs individuals, especially our children, face today is 'to learn how to learn.' Jobs will come and go rapidly. Competing for jobs in the global economy will require the constant modification of job skills and learning new jobs" (Friedman, 2005).

Although billions of dollars have been invested in educational improvements and initiatives, the time has come for creativity, imagination, and inventiveness to be applied to the educational process itself. A renaissance in learning is required. It happened in Europe's historical 14th through 16th century Renaissance period of learning, it happened in India when the British left in 1947, and it happened in China in 1978 with their emergency educational initiatives. It can happen again in the U.S. and Europe, but it will require a new emphasis on education. As you might recall from our discussions in this chapter, there are signs of renaissance activities all around us. Many great universities, such as, The London Business School, France's INSEAD University, Queens University in Canada, Spain's IESE University, and from the U.S.—Michigan, Harvard, Stanford, Pennsylvania, CalTech, MIT, and Northwestern—are building globally focused learning experiences that equip individuals to successfully live, compete, and lead in the new global community and economy. We saw progress being made at the University of Kansas and the opening of the Confucius Institute, as China's Vice-Minister of Education Wu Oidi and Governor Kathleen Sebelius shook hands in agreement that all students need to have global competencies in today's interconnected and interdependent world. In a sense, it was an emotional sight as we stood in a large assembly room overlooking the great plains of Kansas witnessing two peoples, physically miles apart, agreeing to better understand each another in a world of differences—a world where the global economic superpower, The People's Republic of China, and the tiny state of Kansas become linked by dependency on each other. And, let's not forget that small college in Dallas, Texas—Richland College—the first ever community college to receive the *Malcolm Baldrige National Quality Award* for excellence in education. This small community-based college exemplifies the progress and efforts occurring at all levels of the educational process to prepare individuals for life in the global community. What about the thousands of working adults that we discussed in this book who have created a stampede back to evening and weekend classes? I hope this is yet another sign of progress and a renaissance in learning.

It stands as a given that to participate, we must educate. Educate individuals, companies, and entire nations to participate—survive and thrive—in the new interconnected global community and economy of which we are all a part. Simply stated, the emergence of the global knowledge economy has put a premium on learning throughout the world and we must be prepared to participate. "Permanent education is going to be the name of the game in the world of 3 billion new capitalists (the 2006 combined population of China, India, and Eastern Europe)" (Prestowitz, 2005).

Understanding, connecting, and leveraging globalization and "new-age innovation" were discussed in detail in **"Global**

Strategy, Hedgehogs, Martha Stewart, and Others" (Chapter 5). Logic follows that today's organizations must change their strategic plans and business models to incorporate the elements of globalization and "new-age innovation," along with the proper tactics for their execution. In this new global economy, more so than ever before, leaders must turn their organizations into "hedgehogs" that focus on one core product or service market in which others will find competing difficult. Who can I think of as great "hedgehog companies" that have done just this? Starbucks and Martha Stewart Living Omnimedia. Of course, there are many others as well! I often read *Martha Stewart Living* as I sip a Mocha Frappuccino or a cup of that new Rwanda Blue Bourbon coffee.

In **"Governance, Accountability, and Ethics in the New Global Economy: Whose Standards Apply?"** (Chapter 6) we questioned who will establish and monitor fair trade, ethical issues, and human rights. Censorship, governance, accountability and ethics are all topics we'll be hearing more about in the future. Frankly, I don't believe these are subjects anyone is looking forward to tackling, much less dealing with their resolutions. Why? The task of finding "common ground" among even a few of the nations of the world will be daunting. Secondly, there are staggering profits to be made in many of the developing countries where censorship is allowed and governance is lacking—especially with regard to internet communications and intellectual property rights. Much is being done by global organizations such as the World Trade Organization, The World Bank, and the United Nations. There is still a lot of "wink-wink, turn your head, and look the other way" going on in the name of profitability. The world simply cannot be "flat" economically, and "round" when it comes to ethics, governance, and accountability for actions that impact people in our rapidly growing interdependent world community. Whose standards will apply? Who will police the world? To which I will answer—these are good questions. Stand by for more as the major software and internet providers from the U.S. seek a common ground to do business and earn profits "ethically" in The People's Republic of China, where governmental censorship is widespread. Meanwhile, back in the USA, we're wrestling with governmental wiretapping, using data mining surveillance methodologies, and issues brought about by the Patriot Act—all in the name of terrorism! It is really a "wobbly-wheel and jack-in-the-box" world when it comes to governance, ethics, and protecting human and property rights.

"The Standard of Living and Quality of Life Argument" (Chapter 7) discussed the brutal reality that, while globalization may be leveling the world's economic playing field, the world's 4 billion people who live on less than $2,000 per year, and the world's 800 million who live on less that $1.00 per day, are not yet fully participating in the benefits of globalization and the "new age of innovation." On the other end of the spectrum, many—especially those who reside in what has come to be called the "middle class"—worry that their standard of living is being pulled down by the equalizing forces of globalization. The challenge remains that individuals, companies, and entire nations must understand and leverage globalization and "new-age innovation" to successfully reside and participate in the global community.

I am sure it was a surprise, and many of my readers probably correctly asked "who is this guy from Kansas who thinks he can provide a list that represents the solutions to the world's energy shortage (crises if you prefer)?" Well, providing the list and identifying solutions in **"Energy (Crisis?)—Globalization and Innovation at Their Best (or Worst)"** (Chapter 8) is just the first step and perhaps the easy part of the process. So far, as you probably know, many of the solutions have been right in front of us. Many of the solutions on the list I presented in this chapter are underway. Windmill farms are springing up everywhere there is a brisk breeze. A limited number of fuel cell and hydrogen-powered cars and buses are in use in certain parts of the world, but we are still a few years away from these technologies being commercially feasible. Solar panels are providing energy for limited uses, and research continues into making this source of energy cost effective. The use of ethanol and biodiesel fuel is expanding rapidly. Hybrid automobiles are gaining popularity as gasoline prices move above $3.00 per gallon in the U.S. and $7.00 in Europe. Let's hope the pain won't be too bad until catch-up actions can be taken and we've replaced dependency on oil with other alternative energy sources. Based on the research I shared early in this book, the evidence points to the fact that new-age innovative resources in the world (especially in the U.S.) will solve this problem. Check out the list of energy solutions in Chapter 8 again. There are fortunes to be made in profits from the items on the list. Capitalism will drive solutions. It's just a matter of time—which is now the problem. In the meantime, we'll be dealing with some pretty ugly situations, such as Iran, the 3rd largest holder of oil reserves in the world, threatening to restrict the flow of oil if sanctions are brought against it for developing a nuclear capability program. Furthermore, competition will heat up as the U.S., China, India, and much of Europe vie for oil supplies to fuel their existence and growth. I hope you smiled when I listed as a couple solutions to the energy shortage: Sit in the Summer Breeze, Ride a Bike, Wear a Sweater, Work from Home, and Take an Alternative Fuel Powered Bus—I was serious!

"In Transition—It's Not a Pretty Sight, But…!" (Chapter 9*)*, in my opinion, reflects an adequate description of the current state of the world economy and community. Students frequently ask: "What is your opinion of today's economy with regard to globalization, outsourcing, people losing their jobs, continually rising energy prices, and great companies struggling for survival?" The quick answer might be: "It's business as usual. I can't remember a time when there wasn't change and some kind of crises, or perceived crisis." However, the answer must run deeper due to the fact that we're all in the midst of a significant transition to a new global economy, and to a newly interconnected global community. We have not had time to get to know our new neighbors, many of whom we may never see, but whom we will depend on for our well-being and survival. This transition will test our capacity for change and remind us that "when we are through with change, we'll be through …"

****

As I have engaged in research for this book, I am forever amazed at how the long and winding road of history seems to find itself in the future, again and again—as it has with the rise once again of globalization in the 21st century—as China and India continue their return as cultural and "inventive centers" of the world—and, as the U.S. continues its starring role in the global economy as the world's role model for freedom and human rights.

Many individuals, businesses, and entire nations will respond to globalization with imagination, creativity, leadership, and "new-age innovation." Will you be one of them? What more could you ask for? ***The World Is At Your Door! Let it in! It is a door to the future!*** (I'll bet you knew I was going to end with this phrase!)

Finally, I extend my sincere appreciation to each of you and hope you will again be readers of my upcoming books that will deal with living in an extraordinary world where ***every day is tomorrow***.

Never believe that a few caring people can't change the world—for, indeed, that's all who ever have."

Margaret Mead

Appendix A

Strategic Planning Process Road Map (Outline)—"Make-Over"

I. Company/Organization's background

Add the following:

a. Discussion of global impact and status today
b. Discussion of the role innovation plays in the organization
c. Discussion of key "employer of choice" people initiates.

II. Vision Statement

Add the following:

a. A futuristic vision of an organization's global market and industry standing.
b. A futuristic vision of the role innovation will play in an organization's achievement and maintenance of a global competitive advantage.
c. A futuristic vision of an organization's people talent levels, and the roles they will play in innovating new products and services for global markets.

III. Mission Statement

Add the following:

a. Statement regarding the global reach of products & services

b. Statement regarding purpose/intent of innovative products & services

c. Statement regarding expectations from and opportunities for people

IV. Values/Ethics/Social Responsibility Statement

Add the following:

a. Statement regarding global ethical & social (community) responsibilities

b. Statement regarding "good for all" inventiveness direction

c. Statement regarding Code of Ethics, treatment of people

V. Environment Analysis – Internal & External

Add the following:

a. Analysis of global environment from a supplier and buyer perspective

b. Analysis of how innovation will provide competitive advantages

c. Analysis of impact of people trends and impact

d. Apply SWOT (Strengths, Weaknesses, Opportunities, Threats) analysis techniques to above additions to the environmental analysis

VI. Long Term Objectives

Add the following:

a. Establish objective for global reach and position
b. Establish objective for innovation of products & services; cultural change
c. Establish objective for people initiatives

VII. Strategic Directions/Guidance – generic and grand strategies

Add the following:

a. Establish generic or grand global supplier/buyer strategies
b. Establish generic or grand collaborative global innovation strategies
c. Establish generic or grand people strategies

VIII. Implementation Tactics

Add the following:

a. Establish specific measurable global supplier/buyer programs
b. Establish specific measurable product & service innovation programs
c. Establish specific measurable people initiatives

IX. Financial Analysis and Projections

Add the following:

a. Global sales and profitability analysis/projections(country, product line)
b. Cost/benefit analysis for innovation projects; spending objectives
c. Cost/benefit analysis of people programs

X. Key/Critical Success Factors

(Including Scenario Planning/Analysis)

Add the following:

a. Establish key top-level meaningful global outcome objectives
b. Establish key top-level meaningful outcome objectives for innovation
c. Establish key top-level meaningful outcome objectives for people initiatives

XI. Evaluation, Control, Feedback Procedures, and Metrics

Add the following:

a. Establish techniques to monitor, control, and provide feedback on globalization programs, for the purpose of continual improvement
b. Establish techniques to monitor, control, and provide feedback on innovation programs, for the purpose of continual improvement
c. Establish techniques to monitor, control, and provide feedback on people programs, for the purpose of continual improvement

Reference Sources and Notes

Introduction.

Collins, J. (2001). *Good To Great.* New York, Harper Business/Collins Publishers. pp. 90-91; 117-118; 186

Bernanke, B. (2004). Remarks by Ben S. Bernanke, Fuqua School of Business, Duke University. *Distinguished Speaker Series.* Retrieved March 22, 2006 from: *http://www.Federalreserve.gov/boarddocs/speeches/2004/20040330/default.htm.*

Friedman, T. (2005). *The World Is Flat, A Brief History of the Twenty-First Century.* New York. Farrar, Straus and Giroux. p. 5.

Hutto, J. and Mohuidalin, S. (2006). Connecting the Poor. Retrieved April 25, 2006 from *http://www.ppionline.org/documents/Connecting_the_Poor_030106.pdf*

Jobs Tomorrow. (2006, March 18). Gambling on a free-trade deal. *The Economist*. p. 43.

Pocket World In Figures. (2006). *The Economist*. p. 64.

Prestowitz, C. (2005). *Three Billion New Capitalists, The Great Shift of Wealth and Power to the East*. New York: Basic Books. p. 3, 21, 59 & XIV.

Sarfatti, M. (2004). Offshoring Conflicts with National Interests. Retrieved April 10, 2006 from: *http://alum.mit.edu/ne/whatmatters/200408/index.html*

Toyota. (2006, March 27). The Story of the Plant that Never Stopped Growing. Copy Editor, *Newsweek*. p. 9.

Chapter 1 (On the Road to the Airport . . .)

A Brief History. (2006, March 27). A Brief History of Globalization. Time Asia Magazine. Retrieved March 30, 2006 from: *http://www.time.com./time/asia/magazine/Article/0,13673,501060327-1174759,00.html*

A Hall That Beats All. (2006, March 14). *The Kansas City Star*, p. D3.

Bernanke, B. (2006). Ben Bernanke Quotes, *ThinkExist. Com*. Retrieved April 21, 2006 from: *http://en.thinkexist.com/quotes/ben_bernanke/*

Boeing. (2006). The Boeing Company and China. Retrieved March 31, 2006 from: *http://www.boeing.com/companyOffices/aboutus/boechina.html*

Breaking Links. (2006, March 7). Copy Editor, *The Kansas City Star*, p. D3.

Communist Party. (2006). Communist Party. *Wikipedia Free Encyclopedia*. Retrieved April 10, 2006 from: *http://en.wikipedia.org/wiki/Communist_party*

Cooper, J. (2006, February 27). What's Complicating Bernanke's Balancing Act. *BusinessWeek Online*. Retrieved March 23, 2006 from: *http://www.businessweek.com/print/magazine/content/06_09/b3973034.htm? chan=gl.*

Dept. (2006, May 1). Dept. of Early Indicators. *BusinessWeek*. p. 13.

Elliott, M. (2006, March 27). A Backlash Against Globalization. *Time Magazine*. Retrieved April 2, 2006 from: *http://www.time.com/time/asia/magazine/article/0,13673,501060327-1174760,00.html*

Fisher, A. (2006, March 20). Bringing the Jobs Home. *Fortune Magazine*, p. 22.

Fisher, A. (2006, March 27). America's Most Admired Companies. *Fortune Magazine*. p. 71.

France. (2006, April 1). France Faces the Future. *The Economists*. pp. 9-10.

Gates, B. (1999). Insight: Bill Gates, Chief Architect of Microsoft, EBS. Retrieved May16, 2006 from: *http://www.ebstrategy.com/outsourcing/basics/definition.htm*

GENPACT. (2006, April). GENPACT, Global Business Impact. *Fortune*. p. S5.

Global Outsourcing. (2006). The Global Outsourcing 100. *Fortune*. pp S1 – S17.

Graham & Lam. (2004). The Chinese Negotian. *Harvard Business Review on Doing Business in China*. Boston, Ma. Harvard Business School Publishing Company. pp. 38 – 53.

Green Car Congress. (2006). China, Now the World's Second Largest Automaker. Retrieved March 31, 2006 from: *http://www.greencarcongress.com/china/index.html*

Greenspan, A. (2006, May 20). The Practical limits of Globalization. *The Globalist*. Retrieved on March 23, 2006 from: *http://www.theglobalist.com/DBWeb/StoryId.aspx?StoryId=3936*. p. 1 & 3.

Greenspan, A. (2005, March 10). Remarks at the Council on Foreign Relations: *Globalization*. New York, N.Y. p. 6.

Growth--Poverty. (2004). Growth, Poverty, and Equality: Eastern Europe and the Former Soviet Union. Retrieved June 1, 2006 from:

http://siteresources.worldbank.org/INTECA/Resources/overview-poverty-en.pdf

Heffes, E. (2004, September). Offshoring: And the Winner Is… *Financial Executive*. p. 31.

How Many, (2006). How Many Will Go Hungry on World Food Day? Retrieved on April 6, 2006 from: *http://www.mindfully.org/Food/2003/Hungry-Food-Day16oct03.htm*

IAOP. (2006). The Global Outsourcing 100 for 2006. International Association Outsourcing Professionals. Retrieved March 8, 2006 from: *http://www.outsourcingprofessional.org/content/23/152/1197/*

IMF. (2006, May 27). World Economic Outlook. *International Monetary Fund.*

Infoplease. (2004). World's 30 Busiest Airports by Passengers and Cargo, 2004. Retrieved April 21, 2006 from: *http://www.infoplease.com/ipa/A0004547html*

International Monetary Fund. (2006). The International Monetary Fund (IMF). Retrieved April 21, 2006 from: *http://en.wikipedia.org/wiki/IMF*

Krames, J. (2005). Jack Welch and *The 4E's of Leadership*. New York, The McGraw Hill Companies. p. 131 & 138.

Lechner, F. (2001). Book Review: *The Lexus and the Olive Tree: Understanding Globalization.* Anchor Books. Retrieved January 4, 2006 from: *http://www.sociology.emory.edu/globalization/reviews/friedman.html*. p. 1.

Leeb, S. (2006, March). "What They're Thinking." *The Complete Investor.* Volume 4, Number 3. p. 11.

Leeb, S. and Smith, G. (2006, Winter). Welcome to the era of "constrained discretion." *The Complete Investor.* p. 1 – 2.

Lynn, B. (2005) *End of the Line*. New York: Doubleday/Random House Publishers. pp 7 – 9.

Offshore Outsourcing. (2006). Offshore Outsourcing. *Free Dictionary by Farlex*. Retrieved May 21, 2006 from: *http://encyclopedia.thefreedictionary.com/Offshore+outsourcing*

Palley, T. (2006). The Economics of Outsourcing. *Counterpunch Website*. Retrieved March 30, 2006 from: *http://www.counterpunch.org/palley03142006.html*

Prestowitz, C. (2005). *Three Billion New Capitalists, The Great Shift of Wealth and Power to the East*. New York: Basic Books. p. 3, 21, 59 & XIV.

NOW. (2005). Rich World, Poor Women: Understanding Globalization. Retrieved October 17, 2005 from: *http://www.pbs.org/now/politics/globaldebate.html*

Oppenheimer, C. (2006, May 5). Gutenberg Meets Bill W. *Kansas City Business Journal*. Special report, PIA MID AMERICA. pp. 1-2.

Pocket World In Figures. (2006 Edition). *The Economist*. pp. 26 & 70.

Scott, L. (2005, June 3). Remarks of Lee Scott, President and CEO, Wal-Mart Stores, Inc., at Annual Meeting of Shareholders. Retrieved March 14, 2006 from *http://www.walmartfacts.com/docs/1078_walmartannualreport2005*

Semico. (2006). Semico Research: Market Analysis. Retrieved April 21, 2006 from: *http://www.semico.com/ studies/docs/toc450.pdf*

Software Engineer Salaries in India and China. (2006,March 19).Press Release, *Mercer Human Resource Consulting LLC*. Retrieved April 2, 2006 from: *http://blogs.borland.com/davidi/archive/2006/03/19/23827.aspx*

Stock Exchanges. (2006). Stock Exchanges: Worldwide Links. *Metasite.net*. Retrieved March 19, 2006 from: *http://www.tdd.lt/slnews/Stock_Exchanges/Stock.Exchanges.htm*

Teitelbaum, M. (2004). Paul Samuelson on offshore outsourcing. *Corante Website*. Retrieved March 30, 2006 from: *http://outsourcing.corante.com/archives/2004/11/30/paul_samuelson_on_offshore_outsourcing.php*

Thottam, J. (2004, November) Think Globally, Act Locally. *Time Magazine* (Board of Economists). p. A19.

United Nations. (2006). The United Nations. Retrieved April 21, 2006 from: *http://en.wikipedia.org/wiki/United_Nations*

UPS. (2006). The UPS Store. Retrieved May 6, 2006 from *http://www.theupsstore.com/*

UPS Sets $1 Billion+. (2006, May 17). UPS Sets $1 Billion + Expansion of Global Air Hub. *UPS Press Release*. Retrieved May 18, 2006 from: *http://ups.com/pressroom/us/press_releases/press_release/0,1088,4684,00.html*

Weber, J. (2006, March 6). From Dinosaur To Dynamo?*BusinessWeek*. p. 70 – 72.

Weber, J. (2006, March 27). The Yankees Are Coming! *BusinessWeek*. p. 40.

World Trade Organization (WTO). (2005) Membership and What Is the WTO. *The WTO*. Retrieved March 24, 2006 from:

http://www.wto.org/english/thewto_e/thewto_e.htm#members

World Bank. (2006). Doing Business, Economy Rankings. *World Bank International Finance Corporation.* Retrieved March 24, 2006 from: *http://www.doingbusiness.org/Economy/Rankings/*

World Bank, What Is. (2006). *World Bank Organization.* Retrieved March 24, 2006 from: *http://www.doingbusiness.org/Economy/Rankings/*

Chapter 2 (Artistic and Creative Visions . . .)

Annenberg Learner. (2006). Renaissance: Exploration and Trade. *Annenberg/CPB/Learner.org.* Retrieved April 14,2006 from: *http://www.learner.org/exhibits/renaissance/exploration.html.*

AutoBlog. (2006). Volvo Demos Self-Parking for the (Future) Masses. Retrieved June 4, 2006 from: *http://www.autoblog.com/2006/06/01/video-volvo-demos-self-parking-for-the-future-masses/*

Boeing. (2006). The Boeing Company and China. Retrieved March 31, 2006 from: *http://www.boeing.com/companyOffices/aboutus/boechina.html*

Clinton, H. (2005). Remarks by Senator Hillary Rodham Clinton to the Aspen Institute, July 10, 2005. Retrieved April 16, 2006 from: *http://www.aspeninstitute.org/site/c.huLWJeMRKpH/b.1097563/k.1CD3/Senator_Hillary_Rodham_Clinton_at_Ideas_Fest.htm*

Coming of Age. (2006, January 21). *Copy Editor. The Economist*, pp. 10-11.

Digital Strategy. (2005). Digital Strategy: Glossary of Terms. Retrieved May 18, 2006 from: *http://www.digitalstrategy.govt.nz/templates/Page_60 .aspx*

Donald, J. (2006). Starbucks Special Report, *CBS 60 Minutes News*, April 22, 2006.

Einhorn, Bruce and Elgin, Ben. (2006, January 23). The Great Firewall of China. *Business Week.* p. 60

Friedman, T. (2005). *The World Is Flat, A Brief History of the Twenty-First Century.* New York. Farrar, Straus and Giroux. p. 5.

Immelt, J. (2005, August 1). Quote found in Get Creative: How to build Innovative Companies. *Businessweek.* p. 66.

Jana, R. (2006, May 1). Innovation. *BusinessWeek.* p. 16.

Jimmy Carter's Town Hall. (2005). Jimmy Carter's Town Hall Meeting with the American University's Community. Retrieved May 19, 2006 from: *http://www.american.edu/media/speeches/carter.htm*

Kahn, J. (2006, June). Nano's Big Future. National Geographic. P. 100-119.

KCAI. (2006). Kansas City Art Institute. Retrieved from: *http://en.wikipedia.org/wiki/Kansas_City_Institute*

Kelly, Tom and Littman, Jonathan. (2005) *The Ten Faces of Innovation.* New York: Currency/Doubleday, 2005

Lafley, A.G. (2006, January). P&G's Top Secret Design Board. *Business Week.*

Lohr, S. (2006, February). Talent, Not Costs, Is Why Research is Going Global. *Kansas City Star.* February 17, 2006. p. C2.

Martin, R. (2006, January). Ideas and Viewpoint. *BusinessWeek.* p. 102.

Nussbaum, B. (2005, August). How To Build Innovative Companies, *Business Week,* Special Report. p. 62.

Porter, M. and Stern, S. (1999). The New Challenge to America's Prosperity: Findings from the Innovation Index, *Council on Competiveness Report.* Washington, D.C., Chapter 2, p. 25

Prestowitz, C. (2005). *Three Billion New Capitalists, The Great Shift of Wealth and Power to the East.* New York: Basic Books. p. 3 & XIV.

Rieke, O. (2006, January 19). As I See It: Creativity Will Secure Our Future. *Kansas City Star,* p. B8.

Schwab, K. (2005). Global Competitiveness Report 2005-2006. Released September 28, 2005. Retrieved from: *http://www.weforum.org/site/homepublic.nsf/Content/Global+Competitiveness+Programme%5CGlobal+Competitiveness+Report*

Vedres, Andras, *Innovative Characteristics of Countries,* Speech and paper, May 17, 2005 before Hungarian Institute of Innovation, p. 3.

Wikipedia. (2006). Renaissance. *Wikipedia Free Encyclopedia.*Retrieved April 14, 2006 from: *http://en.wikipedia.org/wiki/Renaisance*

World's Most Innovative. (2005, August 15). The World's Most Innovative Companies. Businessweek. p. 64.

World's Most Innovative. (**2006**, April 24). The Worlds Most Innovative Companies. *Businessweek.* (Online advanced copy). Retrieved April 14, 2006 from: *http://www.businessweek.com/magazine/toc/06_17/B39810617innovation.htm*

ZAP. (2006). ZapWorld (ZAP Co.) Website. Retrieved April 2, 2006 from: *http://www.zapworld.com/cars/smartCar.asp*

Chapter 3 (The Cost of Labor Is Four Times . . .)

Carson, J. (2003, October 24). Manufacturing Payrolls Declining Globally: The Untold Story (Part 2). *U.S. Weekly Economic Update,* AllianceBerstein Sponsored Study.

Conrad, R. & George, N. (2006, March 8). Advisory, *Personal Finance*, Volume XXXIII, Number 5. p. 10.

Deloitte. (2005). China in 2005 – Navigating Risks I in A Land of Opportunity. *ITC World Trade Series.*

Elliott, M. (2005, June 27). A New China Rises. Time Magazine, p. 30 – 31.

Engardio, P & Rober, D. (2004, December 6), The ChinaPrice. *Business Week*. p. 104.

George, N. (2006, May 10). Getting Down To Business: When it comes to China, it's just business. *Personal Finance*. p. 2.

Heffes, E. (2004, September). Offshoring: And the Winner Is… *Financial Executive*. P. 34.

International Trade Council. (2005, May 24). Meeting held in Kansas City, Doing Business in China. *2005 ITC World Trade Series*.

Rifkin, J. (2004). *The End of Work*. New York. Tarcher/Penguin. pp. xxii – xxiii.

Roberts, D. (2006, March 27). How Rising Wages Are Changing The Game In China. *BusinessWeek*. p. 32 – 34.

Shenkar, O. (2005). *The Chinese Century*. Upper Saddle River, New Jersey. Pearson Education Inc, Wharton School Publishing. pp. 66, 114, 118, 165, 174.

Wal-Mart Fact Sheets – Wages. (2005). Fact: *The majority of Wal-Mart's hourly store associates in the United States work full-time.* Retrieved March 15, 2006 from: *http://www.walmartfacts.com/newsdesk/wal-mart-fact-sheets.aspx#a136.*

Welch, J. (2004). *Winning*. New York. Harper Business. pp. 344 - 345.

Woodard, B. (2000). *Maestro*. New York. Simon & Schuster. pp. 198 – 199.

Chapter 4 (Education – The Great Equalizer . . .)

Award Winner. (2005). Baldrige National Quality Program: 2005 Award Winner. *Informational Release* by Richland College, March 2006.

Backgrounder. (2006). Backgrounder: Confucius Institutes. Retrieved May 5, 2006 from: *http://english.people.com.cn/200604/29/eng20060429_262201.htm.*

Bessier, E. (2006, April 27). Confucius Institute on KU Campus. *Johnson County Sun*. Retrieved May 5, 2006 from: *http://www.zwire.com/site/news.cfm?newsid=16544310&BRD=1459&PAG=461&dept_id=155725&rfi=6*

Broder, D. (2005, December 26). U.S. Inventiveness. *The Kansas City Star*. p. B5.

Carnevale, A & Porro, J. (2004). Quality Education: School Reform for the New American Economy. Retrieved April 30, 2006 from: *http://eric.ed.gov/Ericwebportal/home.portal*

Finder, A. (2006, March 26). In Reversal, Graduate School Applications from Foreigners Rise. *The New York Times*. Retrieved March 26, 2006 from: *http://www.nytimes.Com/todaysheadlines*

Friedman, T. (2005). *The World Is Flat, A Brief History of the Twenty-First Century.* New York. Farrar, Straus and Giroux. p. 303 - 305.

Intro. (2005). Introduction to the "Confucius Institute Project." Retrieved May 5, 2006 from: *http://English.Hanban.edu.en/market/HanBanE/412360.htm.*

Lieberthal, G & Lieberthal, K. (2004). The Great Transition, *Harvard Business Review on Doing Business in China.* Boston. Harvard Business School Publishing Co. p. 4-5.

MU Considered. (2006, May 14). MU Considered for Qatar Campus. *The Kansas City Star.* P. B2.

Pocket World In Figures. (2006 Edition). *The Economist.* p. 77.

Prestowitz, C. (2005). *Three Billion New Capitalists, The Great Shift of Wealth and Power to the East*. New York: Basic Books. p. 29.

Schlosser, J. (2006, March). Infosys U. *Fortune Magazine*. pp. 41-42.

Study In U.S. (2006). Study in the United States. Retrieved May 15, 2006 from: *http://www.usastudy/guide.com/studyinus.html*

Weird News. (2006, March 18). *"fyi,"* Copy Editor, *The Kansas City Star*. p. F1.

Welch, D. (2006, April 10). Twilight of the UAW. *BusinessWeek*. p. 62.

Chapter 5 (Global Strategy, Hedgehogs, . . .)

Award Winner. (2005). Baldrige National Quality Program: 2005 Award Winner. *Informational Release by Richland College*, March 2006.

Collins, J. (2001). Good To Great. New York, Harper Business/Collins Publishers. pp. 90-91; 117-118; 186.

Hamm, S. (2006, April 3). Innovation: The View from the Top. *Businessweek.* p 52.

Healthfield, S. (2006). Build a Strategic Framework: Mission Statement, Vision, Values. *Human Resources Newsletter*. Retrieved March 19, 2006 from: *http://humanresources.about.com/cs/strategicplanning1/a/strategic plan_2.htm*

Kanellos, M. & Spooner, J. (2004). IBM Sells PC Group to Lenovo. *C/Net News.Com*. Retrieve March 27, 2006 from: *http://news.com.com/IBM+sells+PC+group+to+Lenovo/2100- 1042_3-5482284.html*

Mission Statement. (2006). Mission Statement. *Center for Business Planning*. Retrieved May 15, 2006 from: *http://www.businessplans.org/Mission.html*

Offshore. (2006). Offshore Outsourcing Basics: Case Study: General Electric. *E-Business Strategies*. Retrieved May 16, 2006 from: *http://www.ebstrategy.com/outsourcing/basics/definition.htm*

Schlosser, J. (2006, January). Star Power. *Fortune*, p. 66.

Schultz, H. (1997). *Pour Your Heart Into It*. New York, Hyperion. pp. 103 & 331 - 333

Stewart, M. (2005). *The Martha Rules*. New York: Rodale, Inc. p. 98 -108.

The Ranking. (2006, April 3) The BusinessWeek 50: The Top Performers. *BusinessWeek*. p. 90 & 104.

Welch, J. (2004). *Winning*. New York. Harper Business. pp. 166 - 188.

Welcome Home. (2005). Welcome Home Martha: *A Live Chat with Martha:* March 14, 2005. Retrieved May 15, 2006 from: *http://www.marthastewart.com/page.jhtml?type=learn-cat&id=cat19846*

Wikipedia, the free encyclopedia. (2006). Scenario Planning. Retrieved March 27, 2006 from: *http://en.wikipedia.org/wiki/Scenario_planning*.

Chapter 6 (Governance, Accountability, and Ethics. . .)

Alm, R. (2005, April 5). U.S. Shuns Ruling on Internet Gambling. *The Kansas City Star*, p. C1.

Conrad, R. & George, N. (2006, March 8). Advisory, *Personal Finance*, Volume XXXIII, Number 5. p. 10.

E.F.F.(Electronic Frontier Foundation). (2006). The USA Patriot Act. Let the Sun Set on Patriot. Retrieved March 12, 2006 from: *http://www.eff.org/patriot.*

Europe Warns of Sanctions. (2006, March 15). Copy Editor, *The Kansas City Star*. p. C1.

Friedman, T. (2005). *The World Is Flat, A Brief History of the Twenty-First Century.* New York. Farrar, Straus and Giroux. p. 5

How Has the Onset of the Electronic Age Affected Intellectual Property. (2005, October 16). Beginners Guide to Entrepreneurship. Beginners Guide Staff. Retrieved March 17, 2006 from: *http://beginnersguide.com/entpreneurship/intellectual-property/what-is-intellectual-property.php*

Isikoff, M. (2006, March 13). What Ever Happened to the Civil Liberties Board? *Newsweek*. p 6.

Klug, F. (2006, February 15). Internet Firms Criticized as Allies of Chinese Censorship. *Kansas City Star*, p. B3.

Lieberthal, G & Lieberthal, K. (2004). The Great Transition, *Harvard Business Review on Doing Business in China.* Boston. Harvard Business School Publishing Co. p. 25.

No Questions Asked. (2006, January 21). *Copy Editor. Economist.* p.43.

Taiwan: Desperate Chen. (2006, January 21). *Copy Editor. Economist*. pp. 43-44.

Volcker, P. (2001, April 30). *Globalization and the World of Finance*. Speech given for the Annual Hutchinson Lecture, University of Delaware. p. 3.

What is Intellectual Property. (2005, October 16). *Beginners Guide to Entrepreneurship*. Beginners Guide Staff. Retrieved March 6, 2006 from: *http://beginnersguide.com/entpreneurship/intellectual-property/what-is-intellectual-property.php*

Chapter 7 (Standard of Living / The Quality of Life . . .)

100 Best. (2006, January). 100 Best Companies to Work For. *Fortune.* P. 71

Best Jobs. (2006, May). 50 Best Jobs. *Money*. pp. 97 – 104.

Elliott, M. (2005, June 27). A New China Rises. *Time Magazine*, p. 34.

Forbes. (2006). The World's Richest People. *Forbes Magazine.* P. xx

GM, Ford Sales Down. (2006, April 4). Briefcase: GM, Ford Sales Down. *The Kansas City Star*. p. D3.

How Many, (2006). How Many Will Go Hungry on World Food Day? Retrieved on April 6, 2006 from: *http://www.**mindfully.org/Food/2003/Hungry-Food-Day16oct03.htm***

International Living. (2006). 2006 Quality of Life Index. Retrieved on May 11, 2006 from: *http://www.internationalliving.com/qol06/index.html*

LeMoult, C. (2006, April 23). These Houses Are Little in a Big Way. *The Kansas City Star*. p. D10.

Palmer, P. (1990). *The Active Life*. Harper San Francisco. pp. 125 – 125.

Wallechinsky, D. (2006, April 23). Is the American Dream Still Possible? *The Kansas City Star: Parade Magazine*. pp. 4 – 5.

Welch, J. (2004). *Winning*. New York. Harper Business. pp. 340 – 344 & 354.

World Bank, What Is. (2006). *World Bank Organization.* Retrieved March 24, 2006 from: *http://www.doingbusiness.org/Economy/ Rankings/*

Chapter 8 (The Energy (Crises?) . . .)

Alternative Investing. (2006, April 18). Briefcase: Alternative Investing. *The Kansas City Star*. p. D3.

Appenzeller, T. (2006, March). The Coal Paradox. *National Geographic*. pp. 96 – 101.

Aston, A. (2006, March 6). Hear Comes Lunar Power, *Business Week*. pp. 32 - 34.

Baldacci, D. (2005). *The Camel Club*. New York. Warner Book Group. p. 310.

Carpenter, A. (2005, October). *Andy Carpenter's Making Money*, Phoenix, p. 8.

Dawson C. & Welch, D. (2004, October 11). Reinventing The Wheels. *Business Week*. pp 153-156 & 176.

Earnings Digest (2006, February). *Kansas City Star*. P. C2.

Edmunds Top 10 Lists. (2006, February), Top 10 Most Fuel-Efficient Cars in the U.S., *Edmunds*. Retrieved March 15, 2006 from: *http://www.edmunds.com/reviews/list/top10.*

Elphinstone, J. (2006, April 4). Exxon boots Wal-Mart from top of Fortune list. *The Kansas City Star*. p. D8.

Emerging Market. (2006, May). Emerging Market Indicators: Petrol Prices. *The Economist*. p. 102.

Ethanol: Life after subsidies. (2006, February 11). Copy Editor. A Much Maligned Alternative to Oil Comes of Age. The Economist. p. 60-61.

Everly, S. (2006, March 24). Canada Crude: Is This Our Fuel Fix. *The Kansas City Star*. pp. A1 & A6.

Friedman, T. (2006, May). Relations With Beijing: China's Real Business Isn't In Washington. *New York Times.*

Geothermal Energy. (2006). Geothermal Renewable and Efficient Energy. Retrieved May 12, 2006 from: *http://geothermal.getfast.info/geothermal/geothermal_enrgy.html*

Kraske, S. (2006, May 12). Cleaver wants congressional fuel efficiency. *The Kansas City Star*. P. A4.

Norris, Floyd. (2006, February 6). High Profits, Sluggish Investments. *New York Times*, p C1.

Nuclear Energy. (2006). Nuclear Fusion. Retrieved from: *http://www.answers.com/topic/nuclear-energy*

Nuclear Power. (2006). Nuclear Power Plants. *Wikipedia*. Retrieved May 31, 2006 from: *http://en.wikipedia.org/Wiki/Nuclear_power_plant*

Oil and Gas Journal. (2006). *Energy Information Administration.* p. 10.

Parfit, M. (2005, August). Future Power: Where Will the World Get Its Next Energy Fix? *National Geographic*. pp 2-31.

Petit, C. (2006, April). It's Scary, It's Expensive, It Could Save the Earth. *National Geographic*. p. 56 – 63.

Quick Guide to Dams. (2006). Dam facts and figures: A Quick Guide to the World of Dams. Retrieved May 13, 2006 from: *http://www.panda.org/about_wwf/what_we_do/freshwater/our_solutions/policies_practice.*

Renewable Energy. (2006). Renewable Energy is Off and Running. *BusinessWeek*. p. 61.

Sprint . . .Wind Farm. (2006, April 29). Sprint Soon to Rely on Wind Farm. *The Kansas City Star*. p. C1.

Thermoelectrics. (2006, March 18). Every Little Bit Helps. Copy Editor. *The Economists.* p. 78

U.S. Energy Information Administration. (2006, March). Retrieved March 13, 2006 from: *http://www.tonto.eia.gov/oog/info/hopu.asp*

Volcker, P. (2001, April 30). *Globalization and the World of Finance*. Speech given for the Annual Hutchinson Lecture, University of Delaware. p. 2.

What's Hot. (2006, April 6). United States is Addicted to Oil, According to President Bush. *The Kansas City Star*, p. D3.

What Is Fusion. (2006). *What Is Fusion*. Retrieved May 30, 2006 from: *http://fusioned.gat.com/images/pdf/what_is_fusion.pdf*

Yahoo News. (2006, Mar 7). Global wind energy capacity seen tripling by 2014. *Reuters.* Retrieved February 20, 2006 from:

http://news.yahoo.com/s/nm/20060307/sc.nm/nm/energy.wind

ZAP. (2006). ZapWorld (ZAP Co.) Website. Retrieved April 2, 2006 from: *http://www.zapworld.com/cars/smartCar.asp*

Quinn, J. (2006, April 24) The Price of Our Addiction. *Newsweek*. p. 45.

Chapter 9 (In Transition, It's Not a Pretty sight . . .)

Associated Press. (2006, January 11). VW Slashes Jobs. As reported by the *Kansas City Star*, p. B3.

Bergheim, S. (2006). Current Issues: Global Growth Centers. *Deutsche Bank Research*. Retrieved February 12, 2006 from: *http//www.dbresearch.com*.

Block, S. (2006). Europe: Investors See Happier Returns. Keep Media, *USA Today*. Retrieved April 10, 2006 from: *http://www.keepmedia.com/pubs/USATODAY/2006/04/07/1378068?ba=a&bi=2&bp=7*

CIA Global Trends. (2000). CIA Global Trends 2015. Retrieved May 19, 2006 from: *http://www.cia.gov/cia/reports/globaltrends2015/index.html*

Clinton, H. (2005). Remarks by Senator Hillary Rodham Clinton to the Aspen Institute, July 10, 2005. Retrieved April 16, 2006 from: *http://www.aspeninstitute.org/site/c.huLWJeMRKpH/b.1097563/k.1CD3/Senator_Hillary_Rodham_Clinton_at_Ideas_Fest.htm*

Collins, J. (2001). *Good to Great: Why Some Companies Make the Leap, and Others Don't!* New York: Harper Collins Publishers. pp. 186-187.

Colvin, G. (2006, April). Dial Down the Expectation. *Fortune*. p 47.

Easton, T. (2005). Competiveness Rankings. *Fact Book*, Retrieved February 12, 2006 from: *http://www.CIA.gov/publications/factbook*.

Frank, B. (2006, February 27). When The Bounty Isn't Shared. *Business Week*. p. 104.

Hoovers. (2006). Volkswagen AG. Retrieved from: *http:///www.hoovers.com/free/co/news.* pp. 1-10

Immelt, J. (2004, April). *The Innovation Imperative*. Speech given for the 2004 Robert S. Hatfield Fellow in Economic Education Program. April 15, 2004. Cornell University. Ithaca, New York.

Jubak, J. (2006). The New Risk from China: Deflation. *Jubak's Journal*. p. 1. Retrieved from MSN Money, January 31, 2006. *http://moneycentral.msn.com*.

Loomis, C. (2006, February). The Tragedy of General Motors, *Fortune*, p. 62.

Mander, J. (2003). Speech by Jerry Mander: *World Affairs Council*, San Francisco 4/2/03. Retrieve 5/18/06 from *http://www.ifg.org/jerrywac.htm*

Mateja, J & Popely, R (2006, February 6). General Motors, *Kansas City Star*, pp C1 & C5.

Naughton, K. (2006, March 13). Detroit Muscles Up. *Newsweek*. p. 41.

Pocket World In Figures. (2006). *The Economist*. p. 70.

Stewart, M. (2005). *The Martha Rules*. New York: Rodale, Inc. p. 182.

Veal, J. (2006, February). Governance Models for Entrepreneurial or Closely Held, Family-Owned Companies. *Directors Monthly, NACD*. p. 20.

Welch, J. (2004). *Winning*. New York. Harper Business. p. 341.

ZAP. (2006). ZapWorld (ZAP Co.) Website. Retrieved April 2, 2006 from: *http://www.zapworld.com/cars/smartCar .asp*

Conclusion

Friedman, T. (2005). *The World Is Flat, A Brief History of the Twenty-First Century,* speech at the 2005 National Book Fair, Washington, D.C.

Prestowitz, C. (2005). *Three Billion New Capitalists, The Great Shift of Wealth and Power to the East*. New York: Basic Books. p. 3, 21, 59 & XIV.